WITH
EVERY
GREAT
BREATH

Also by Rick Bass

Fiction

Nonfiction

WITH
EVERY
GREAT
BREATH

New and Selected Essays, 1995–2023

RICK BASS

COUNTERPOINT

BERKELEY, CALIFORNIA

With Every Great Breath

First Counterpoint edition: 2024

Library of Congress Cataloging-in-Publication Data
Names: Bass, Rick, 1958-
Title: With every great breath : new and selected essays, 1995-2023 / Rick Bass.
Other titles: With every great breath (Compilation)
Description: First Counterpoint edition. | Berkeley, California : Counterpoint, 2024.
Identifiers: LCCN 2023041699 | ISBN 9781640096301 (hardcover) | ISBN 9781640096318 (ebook)
Subjects: LCGFT: Essays.
Classification: LCC PS3552.A8213 W58 2024 | DDC 814/.54—dc23/eng/20231011
LC record available at https://lccn.loc.gov/2023041699

Jacket design by Farjana Yasmin
Jacket illustration © iStock / Shemelina
Book design by Laura Berry

COUNTERPOINT
2560 Ninth Street, Suite 318
Berkeley, CA 94710
www.counterpointpress.com

Printed in the United States of America

1 3 5 7 9 10 8 6 4 2

Carter

We are miners / hard rock miners
to the shaft house / we must go . . .

—COWBOY JUNKIES,
"Mining for Gold"

CONTENTS

Selected Essays

New Essays

SELECTED

ESSAYS

INTO THE FIRE

I'M RUNNING THROUGH A FIELD WITH MY BEST FRIEND, a man I went to high school with. We're on the outskirts of Houston, it's nighttime, and we can see the fire in the distance. It's a hay barn at the far end of a field that's caught fire, and the barn is burning, as are the bales of hay in it. The loose bales in the stubble field are aflame, and the groves of trees at the back edge of the field are burning too. My friend, Kirby, is a volunteer fireman now for little Spring, Texas, which is a pretty suburban community (not that long ago, the area was woods) nestled in amid and among the concrete and chaos of Houston. Kirby is dressed in his full turnout gear—his firefighting equipment—as am I, in a borrowed suit; I just happened to be hanging out in the station when the call came, and there was an extra set. We have to run across a golf course, a driving range actually, to get to the fire—another station is already there, we can see the red-and-blue lights—and as we run huffing through the humid night there are little pissant golf balls like mushrooms everywhere, which we keep stumbling on. It seems like it's a mile to that fire and as if the whole western horizon is ablaze. The turnout gear—helmet, big-ass boots, air tank, bunker coat, rubber overalls, giant gloves—feels like it weighs about seventy pounds. It feels like we'll never get there, or that if we do, we'll be too tired to fight the fire and will just have to stand there gasping and sucking air at the edge of the fire, burning ourselves, legs and lungs aflame. Probably when we were eighteen we could have just cruised on out there in forty seconds flat, never even breaking into a pant, but twenty years ago of course we would have been more interested in breaking apart order and structure than trying to weave it back together or keep it from burning down.

Now we are finally drawing closer to the mega-fire—we're drenched with sweat inside our heavy rubber boots—we've divoted the hell out of that golf course, tromped its sand traps, so that in the daylight it will probably look like a herd of wild horses ran through—and with the flames' backlighting we can see the stick figures of other firefighters moving in and through and among the flames, working with shovels and axes and hoses. There's smoke and steam, and at night it looks like an evacuating village, elemental. It seems to be calling us.

There are a lot of firefighters on this one. The barn was a goner a long time ago; the trees are goners too, flames searching for the sky, but they have nowhere else to go, nothing else to burn—a city of concrete lies beyond them, with fire hydrants on every corner—and the burning hay bales and the burning field stubble smell good.

The fire's been going on a pretty good while—maybe an hour, before we received our call to come help close it out. It's December, nearing Christmas and New Year's—prime time for firefighters, along with, of course, the Fourth of July and Halloween—all those candles and burning pumpkins! What started this fire was probably either someone trying to collect the insurance money, or a homeless person just trying to find a place to hang out and stay warm. Maybe they built a little fire with which to make coffee. Maybe a cigarette fell in the hay. Either of these explanations is just as likely—or it could have been kids—eighteen years old, perhaps—just out fucking around. In December like this, it was almost certainly a human-caused fire, some errant excess of social imbalance, some fringe unraveling or deterioration, and now the firefighters are here to snip off that excess and snuff it out and smooth it over. It may seem like a cliché, and you may, when the talk turns to firefighters and especially volunteers, hear the easy stereotype, the armchair assumption of "hero complex" or "boring home life—needs excitement."

It's not this way at all. Perhaps for a handful of them it is that way, but far more common, I think, are the ones who do it for the same reasons that any of us do whatever it is we do, or dream of doing: the act of it, the doing, achieves a fit and an order with the rhythms and essence within. You run across fields with them, you race around town with them from call to call, and pretty soon you realize that it's just the way they are. You start to view them not as individuals but as a force, summoned and directed by nature, like the fire itself; that in a world with fire, there must also exist a force that desires for the fires to be put out—and further, that the two forces desire and require each other.

They love to put out the fires, as does, perhaps, a rainstorm. Plus, when it's not dangerous, it's fun. It tips the world a bit sideways—reorders it, makes it new, recharges it. At this particular fire everyone is sweating like racehorses and walking around ankle-deep in smoldering smoke and flame and ashes and coals, some of us wearing masks and helmets, others of us barefaced for a moment in the night air, breathing good cold air and the sweet odor of dry burning grass. We are pawing at the smoking, burning ground with rakes and shovels, breaking apart the hay bales so they will finish burning and we can go home (they flame brightly, like marshmallows, each time we separate a sheaf of them), and because I do not want to upset the rhythm of things—despite the presence of several units, several stations, they are all more or less familiar with each other, by sight if not by name, as would be athletes who trained or competed together—though in this case they have risked their lives together, each time they assemble—I keep my Darth Vader mask on. There must be thirty of us out here, wandering through the night and the flames, each one of us looking to me like any of the others, but they can tell, I know, when I pass near them that I am not of them, and I duck my head and turn my shoulders when I see one of the various captains or commanders, whose job it is in instances like these not to fight the fire hand-to-hand, but to deploy their crew and observe, like a hawk from above, the flow of things—the comings and goings. To them I stand out like the proverbial sore thumb, and though I have permission to be hanging out with Kirby (who is also a captain), I try to steer clear of the men and women who are carrying radios; I try not to interrupt the pulse and rhythm of the thing they have become in their assemblage, a force that is hopefully equal to that of the fire. We hear the phrases "armed forces" and "show of force," but the way I mean it, "force" is more elemental than that. I mean it like rain or wind or desire; like gravity, or oxygen.

I can feel them scowling after me as I careen away from the ones with radios. I strike at the smoldering hay bales, break them apart and rake them flat, soothing order back into the system. I had hoped that in theory everyone would think I was a rookie with another captain's department, one they had not seen in action yet, but of course it did not work out that way: they could all sense or see that I was different, not of them, as if a deer were trying to walk among a gathering of bears, or a moose through a flock of geese, even at night, even amid smoke and flame. I was not an element of their force.

Kirby, picking up on the vibes that are gathering around me—the way my presence is confusing and annoying the various captains—escorts me to the perimeter of the fire, to a still-smoldering section of field that has pretty much already been mopped up. There are puddles of water standing here and there. We walk past the incredible sight of two beautiful red-haired women sitting side by side on a bale of hay that is still burning.

They are resting, their turnout coats opened to their T-shirts, and as the firelight flickers on their faces—red freckles, copper skin—it seems they could be drinking a cup of coffee and talking about any old thing, rather than resting, grimy and damp, having kicked this fire's ass—having cinched or sewn order back into being.

It inflames the senses, firefighting. It argues against chaos, even while it celebrates and marvels at our proximity to chaos. From a distance it just looks like a bunch of men and, increasingly, a few women running around trying to react against and defend something. It looks a little ragged, a little mechanical. From the outside, you don't quite understand that even as you watch the men and women swirl about (dragging hose, swinging ax), a transmutation is occurring: that they are altering themselves from individuals into connected components often equal or superior to the force of the fire itself. You can't really see or feel the magic unless you are right in with them—as if in, perhaps, the eye of a hurricane. From a distance it looks as if they are running behind, playing catch-up, and that the fire is in control. You'd never guess that the opposite is true: that they are in control, and not behind but in lockstep with it, feeding on its energy—that it, the fire, is the thing that allows them to exist, and that as it releases stored energy in the burning, it makes that much more energy available to them for them to bend and shape and alter and turn and compress and redirect.

You need to almost go right into the center of the fire to see this.

———————

Going into the fire of course is the worst thing in the world you can do, the last thing you should ever consider doing. The absolute best thing civilians can do is to melt and disappear, to draw way back—to become invisible, if possible—and let the two forces sweep in against each other. This is hard to do. We each have in us an innate longing for spectacle and drama, for an arousal of the senses—as wire desires electricity, as wood desires rot or flame—and when the trucks race past, or the smoke billows from the building across the street, we are drawn to it like angels, or moths; we gather, we get in the way, we clog things up. There is something godlike in the way the firefighters hurl themselves at the fire and shut it down cold—something monstrous, too—and wherever they go, people are following behind them, clinging to the charred edges of the event, gawking and getting too close to the giant hoses and the crumbling, crashing-down walls of things, so that the firefighters can hardly ever concentrate purely on the task at hand—aligning their undiluted force squarely against that of the onrushing fire. Always, it seems, they are anxious to make that leap from human to godlike, forgetting about the people behind them—the spectators, the traffic—and hurling themselves instead completely into the matching of the fire's force—but always, it seems, there is energy that must be expended by them, wasteful energy, patrolling their flanks, and keeping humans from edging too close, or even following.

I often wonder where such individuals come from. It—firefighting—is both an art and a science. It remakes the individual. In the instance of my best friend, Kirby, it is a marvel to see. This is not the place for such stories, but suffice it to say that twenty years ago he, we, were masters of—what? Shall we call it unraveling things, and pause there? (Matches were not involved, but might as well have been.)

The fires have transformed him—they have found him and summoned and recast him. I do not know why. It is tempting to think that for each of these firefighters there is some space within them waiting to be ignited when the fire, or the beckoning, sweeps over them—and that either you have this place in you or you do not.

I think this is how it is. Plenty of people have hidden or buried or held deep within them the desire for order, sometimes extreme order, just as plenty of them have the opposite desire. There are also plenty with a desire for beauty, and no small number who are enraptured these days with the stupid, the insipid, and the plain plug-ugly.

But it is not that simple. There are only handfuls of them here and there who love to wade into fire, and if you ask them, not a damn one of them, not even Kirby, can tell you exactly or even satisfactorily why they do it. And in observing them one of the things you pick up on pretty quickly, if you're in close enough, is that, unlike many other things, there seems not to be so much a joy or a pleasure in the doing (if anything, they appear to be in a zone of near-hypnotic, inhuman trance), but rather a deep sweetness of relief and fullness in the after of it. The pleasure of pulling off dirty turnout gear, dirty boots. Looking forward to a cleansing shower.

It's not very Zen. Or hell, maybe it's real Zen. But I don't think so.

————————

Sometimes one fire—the excitement of it, the sensation of it—will seemingly ignite others in the same area, days and even weeks or months later, like some kind of delayed fuse. Even if the first one was accidental, non-arsonous, something will often have been released—something latent—in a handful of individuals, sometimes only one or two, within that community; pining and lonesome for the return of that kind of excitement, hungry to have the senses felt that deeply again (and perhaps cherishing the relief of the aftermath, as the throbbing senses cool and return to normal)—that individual or individuals will then set a fire or fires, seeking to lure or beckon the firefighters' return.

And always, they come. Occasionally it will be one of the

firefighters themselves who has set the fire—the bad seed getting in among them and somehow confused, seeking to simultaneously both create and destroy the very thing that gives them purpose, the very thing that calls and shapes and alters them—but seeking, in a kind of gluttony or instant gratification, to elude or shortcut the rules.

But the men and women in the fire departments are extraordinarily good at sniffing out this kind of firefighter: of determining, as if with ESP, when such a hybrid or renegade is in their midst. They sense it perhaps as the magma flow of a volcano senses the presence within it of a floating chunk of boulder—that which has not yet completely given itself over to the rest. They sense it, by and by—soon enough—when they are fighting fire side by side with such an individual, and they can sense it coming from that person when they are back at the station watching a football game on the television. They can feel it and hear it and see it coming off in waves, as if that individual in their midst is not at peace but aflame, or at least smoldering. They can sense soon enough, by the way he does not fit the rhythm that is their force, that he is the one who is setting the fires in order to be drawn to them and engaged by them, and because this goes against both the code of ethics and the code of physics—the law of nature that lets them and the fires exist in the same universe—they turn him in, or drum him out. They can sense it, suddenly—can see it—as if the message is writing itself in some awful hieroglyphics across the perpetrator's body.

It is elemental, the way they find out; it is the way animals, who have been here in the world so much longer than we, communicate. They are never wrong.

It is as if their existence, their integrity—the purity of their desire and being—has been threatened near unto extinction, by the presence of one such among them, and it is as if that one has willfully been gambling their lives, rolling the dice, oblivious to the risk that's being run: the threat of this stranger among them putting their life on the line for mere joy or pleasure—risking a child's father, a woman's husband, a mother's son, or a husband's wife. Rolling the dice.

There was once one like this whom Kirby found out about—not in his department, but in a nearby unit. Such is the hatred among the fraternity, or family, of firefighters that even he, my best friend, cannot or will not speak to me of him. His voice deepens and his words thicken with rage and wonder; he shakes his head: *No, never mind.* It strikes me that it, the firebug among them, is like the metaphor, or transformation from metaphor to reality, of their fear, their foe—a building, a structure of integrity and order—burning from within.

It's rare. Much more common—infinitely more common—are the grass fires, electrical fires, and cookfires out of control; the propane heater fires, careless-with-matches fires, industrial fires, chemical fires, fires started by the friction of two dry branches rubbing together, fires started by lightning, fires started by oily rags, by fireworks, by hot mufflers, by magnifying glasses, by cigarettes. People fall asleep smoking in bed and immolate themselves by the dozens, even hundreds, each year. Sometimes they do it in high-rise hotels and take out dozens or hundreds with them in a single night. Archaeologists excavating the ruined cities of the future might mistakenly believe, viewing the remains, that fire still played an important part in the culture or religion of these times: that sacrifices were still common, and that at any given time in these ghost cities there would have been fires raging, consuming.

But they would not be able to catch the sound of the fire engines racing toward those fires in their archaeological diggings: would not be able to measure the sweat and fury and muscle-cost of the firefighters manning the water-taut hose lines and swinging axes, shouting instructions: the tension and determination and purity of focus as taut as the fire was loose and raging.

Things being cast anew, or tautened and strengthened, by the fires—the archaeologists would miss that. The order that the fire-fighters cannot restore in the fires' consumption sometimes gets turned within them, as if with an overflowing, or excess. They come to rely (and be incorporated by) lists and repetition. They can enumerate danger better than anyone—have observed and learned the vertical and horizontal components of it (as if it is thick, like nests of snakes or hives of bees), behind the walls of things, just beneath the skin of the earth, waiting to be peeled back or released by a simple nick or a cut. Their minds are wired taut with understandings of possibility and cause and effect. They break the world down into three components: fuel, oxygen, heat.

When they relax, they do so deeply. Their family lives, rather than becoming weakened by the attention to and obsession with a thing and the time spent at the station, often instead become strengthened. The weave and rhythm of their profession becomes similarly the fabric of their other family, their blood family. You will notice in most of them a celebration of order and structure. They're big on picnics and cookouts, circuses, trips to the beach, parades, rodeos, trips to the zoo—that kind of thing. They have a ferocity for life, even in the midst of what can be a physically and intellectually desensitizing, unstimulating environment: the late twentieth-century suburban landscape, and beyond that, the decaying cores of the urban interior.

They tend to be aware, too, of how thin the crust or skin of the earth is. Nick it, and fire issues forth. Generalizations are easy and hence dangerous, but I could not help noticing that the "thinkers"—the captains and lieutenants—often tend to be if not fundamentally at least peripherally religious—stolid to near-stolid churchgoers—while the more physically responsive firefighters, the ones who are not so much interested in plotting or strate-gizing but instead like to hurl themselves at and against the fire according to the captain's or lieutenant's directions, are usually

reckless to an extreme, living what might be called a compromis-
ing or high-risk lifestyle: drinking hard, smoking hard, driving
fast—acknowledging the nearness of death and disorder by their
actions, every bit as much as the churchgoers.

Hanging out with a firefighter, you learn to see the city not as
some artificial and completely controlled system, but as an organ-
ism: as a pulsing, supple, almost living thing, responsive to the
world. Sometimes things in a city burn because they are meant to
and need to—rotting timbers, rat-chewed wiring systems—and
other times, as in cases of arson, the fires pop up in what seems to
be an illogical response, like cancer, done purposely and malig-
nantly to harm the good cells in a body and bring them to ruin.

It's amazing how much of a good-sized city is burning at any
one time, and even more amazing how much of a city has burned,
cumulatively, in the past: as if the scars of fire overlay every inch
of the earth, rural or urban, several layers deep; as if the skin of
the earth is burning daily, a necessary way of replenishing and
invigorating itself, as our own cells are said to do every two or
three days. Riding around the city with Kirby, I was almost disbelieving as he pointed out various structures that had burned.
I thought it was a joke at first, a parody of a firefighter's view of
his or her city, but it was actually the way he saw it. As if with
an X-ray vision of history, he seemed to look right through the
glossy surface, the skin, of new paint jobs and newly constructed
exteriors and still see hidden within the ghosts of old fires, like
opponents with whom he had once done battle. It seemed that
at any given point there would always be, somewhere within his
range of vision, at least one building and usually more where a
fire had occurred during his ten years on the force. We all have
our lenses for viewing the world. *How many memorable localities in
a river walk!* wrote Thoreau. *Here is the warm wood-side; next, the
good fishing bay; and next, where the old settler was drowned when
crossing on the ice a hundred years ago. It is all storied.*

We all see the world through different lenses, according to our various knowledge and life experience. Doctors, farmers, writers will often look at a landscape and its inhabitants each in a way slightly different from the other, and in so doing, come up with different translations or interpretations, different perceptions, about that place. Kirby's lens is fire. There is only that which has burned in the past, or which is at risk in the future. There is also a very small portion of the world—within the range of his roving gaze—that is, for the moment, for the time being, safe: secure.

The stories with which Kirby sees his city almost all involve fire. We cannot drive past a place, it seems, without his having a story—as if they are latticed between the walls of structures, waiting to be released by fire—or as if the stories are the skeletal system of a structure: not timber and steel and stucco and concrete, but stories, with humans living within them like ants. He was not inhumane as a teenager—no more than most—but it seems that the firefighting has made him more humane, more understanding of and attentive to the stories within the latticeworks. As a writer, it's a little fascinating to me, the way we went different directions after high school—he, to marriage and children almost immediately, and to an increasingly fine and responsible job with a suit and tie and office and secretarial staff, appraising urban structures not for fire-worthiness, or fire-proofness, but for tax assignations—while I went in what I thought was a different direction, writing stories and novels and hanging out in the woods. Now I am noticing that our paths did not really diverge at that significant an angle: that he sits at his desk in his day job, high above the city, and runs his evaluation sheets, his analyses, through the computer—but at night, or even in the day, when the dispatcher's horn sounds, he becomes more sensate, more alive, and he rushes to the fire eagerly. And in moving toward that fire—one after the other after the other—and in the fighting of it, he is as passionate and engaged not just with the process but with the stories and lives of the structure's inhabitants—as much so as any writer could ever hope to be about the characters housed within one's story—and I watch this, and try to learn from it. I try to imagine all characters as inhabiting invisible or hidden stories lattice-worked around them, both constraining and supporting them, which can then be released around them—the walls falling away—by fire. In ways that no writing class has yet been able to impress upon me, I begin to think about structure—about what it is—and about the forces that tug and pull at it.

I wonder what it must be like for Kirby's coworkers to hear, in their air-conditioned offices, the squelch and bawl of his beeper down the hallway; what it must be like to see him emerge from his office like a hornet from its nest—to leave them and hurl himself out into the hot flames of Houston—hot sky, hot concrete, hot chrome.

Certainly his wife, Jean Ann, has mixed feelings about it with regard to her and Kirby's security, as well as that of their two children, and Kirby's daughter from the first marriage—her stepdaughter, my goddaughter. Jean Ann knows full well that it's a big part of what makes him be alive, what makes him be Kirby, what makes him not just the man but the force she married—but she cannot help but also know full well that he is rolling some kind of dice each time he goes out the door—not just for his own sense of being alive, but to help other people in dire straits—strangers, even—and it seems that she walks well a fine line between the two territories; that their marriage has a sharpness and defined clarity to it, a being-in-the-moment quality that may or may not be connected to the firefighting, though it is hard to imagine how it is not, at least in part. It's impossible for me to watch him go briskly out the door of his home, or out of the fire station, and not think of the Neil Young line: "The same thing that makes you live will kill you in the end"; just as it is impossible for me not to approve and be happy for my friend, and my goddaughter's father, that he has this thing to be on fire and sensate about.

However, it sometimes seems almost like a kind of entrapment—the way he attaches his sympathy to the victims of the fires—the victims, indirectly, of his passion. He thinks he keeps it at arm's length, as do most of the other firefighters, but an arm's length is not very far. Some firefighters seem to have no trouble at all shutting out their concerns and sympathies for the lives of the burned—if I am not mistaken (and quite possibly I am), some of them seem sometimes to almost relish the act of putting up that barrier and not letting sympathy invade, diluting the purity of what it is they do and the fervor with which they do it.

But with Kirby it is not that way, and in the years that I have known him I can see that it has made him more aware of and sympathetic toward structure, and the strength and solace it can give, the support it can have to offer, to people's lives.

So as not to miss any of the calls, I'm hanging out at his house through the Christmas holidays. The baby girl, Payton, two, is doing all sorts of cute things, and Jean Ann is pregnant with their second child. Kirby gets to keep his other daughter, Kirby Nichole, on Wednesdays as well as alternate weekends and like any parent often is aware of the interval of time, sometimes down to the hour, of how long it is before he'll see her.

There are Christmas presents wrapped and set beneath the tree and stockings hanging from the mantel. It doesn't seem like that long ago that we were young. Kirby is telling me a little about firefighters' philosophies—not so much about the cross-grid, the latticework, horizontal and vertical, of technical data (the boiling point of ethyl glycol; the incineration point of phosphene gas; the counterclockwise threading of metric and standard lug nuts; the carrying capacities, in units of amperage, voltage, and wattage, of city power lines). Rather, he's filling me in on the invisible stuff, the important stuff, about how firefighters get along in the world: not so much about what things are like inside the burning structures they fight, but instead, more about what things are like inside the men and women who do the fighting.

We're all just sprawled around on the couch, drinking Cokes and eating hamburgers and chips and watching the baby play. We watched a television show I didn't know existed—I don't have one—*ER*, about emergency room stuff. Kirby scoffed at the inanity of the situations, bent and warped and altered from real life to fit some feeble notions of drama—and after that, a movie we'd rented, *Robin Hood*. It was pretty mainstream, pretty stable and secure. It was as mainstream as I'd tasted in a long time. It tasted good. It was nighttime and we could feel the temperature dropping, could hear the bare branches clacking and waving in the cold front that was moving through the city, riding in like a wave or a gift: a crispness, a coldness, that seemed of course appropriate to Christmas. It would definitely bring fires, and the feeling I got as we sat there watching the movie and waiting for the dispatcher's horn to sound was that this was not a bad thing. Kirby didn't want anyone's stuff to burn up, nor did he want anyone to get hurt, but I have been around captive falcons right before they go hunting, and bird dogs in the morning before they are turned out into a field, and there was that same calm, steady kind of confidence and anticipation, knowing that the call was going to come, and that he would once again get to test and engage himself against the thing he was evidently meant to do.

"Two things," he said, "piss off a firefighter more than anything else. Number one, not having a smoke detector in every room in the house. You don't have to carry out but one burned-up corpse—one charred kid. One's enough. A smoke detector's as simple as it gets. A fire starts, you hear the alarm, and you and your family wake up and walk outside to life. They cost five bucks and if you can't afford 'em the fire department will find a way to get you some.

"Number two gripe is the folks who think a fire's a form of entertainment—as long as it's not their house that burns up." He shook his head. "These silly dumbasses who feel compelled to come get in the way and gawk, or complain, or hell, criticize . . ." So I get to see that part of my fire-altered friend, too. The fires, and the fighting of them, have made him more compassionate to the lives of people in need—but he has been stretched and drawn in the other direction, too, so that he's lost tolerance for stupidity, carelessness, complacency. I see how important it is to him, this thing he volunteers to do, and how the worst possible thing any-one could ever do would be to accuse a volunteer firefighter—or any other kind, for you do not go into a burning building thinking about your salary, if you have one—of not trying hard enough.

It would be such a mistake on the part of the layman to un-derestimate how much they love to fight the fire; it would be such a mistake, too, to underestimate the feelings of relief they savor after they have put the fire down.

We are clean-scrubbed and fresh-dressed from the earlier fire; our smoky, charcoal-smeared clothes are out in the utility room. The washer and dryer are almost always going at his house. I can still smell a little of the smoke on me, but it feels good to be clean. Kirby says that in a long and hot fire the insides of your nostrils will cake black with carbon and that the ebony crust of it, the burned lining, will come tumbling out in fragments for days afterwards, and I wonder what the readers of his tax evaluations must think if they find those black crumbles caught between the pages, like dust from a bag of briquets.

The temperature's dropping fast. We know there's going to be another fire tonight. And about two-thirds of the way through the movie, the call comes.

It's interesting to me the way Kirby and Jean Ann look at each other, as they're listening to the dispatcher's description of the fire, and the summons. It's as if, in the listening—independently but together—each is acknowledging the connection they have to each other, and to the fire—as if there are three things in the room, each with a different relationship to the other: and that each time that fire call rings, these connections and obligations—Kirby to Jean Ann, the fire to Kirby, Jean Ann to Kirby—must be acknowledged.

The dispatcher says that it is a structure fire (a building) and that it is "fully involved," which means that it is really rocking. Kirby is ready to go but is listening intently: he doesn't want to miss the coordinates. The dispatcher gives the street address. "That's right near my mother's apartments," Jean Ann says. Then the dispatcher gives the name of the apartments, which are her mother's.

"Call her," Kirby says, as he and I are leaving. In an instant Jean Ann has, though there is no answer.

It seems to take a long time: a minute to the station, a minute or maybe two or three to get into the station, packed up and suited, and back out. Kirby and I ride in his fire chief's truck with the siren and lights on. This fire is less than half a mile from the one we were just on and it seems to me that they want to pop up in certain areas like toadstools after a rain: that there is sometimes perhaps some itch beneath the surface that desires the fires and does all it can to summon them, even to the point of encouraging mistakes and clumsiness.

We reach the apartments after four or five minutes of hard driving. We enter the dark complex—we can see smoke, and flames—and try and navigate the swirled street patterns, as if in a maze, that will lead us toward that orange glow in the sky. Every left and right turn we take, Kirby says, is taking us toward Jean Ann's mother's apartment—but finally, at the last fork, we see the fire and the other engines and firefighters—we see the burning apartments—and we turn right, where Jean Ann's mother's apartment lies just to the left.

There's nowhere to park without getting in the way of the pumper trucks and their hoses, so Kirby bounces the truck up over the curb and sets it in the grass across the parking lot from the burning buildings, which are an awful sight: tongues of flame racing along the roof eaves, orange fireballs glimpsed through the blackened windows within, and so much thick gray poisonous-looking smoke.

The man who lives in the corner apartment where Kirby has parked his truck on the grass has been peering at the spectacle from behind drawn curtains—all the lights in the complex have been turned off by the firefighters to prevent their being electrocuted as they prepare to enter the flaming structure—and now as we climb out of the big red truck he comes storming out in a rage, furious that we've encroached upon his territory.

He's a little old man with a chip on his shoulder so perversely large that it appears he might have been lying in wait his whole life for Kirby to come driving up and park on his lawn, or rather on the fragment of a corner of the lawn outside the apartment he's renting. He comes hurtling down the slope in his boxer shorts and T-shirt and house slippers, cursing like a banshee—calling out, among other things, "Hey cowboy! Hey cowboy!" He launches himself at Kirby, becomes airborne, like a flimsy paper kite or some tiny Styrofoam toy glider, but falls short of his mark, so that he's rolling around on the ground, still cursing, and now he's on all fours, laboring to get up, so that it looks (and sounds, strangely enough, given the fervor of his exclamations) as if he's praying to Kirby.

Kirby's adrenaline is up—I can tell he's seen a lot, but doesn't know quite how to take this. He stares at the old geezer (who is now upright and kicking with vigor the tires of Kirby's truck with his house shoes), and then shakes his head as if to refocus, and turns and disappears into the center of the fire to find an assignment, something he can do before his men get here. He hands me a walkie-talkie so that I'll look official and tells me to patrol the perimeter and try to keep spectators—of which there are dozens—as far back as possible.

Despite the flames, it's dark, and now in their tinted fire-hat face shields and heavy turnout gear, the firefighters all look the same. There is a tremendous force of energy encircling the fire, the hopeful presence of frantic, industrial might: powerful portable generators humming on all the trucks, and radios squelching and squalling, and different teams of firefighters running in ordered directions to various sections of the burning complex, their boots heavy on the pavement and across the sodden lawn as ribbons of water surge from taut hoses and cascade onto the flames, slowing their spread but not yet shutting them down.

Walking in circles around the burning apartment, trying not to hyperventilate at the spectacle, the most dominant impression beyond the speed and power with which things are happening is that this is not some drama staged for the screen in Hollywood but is that seemingly rarest of things, the real thing—and you can see what a living thing, what an awful animal, the fire is. You can see it bulging and writhing; you can tell how, when they apply water to one end, the fire hunkers down in that spot but almost simultaneously billows larger somewhere else.

It's so fucking big. The men and women running into and around it are so tiny.

The suit's heavy as lead. I'm tired just from my frantic circling. When I tell spectators to "get back, please," they ignore me, as if my words of politeness were some insignificant breeze, so that on the next lap I have to shout at them, "Get the fuck back, motherfuckers"—trying to break the spell of hypnosis that is being cast upon them (they are edging ever closer to the fire, drawn, faces upturned), and to replace it, jolt it, with fear.

Some of the firefighters are entering the burning rooms, attacking the fire directly, while others of them are being deployed into those apartments that are smoke-filled but not yet burning and are searching those rooms for the young and the elderly, or anyone who might have been felled by the smoke, which is usually what kills the victims, rather than flames or heat. You always check the closets, and under the bed; a lot of times, kids will hide when they're scared, just waiting for the trouble to pass. And they're sure not going to come out and say "Hello, here I am" when some big-booted stranger in a dark mask and breathing gear comes stomping through their house, appearing from out of the smoke, swinging a pike staff.

In Larry Brown's wonderful memoir of his firefighting days, *On Fire*, he tells how dogs and cats trapped in a burning house will go get in the bathtub, whether there's any water or not, and how that's always where you find them, dead and curled up, suffocated. Kirby has told me a somewhat similar thing: that if you're trapped in a room that's on fire, or full of smoke, you can open the cabinet under the sink in the bathroom, twist off the U-pipe beneath, and breathe that air, a few minutes' worth of cool air coming from the place wherever it is that the water goes.

It's one thing to read about it in textbooks or to have Kirby tell me about it, in a slow and leisurely storytelling way over a beer or something, and quite another to see it unfolding in fast motion. I keep circling the burning apartments. Now firefighters are up on the roof, cutting vents into it with the machine roars of their Sawzalls—a reciprocating saw—to ventilate the fire, to release heat, to help kill it (when it tries to come rushing through those new vents, they will be there waiting for it, and will attack it)— and other firefighters are still storming into the burning building and smashing at it with their fire tools, evil-looking mauls and pikes. Occasionally I get probing, suspicious looks from some of the officers with radios, and from the firefighters themselves, but they seem able to sense, in that zone or loop of unspoken communication, that whatever I am doing, though not readily explicable to them, is all right and not a menace, but a help.

I cannot impress, in these sentences, the pace at which things are happening—the speed and force with which problems are evaluated and decisions made.

I see Kirby disappear into the back side of the building, manning, with one other partner, a heavy hose. If you don't have enough people on a hose that's too big, it'll lift you off the ground when the water surges through it, like the trunk of an elephant, and smash you against the roof, then thrash wildly, anaconda-like, all over the place, deadly brass nozzle flopping and snapping every which way.

Kirby says that when you get into a blackened, still-burning building—unable to see, because of the smoke (flashlights only make it worse)—you always have to go in with a partner. A lot of the time you're crawling around on all fours and you can't even see your partner, even though in those situations you keep in physical contact with them—never more than an arm's length away, and if for some reason you do become separated, each partner should freeze and then slowly sweep their fire tool (like an ax) in a circle until they bump it against either their smoke-invisible partner, or against their partner's similarly reaching, searching ax. Kirby says that that's about as scary as it gets: as if you and your partner are crawling to certain death, but that you have to go forward and meet it because it's what you are and what you do, and the fire is what it is, and it's not right for one to exist without or unopposed by the other. Of this, Larry Brown has written, "You have to meet the thing, is what it is . . . and for the firefighter it is the fire. It has to be faced and defeated so that you prove to yourself that you meet the measure of the job. You cannot turn your back on it, as much as you would like to be in cooler air."

You crawl on through the fire-gutted, hanging tentacles of

drooping electrical wires, Kirby says, knowing that the power's been shut off but terrified that some well-meaning onlooker, some dipshit, or even some rookie is going to notice that the main breaker's been turned off and will flip it back on, thinking that it's awful dark in there, that maybe the firefighters could use a little light.

Kirby says that when it gets like that, the senses are incredible—that you feel like you're on another planet—an inflammation of the senses, a hyper-awareness, so that if you knew how to, you could almost read Braille through the heavy leather gloves: every cell inflamed and fully maxed out with physical and intellectual receptivity. Of course it's addictive—if you survive it.

Kirby says if you get lost in a house where you're fighting a fire, or separated from your partner and can't find your way out, you can drop to your knees and crawl until you come across one of the braided fire hoses. He says there are nubby arrows in the weave of them that always angle back to the source—that by feeling the fabric of the hose you can tell in which direction the pumper truck and safety lie, and crawl back out.

If you get trapped by smoke and flame—an injury, perhaps—you can take a knife or ax and cut a slit in the fire hose. The water will surge straight up through the slit and spread itself in a fan-shaped hissing spray known as a "water curtain," which can keep the fire from sweeping over that area for a few seconds more.

I'm wishing Kirby hadn't gone into the burning building. All I can see is darkness and flames, darkness and flames. It seems like far more firefighters are going in than are coming out. It seems as if the fire is swallowing them. Sometimes during a fire bats will swarm in great flocks, trying to fly back down the chimney to rescue their young.

I wonder if Jean Ann's ever seen him in a real fire, or only in training fires. (The firefighters relish the destruction of old condemned buildings, because often they can obtain permission to torch them—and in so doing, are given the chance to practice, under controlled circumstances—to perfect their craft.)

On their hips, the firefighters each wear PALS, or PASS—Personal Alert Safety Systems. If the firefighter is motionless for thirty seconds, the device emits a piercing shriek, which lets all the other firefighters know one of their members is down—though finding the source of the alarm can be difficult, with all the other noise of the fire and (hopefully) smoke alarms. The wails of the PASS also bounce off ceilings, walls, and floors, further confusing the firefighters. They're taught to freeze in unison when they hear one, control their breathing, open their ear flaps, and cup their hands perpendicular to their faces to get as accurate a fix as possible. They're expected, when this happens, to change gears, change mentalities, in a split second—to go from thinking in terms of assault and attack to thinking solely of rescue: defense, rather than offense.

The PASS can be self-activated, too, by a firefighter in trouble; you don't have to wait the full thirty seconds to deploy it. The trouble is that sometimes firefighters, caught up in the rush of adrenaline upon receiving a fire call, or entering a burning building, get a severe kind of tunnel vision and, despite their training, forget to activate the PASS. And then when they're lying face down, unconscious from the smoke, it's too fucking late.

It's all darkness and confusion to me, speed and flames. The fire trucks' generators are hooked up to giant fans that are humming and roaring, sawing the night with their sound and killing, or bending and routing, the heat and smoke with their cool winds. I hear someone murmur the word "backdraft." This is the dreaded phenomenon that occurs when a fire, straining against its limits, is compressed by a lack of oxygen but has nonetheless superheated all the materials around it, almost to the point of spontaneous ignition—a bright chrome teapot leaping suddenly into incandescent flame, or a painting on a wall flashing to fire like a match being struck—or an entire room, or an entire building, and the firefighters within, igniting spontaneously in this manner. I hear the word again. I can't tell if they mean that one's occurring, or that the fire is approaching the conditions suited for one. (Blackened windows, pressurized gray smoke leaking from beneath doorways and window cracks, windowpanes rattling and trembling their frames.) All that's required for combustion in a situation like this—the whole building superheated to or beyond the ignition point—is the introduction of even a trace more oxygen, and the mere opening of a door can give the fire access to the welcoming flood of air.

Now the ranks of the firefighters that are surging around me, running in and out of the building, are carrying the message that one of their number is missing, though they can hear no PASS squall. Immediately I look for Kirby, whom I do not see, but a minute later he appears and begins questioning the squad that's missing one. Kirby wants to know where the firefighter was last seen and what he was last doing, and they point to a second story bedroom window that is bright with flame and say that he was going to try to go in above it, through the attic, and ventilate it.

I can't quite follow what's going on after that, but I hear the term "ventilate" repeated, and rather than bringing a hook-and-ladder truck around, Kirby runs up to the back patio of one of the downstairs apartments, lifts one of those big-ass black wrought-iron patio chairs up over his head, runs back out into the yard, takes a couple of frenzied, waltzing spins with it, and hurls it up against the yellow-flame window—and I know that in the morning his forty-year-old back is going to feel that one.

There is another minute or two before word circulates around to us that they found the missing firefighter—that he had gotten dizzy in the heat and smoke up in the attic and had fallen through part of the ceiling and been stuck for a minute or two but that he pulled himself out and got out all right.

The fight continues.

I continue circling the building, urging people back. It is still drawing onlookers and they are still staring hypnotized at it—some of them growing more comfortable with it and edging closer. Kirby says that he likes to fight a hot fire in cold weather and that when it's really cold he relishes going into the burning building, just to warm up.

There are patches of moments where it seems strangely like Mardi Gras: fragments of time and space that rest on the outside of the thing that is going on between the fire and the firefighters— the weave of that thing being cinched tight. On the other side of the parking lot, not thirty yards from the apartment complex that's burning, a fortyish woman in a white terrycloth bathrobe, not very tightly closed, is standing languidly in the darkness of the doorway of her own apartment, watching, smoking a cigarette like a movie star, elbow tucked into one hand, legs crossed, blowing lazy smoke rings as the leaping flames occasionally illuminate her: darkness to light, darkness to light.

Watching Kirby throw that chair through the window reminds me of an image from twenty years ago. There was this pizza restaurant called Major Domo's, just a strip mall restaurant in Houston, but it had a gimmick designed to draw people in: a large plate glass window through which you could watch the chefs, all with baker's hats and white aprons, as they twirled and tossed immense droopy, saggy flying saucers of dough.

There's no explaining the surges and hormonal profiles of adolescent blood. For no reason that we knew of then, and still don't, it came into our minds (watching moths flutter against the street lights, perhaps) to come running up out of the darkness on summer nights and launch ourselves, hurl ourselves spread-eagled, eyes bulging wide and mouths open in expressions of mock surprise, hurtle through the air (dog-paddling as if in space) and then land hard against that great vertical pane of glass, striking it so hard as to make it reverberate within its frame.

I suppose the object was to try to disrupt the pizza-toss—to cause the chefs to pause and stare at us as the pizza, momentarily forgotten, came down on top of them. We never quite got the desired effect, but we did distract them enough to cause a few two-handed saves.

We would hang there against the glass for some fraction of a second as if struck there, like giant tree frogs, before sliding slowly down and then running back off into the night. We struck at random—we might be driving around, bored, and one of us would say, "Let's do a Major Domo tonight"—and the object of the game became, over the course of the summer, to go all the way to the edge: to guess just how hard you could leap against the big plate glass window without crashing through. We never did, though surely we came close, and it used to please us no end to consider how it must have affected the lives of the dough-tossers: the chefs wondering each morning, perhaps—maybe even upon awakening—whether the window leapers would come that night. And tossing the dough, twirling it, but also squinting, peering out into the darkness, watching and waiting. Sometimes it was more fun to not go by there, to not leap—to let the tension build for days, even weeks.

Another thing the captain of the fire department and I would do, twenty years ago, was to pull up at construction sites after school and walk right in among the half-framed timbers of a place, with our own hammers and saws, and begin hammering and nailing—pounding goofy little pieces of scrap wood into goofy little places, or fooling with screwdrivers as if checking the preliminary electrical wiring boxes, and calling out instructions and measurements to one another, always appearing brisk and unquestioning—hurling bullshit to the redline, trying to see where it would max out. Subcontractors were forever coming and going, especially on the larger projects, and even now I can re-member the deliciousness, the sparkling in the blood as we bluffed our way through work—a thing like adrenaline, but goofier—a yearning for chaos, for making a little disorder out of what we doubtless perceived as too much order, too many constraints and boundaries.

Now Kirby pulls burning people out of buildings, saves their lives and properties—hurls himself against the crumbling, burn-ing city as if single-handedly trying to prop it up. The change amazes both of us. I studied geology in college, learned how time carved valleys and mountains and spread the plains flat, but time is no slouch at carving our own lives anew, assembling order of disorder in stretches of time far shorter than millennia.

You can see the fire shrinking as the fighters begin to gain the upper hand. They will always do this—no fire lasts forever—and it's only a question of course how much damage will be done. This fire is disappearing, and as it does, the apartments seem to be losing what made them alive—flaming, raging, reckless—and becoming instead the blackened, gutted husk of a thing. Finally they are only a smoking, sodden ruins, and now there comes the monotony of salvage and cleanup. The firefighters cover ev-erything they can with plastic tarps before moving through the interior, hosing down anything still smoking. This is good firefighting—there's no sense packing up and getting back to the station, tired and dirty, only to have to turn right around and race back out half an hour later because a stray coal or ember found a little breeze and fanned back into flame. It's good public rela-tions work, too, which is always important. Kirby says that little things like that—trying to stack the burned furniture out of the way, or protecting what can be protected in the midst of such carnage—order amid disorder—really helps soften the blow for property owners. You'd be surprised, he says, how much difference it makes to them when they come back to view the damage to notice that someone was thinking about them.

I'm helping carry boxes out from the hollowed, char-blackened apartment. (Investigations will later show that an untended candle started this fire.) The renters are there and one of the shoeboxes of photos, with which they fled, has spilled its photos, and in the darkness they can't find them. We search with flashlights in the bushes below the second story window and find them, drenching wet, but still with the likeness, the images; we salvage them.

Now it is over and the trucks are loading up and pulling away, letting the night fill back in with darkness and silence. The firefighters have shed their coats and glisten with sweat, ghostly like angels in their white T-shirts beneath the suspenders of their fire pants. Char-faced, they guzzle Gatorade and various sugary drinks; they drain their hoses and roll them back up in neat but basic folds. At the station the next day, they will clean them and dry them and refold them into more intricate packages designed for ease and speed of unfolding. They will coil them up in reverse horseshoe folds, straight finish and Dutchman folds; in flat loads and reverse and split lays, in accordion load folds, and in donut roll and twin donut roll folds. They will practice knots, refill their air tanks, and clean the trucks until they gleam again, bright as the fire itself. Once a week they will go to a continuing education class designed to further cram their brains with knowledge that will help them prove counterweights to the fire, and once a month they will go to an all-day training station to stay sharp, whether they have been having any recent fire calls or not, though in a big city like Houston, there will always be fires—some place in it will almost always be burning, and if it is within their territory, they will be rushing to it and grappling with it, as if trying to wrestle it, to press it back into the earth or wherever it came from.

I noticed at these and other fires I attended, as well as at the training sessions, two basic profiles of individuals. No one person will fit any other's profile, but I was struck by how it seemed there were only two types of firefighters. (Perhaps if you draw the parameters loose and wide enough, there are only two types of anything.) There seemed to be the thinkers, like Kirby, who loaded their minds with the vertical and horizontal components of possibility—the ones who are able, through repetition and practice, to throw back the awful and intoxicating tunnel vision that can occur in a fire and can instead look down upon the scene (even when involved in the midst of it), as a hawk might look down on a field from two miles up. These people are generally the leaders—the captains, the chiefs.

There are also what could be called, unfairly in many instances, good old boys—men and women who would work just as hard or harder to save your life and property but who prefer to hurl themselves physically at the fire, under orders and command.

It's possible you could call them thrill seekers—they often moonlight as policemen, security guards, and ambulance drivers—and I think the common denominator these hurlers have with the thinkers is that they desire, have a need bordering almost on addiction, to feel life deeply, sharply—with either their minds or their bodies—and that they also want to do good, for any of a million different reasons.

This specific, unspoken desire in the blood bonds them as close as family; in many ways it reminds me of the unspokenness of animal language. The sudden leap, without transition, from full stop to full start—usually in the middle of the night—when the dispatcher's horn sounds in each of their homes . . . Kirby's told me that many times he and Jean Ann have been sitting on the couch and have paused and looked at each other just moments before their horn goes off, somehow knowing that a fire is burning in their territory, and that a call is coming through.

A leader like Kirby needs hawk vision—needs the ability to

juggle the horizontal and vertical matrices—but he also needs the animal knowledge of the body—the awareness of grace, or its dangerous, confusing absence.

Kirby tells me of one of the first fully involved structure fires for which he was a captain. It was in the home of a trophy big game hunter. The house was full of smoke and visibility was almost nil, save for the flaming heads of rhinos, lions, elephants, kudu. They were fighting hard but were losing ground and at great risk of losing contact with each other. The whole time, Kirby was antsy as hell, for this and other inexplicable reasons, and finally he made the decision to withdraw—to get the hell out. They'd done all they could—they'd been called too late—and it was out of hand.

Thirty seconds after he had all the men out, the second floor gave way—it wasn't a typical wood-frame floor, but poured concrete—and it smashed pancake-flat onto the space where his firefighters had been crawling only seconds before.

Then, as if for punctuation, the fire found the ammo cache, and the fusillade of large-caliber bullets in vast quantities—ordnance—began.

The firefighters turned their attention to the other surrounding homes—spraying them down to keep them cool, to keep them from igniting simply from the radiant heat of the house fire next to them. To someone unfamiliar with firefighting, it must have looked like they'd lost their minds—the house in the center burning more or less merrily while the firefighters hosed the hell out of the unburned ones next to it.

Not that he was always cool or graceful, or possessed of hawk vision. Kirby says that on the first structure fire he ever went out on—a green-ass rookie—he got the tunnel vision so bad that he jumped off the truck (his was the first on the scene), and did indeed run into the wrong house, busting the door down to do so, much to the dismay of the occupants inside. They kept asking him why he was in their house and he told them to never mind that, to help him haul the heavy hose up the stairs to the attic, where he believed the fire was hiding.

It seems like a long time ago, that. He's taken to the profession—his other, alternate, second profession—as if he'd been born for it, fitting comfortably into the huge responsibility of captain, and being named Firefighter of the Year by his district.

We're driving home so he can tell Jean Ann that it wasn't her mother's apartment that burned but the one next to it, and that everyone's all right—driving sweat-stained and grubby with the windows down, the cold December air cooling us as if we still carry the heat of the fire with us—and I think about the notion that Kirby has been ready for this all along, has been made for this, and has just in the last several years stepped into the fit of it.

I'm remembering a couple of other seemingly mindless games we used to play in high school. The first one, I realize in retrospect, presaged the salvage operations of fires and spoke, even then, to the strange duality we all have in varying degrees within us: an attraction to order, and yet an attraction to disorder. The necessary way the two must bind together.

I can't believe we used to do this, but when there was a girl Kirby was dating, we would sometimes sneak into her house while she and her family were out to dinner. I might as well call it what it was, breaking and entering, for almost always we'd slither in over a windowsill, or find a key under a doormat.

Once inside (after the requisite trip to the refrigerator), we'd completely rearrange the bedroom of the girl who was the object of Kirby's affections. I don't mean in a disorderly way; far from it. We'd just rotate things. If the bed were on the north wall, for instance, we'd move it neatly to the east wall, and move the chest of drawers to the south wall, and so forth, a neat and precise reordering of things. It is no small miracle that we didn't get our asses shot off. This was in the 1970s, right in the last tiny seam of time when you could still do something like this. Still, we were lucky.

The second thing I'm remembering speaks ever more closely to the fireman Kirby was to become. There was this game we would play in our biology class that we called "Penetrations." Back then, it seemed to have no logic, but the way we played it—and God knows how we created it in the first place; we just started doing it one day, as if in a trance, or a dream—was to see which of us could, during the middle of lecture, walk up the closest to the front of the room, where the teacher (order! authority!) was lecturing. The goal was to get all the way to the center—to go all the way to the blackboard without being questioned or challenged.

The tension was incredible. I would get up from my seat and walk a few steps forward, then turn and go back to my seat. The point of my forward penetration then became the mark for Kirby to meet and surpass. He'd wait several minutes, then go as far as he dared.

You couldn't pretend a pencil had rolled off your desk, or be throwing away a piece of trash. You just had to go for it—had to walk up there barehanded.

It was strangely hypnotic, between the three of us—the teacher and Kirby and me. There's no telling now what she thought. We didn't say anything, weren't disruptive, were good students. Often she'd fix her icy blue eyes on whichever of us was daring to come forward, and we, like somnambulists, one at a time, would watch her. She never spoke a word to us about it. I can still remember the strange, unarticulated power of it; the thrill, too, of getting right in close to the heart of a dangerous thing.

That good flushed feeling in the blood, afterward.

———————

We pull up in Kirby's drive. He's saved a baby before, has seen dead people before, has seen people burned up and perforated and lanced and crushed. He's burned himself badly—his body is mottled with ember scars, like constellations—and has torn a knee, twisted an ankle, broken a shoulder, etc., etc. So far, he's always come back from a fire.

I can feel the relaxation. I can feel the charged new ends of things, the senses whittled sharper. It's very relaxing, very nice.

It's 3:00 a.m. The lights at his house are the only ones lit on the street. Lit up like that, his house looks like a castle.

Jean Ann meets him at the door, as she has hundreds of times, and he meets her.

It's not about being a hero. It's about being alive. It's about being the counterweight to a thing: about being connected to some force that's out there.

We shower, then sleep lightly, waiting for more. He's different from how he was in high school. The fire has altered him.

THE RAGE OF THE SQUAT KING

BACK WHEN I WAS A COMPETITIVE WEIGHTLIFTER, there was a man we revered greatly, who was the world's strongest squatter.

The squat is a lift that combines brute strength in equal measure with technique. You place the bar, loaded with its ponderous weight, across your back. You lift it up out of a rack and take one and a half or two steps backward. You wear a thick leather belt cinched tight around your belly, to keep your intestines from blowing out under all the pressure, and you wrap your knees tightly with elastic bandages to keep the somewhat fragile, intricate arrangement of ligaments, tendons, and cartilage from uncoiling, snapping and spraying out everywhere like the broken springs from a Swiss watch—but that's all the support you get. Other than that, you're on your own.

You sink down into a crouch, with that weight on your back. It's heavy. It tries to keep driving you down, all the way down.

My lifter friends and I would occasionally see Fred Hatfield, the champion of this lift—aka "Dr. Squat"—perform his greatness on television, on obscure Saturday afternoon sports specials.

He would snort and do this odd little shuffle step, and then rush out to the bar that rested waiting for him in the squat rack. He'd be howling and huffing and puffing, rolling his eyes and his head like a Chinese dragon.

He would run up to the bar and grab it and shake it, get

under it and maneuver his back beneath it, wriggling himself into position—not unlike someone taking pleasure in his lover's embrace—and then he would lift the weights free of the rack and back out with the horrible weights draped across his back, the iron bar bending and bouncing, there was so much weight on it. He would plant his feet, look skyward, huff twice more, a third time, and then he would go down.

His mouth would open in a groan as he sank, and his eyes would roll and bulge as if about to pop. Veins would explode into view everywhere, not just in his arms and legs and shoulders, chest and neck, but in his face, in his hands, across his nose, *everywhere*, with his face turning red and then purple, his knees and elbows quivering.

And then the weight would begin going back up—being driven slowly, infinitesimally, upward again.

Twenty years later, I decided to track him down—to see if he was still squatting. I visited him at the headquarters of the World Wrestling Federation in Stamford, Connecticut, where he had taken a job training the wrestlers how to get bigger and stronger.

When I enter his office, my first thought is how very much he seems not to belong in this place, this building, with its well-dressed executives walking down the silent carpeted hallways. He's dressed in a white sweat suit and tennis shoes, a red T-shirt, and wears a blazing pink baseball cap with the words SIMPLY THE BEST on it. He looks trim, almost nautical. He's neither tall nor short, nor is he really either heavy or light.

We walk past office after office of accountants and public relations folks—so many young, pale, skinny white men, all the same age, all slightly skittish as we pass, and all seeming to fail to exude—is it presumptuous to say this?—any semblance of spirit whatsoever.

"The pencil-necks," Hatfield mutters under his breath. He shakes his head. "Let's just say I don't have very much *corporate acumen.*" He's rolling off the balls of his feet, rising up on his toes with each step, and maybe it's just that the gearing of his body is all wrong for him to be walking without any burden.

In his office, he has a computer perched before him, a big one, such as you might use to pilot an airliner. He prints out his résumé or rather a twenty-page partial résumé for me, and though it would be interesting were it someone else's—a kind of a caricature of some kind of superman—I scan it somewhat impatiently.

Gymnastics champion, soccer champion, author of sixty books, strength consultant to world class athletes such as Evander Holyfield and Hakeem Olajuwon; schooled in Naval Communications, Pensacola, Florida, for top-secret and crypto-clearance with the Office of Naval Intelligence . . . Taught statistics at Newark State College, 1972–1973 . . . Computer programmer for Pratt and Whitney Aircraft, enlisted as U.S. Marine Corps decathlete, cross-country . . .

"Did you ever have the feeling that this lift—the squat—was designed perfectly for your body?" I ask him. "That you had the perfect leverage and musculature for it?"

Hatfield doesn't really bristle, but I've touched some nerve, way down there. "Everybody thinks I excelled because of a God-given gift," he says, his voice a bit thick with emotion. "Obviously, I had the genetics. But my genetics alone weren't enough to get me beyond a certain level." He shrugs. "I spent several years squatting around only five hundred fifty pounds. I was *wallowing* in mediocrity. And I decided: Hey, enough is enough. I'm going to develop my *own* science."

He punches away on the computer, drawing up data.

"I began the arduous task of categorizing all the various factors that could affect strength," he says. "I fashioned a working definition of strength as ability to exert musculoskeletal force"—he's speaking carefully now, reading from his computer screen—"given existing constraints stemming from: Structural, Anatomical, Physiological, Biochemical, Psychoneural/Psychosocial, External and Environmental factors."

"Is that all?" I ask, like a smart guy, standing there in the shadows of five hundred pounds, but Hatfield either doesn't hear me or ignores me.

"I cataloged thirty-five or forty different factors which must be accounted for to truly maximize strength," he explains. "I used eight different ranking technologies and applied multiple-factor analyses . . . in the statistical sense of the word.

"Significant factors affecting a squat include muscle fiber arrangement, musculoskeletal leverage, freedom of movement between muscle fibers, sensitivity of glandular functions . . ."

"This is very enlightening," I tell him.

Hatfield corrects me. "It's revolutionary," he says.

"I considered *each point* along the ATP/ADP glycolytic pathway," he says in a quieter voice—almost conspiratorial. "I made graphs of the various percentages of the energy-delivering processes over time—CP-splitting, ATP-splitting, oxidation, glycolysis. I thought"—Hatfield's almost whispering—"how will I be able to exert maximum force and how can I *augment* that application? And that, my friend, is why I broke world records.

"There is a place you go to," Hatfield tells me, speaking carefully, precisely. "Call it out-of-body experience, call it state of mind, call it whatever you want—that is not achievable except by the most intense and pure focusing of your passion. And only after years of intense concentration are you able to reach this zone. It's a place where the movement of your lift becomes perfect; it's not even a part of your consciousness. You're simply at one with the weights on your back: you're part of the iron, and it's part of you. You go down, and you come up."

Hatfield leans forward, as if delivering a promise. "You could literally blow a muscle out in the process, and you'd never know it. You can't hear the crowd screaming. You never feel the sweat that is dripping down into your eyes. *Nothing.*

"And then all of a sudden you're done, and you've broken a world record by over a hundred pounds—and you literally cannot remember having done it.

"I got to the point where I was able to enter that state *at will*," he says.

———————

Hatfield grew up in an orphanage, in Cromwell, Massachusetts, where he was sent with his three older sisters when he was seven.

"Certainly I knew from that early age that I was not the same as the other kids. They all had mothers and dads, and all I had was seventy-two non-sibling *rivals* more than anything else. You had to fight for seconds at the dinner table. You had to fight for just a little affection from your counselor. But it was kind of a strange relationship, because on the one hand there was that inadvertent rivalry, and on the other hand, there was a sense of protectiveness and camaraderie and shared passion amongst all of us."

Fred and I take the elevator to the top of the WWF building and walk out onto the rooftop patio. It's a hot, hazy summer day, but there's a good wind blowing, up high like that, and it's a nice patio, with picnic tables and a view of the Long Island Sound, sailboats in their slips, blue water, and forests and hills beyond, steeples and rooftops visible through the trees.

"There's my home, out there," Hatfield says, pointing across the bay to a steeple rising from the woods on the farthest hill. "We live right there," he says, with a pleasant, almost childish satisfaction. I like how long Hatfield stares out there, and the comfort I sense it fills him with. He stands there looking out across the water just a hair longer than you or I might.

Next, he takes me down to the gym that's available for WWF employees. It's a nice gym, of course, with a leg press, a squat rack, and a modest amount of iron. Dumbbells, barbells, etc. But it's obvious Hatfield doesn't train here. It doesn't have enough weight, and more importantly it doesn't *feel* quite right. It doesn't have that lingering echo of grunts and groans and shouts. Hatfield admits that he trains at home now—he tried to work out here, but there were a few problems, not the least of which were technical. He points out with pride the powerlifting platforms he designed—"floating platforms," he calls them, built out of polyurethane and hard rubber interlayering, to cushion the floor against the heavy weights being dropped on it, as happens at the end of a heavy deadlift, or any Olympic lift.

Hatfield explains that the whole building is a concrete frame, so that it's rigid, and that even with his floating platforms, the whole building would shake whenever he was working out with his heavy weights. It made the pencil-necks and the "B-B's" (as he calls them) nervous, but the most significant complication was that it kept shutting down all the computer systems. At the end of one heavy lift, the building shook so hard it did about fifty thousand dollars worth of damage to the computers, and they were down for a week.

"I don't have very much corporate acumen," Hatfield says again.

In the orphanage, it wasn't as if everyone was chosen except for young Fred. That might be too horrible to imagine—seventy-two other orphans being selected for adoption, while year after year, strange Fred, young Fred, and then not-so-young Fred was bypassed, every time. That might be too much for any human body, cell-split or not, to stand up to, though who knows what the real outer limits are? Would he have gone on to squat past his record eleven hundred pounds, to twelve or thirteen hundred pounds? Probably not. Surely his record is very near the outer limits.

Several kids from the Home were adopted. And Fred had his chance.

"It was a family from New Jersey," he says. "These people had a rich grandfather. In fact, as I understand it, the grandfather—I'm remembering things that haven't been in my mind since the time I was twelve—he had something to do with the machinery that Friendly's Ice Cream used to make ice cream. He invented all that stuff."

They chose Fred, this strange young bull, to go with them on a trip across the country that summer—to take him out on a test run, a ninety-day trial.

Except they didn't want to take Fred's three sisters, who were also in the Home—one younger, nine, and two older, thirteen and fourteen. Fred was twelve.

He went anyway. Just to say he'd been. And to check it out: to give it a chance.

They drove west in a big brand new 1955 Cadillac, a yellow hard-top. The deal was that the grandfather, who wasn't going on the trip, would let the mother and father take his Caddy on this trip if they brought the grandmother along with them. There was a daughter, too, who was Fred's age.

They left New Jersey and went through Pennsylvania. Fred remembers that, because it was the first time he'd ever seen an oil well. And even though they didn't have any air conditioner, they drove in the day and stopped at motels in the evenings. There weren't many superhighways back then, if any, so they went through a lot of small towns. It was all new to Fred, stuff that he'd never seen before, maybe never even dreamed before, and it must have wedged in his mind like a crack of light: must have pried open some spaces inside him, like roots spreading, and tried to let something else in. Some abatement of the franticness and rage, though perhaps it only allowed in oxygen, which enabled the flame to burn brighter.

"We stopped at all the typical tourist places," Fred says. "The Painted Desert, the Grand Canyon . . . We drove through Yosemite, including the tree, which was almost impossible to do, with that big brand new Cadillac . . . There was only about one inch on either side of the car."

It didn't work out. Fred rode in the back seat and knew, they all knew, it wasn't going to work out. He sat back there with the daughter, this quintessential American family, and surely they must have been able to sense even then his otherness, his animal-ness—his hot raw heart burning in the back seat of their car like a lump of lead that has just. been pulled from a bed of coals.

"We were driving across the desert," Fred says. "I remember the guy was driving, the father—his name was Emmett Huntz—and I had my arm out the window with a little piece of paper in my hand, and it was flapping in the breeze, making a horrible racket, and I was doing it just to piss everybody in the car off.

"And all of a sudden Emmett was swerving the car wildly like this!"—Hatfield waves his arms, flaps them like a stork's wings.

"Well, I come to find out I had my arm out the window so far that it was about to get taken off by this bridge that we were passing!

"It became very clear to me that I didn't want to have any part of this family," he says. "And I missed my three sisters, who were at the orphanage *without me*. I felt sort of a sense of protectiveness, and I said, 'There's no way these three girls are going to grow up without my influence.' And so I opted to go back to the orphanage."

———

You mention the squat to Fred Hatfield, and the old lifter will talk to you about concentric strength, static strength, and eccentric strength; about starting strength and explosive strength. He will talk about tissue leverage (interstitial and intracellular leverage stemming from fat deposits, sarcoplasmic content, satellite cell proliferation and the accumulation of fluid). Extent of hyperplasia (cell splitting). Stroke volume of the left ventricle. Ejection fraction of the left ventricle. Motor unit recruitment capacity.

"Do you ever get under a heavy weight," I ask him, "and find yourself thinking, 'I can't get this today?' And if so, what do you do?"

There is a long pause while Fred searches his memory valiantly for a time when he might have been mortal.

"If I ever have felt that," he says finally, speaking very carefully, "it was only extremely occasionally. Offhand, I can't remember any."

"Have you ever had to scramble, to continue training?" I ask him. "Have you ever been in a situation where you didn't have access to a good gym?"

Hatfield rejects that notion out of hand; bats it away.

"You have to learn to take control of your life!" he cries. "You have to ensure that doesn't happen!

"Only a fool would go into the desert without water!"

"Have you ever felt *passion*, Rick?" he asks me later. "Do you know what it is?"

"Well, yes," I begin, "I've—"

"Passion," says Dr. Fred Hatfield. "Allow me.

"Passion," he says, "is not *'the need to achieve.'* Instead, it is a burning desire to exceed *all* bounds!" He pauses, then says, "*It is not a 'commitment to excellence;' rather, it is utter disdain for anything less!*

"NOT *'setting goals,'*" says Dr. Squat. "*Goals too often prescribe performance limits!*"

There is a stern pause.

"*There is* not *force of skill or muscle.* Rather, it is the *explosive, calamitous, force of will!*"

It should not surprise a gentle reader that just a few weeks before my visit, at the age of fifty, he broke the record for the one-hundred-ninety-eight-pound bodyweight class, with a squat of eight hundred sixty pounds.

Hatfield drives me out to his house, where I meet his friendly and hospitable wife, Joy, who also used to be a competitive powerlifter. I look at pictures of their children and pet their dog T-Bone, who they adopted from a pound. He's a fine dog; it's a fine nuclear family.

On the drive back, we get caught in a traffic jam. Hatfield's driving. I ask him if he has any secret rituals in preparing for a re-cord squat, such as the eleven-hundred-pound lift that he and Joy referred to as "The Giant Squat." Once more, Hatfield referred to being able to "go to another place."

"There's a place within each person's mind where there is no pain, no negative force," he tells me once more. "Where only pos-itive forces dwell. And that's the place I need to be, to put that kind of weight on my back and have the capacity to ignore the sound of the crowd, and the pain; the fact that my shoelace is untied, or that the judge is picking his nose—or any of the other disconcerting cues in my immediate environment. Those things must be completely ignored in order to execute the task at hand, which is nothing more than sheer movement: going down, and coming up.

"I can't feel anything, I can't see anything—and yet I must feel and see everything, at the same time. And it's a matter of pure movement, with no other sensations creating distracting noise."

The jackhammers blast away, up ahead of us. Cement mixers groan and growl and roar. It's some kind of construction ahead, instead of a wreck, or perhaps it's both. Hatfield jerks in his seat, as if willing himself to be free of the jam. "I don't know what happened with this traffic," he says. "Aw, *Gawd*," he huffs. "We're only half a mile from our exit."

The jackhammers chatter louder. "It's right *there*," he says, "the exit that we're trying to get to." He exhales. "In sight of it!" he says. Blows out steam; rocks, fidgets.

To try and calm him down, I brag on that dog of his—that sweet hound, T-Bone.

Hatfield looks uncomfortable for a minute, uncertain.

"I wouldn't know the first thing about what constitutes a good dog," he says finally. "If it'll not crap on my rug, I like it." He laughs nervously. "That's why T-Bone is still there. And he loves kids, too. We got him at the pound when he was less than a year old."

"First dog you've ever had?" I ask.

"No, out in California, we had a couple of Lhasa apsos. They were fine, you know? They weren't real nuts about being on a leash, but other than that, they were fine. Then we moved to a bigger house, and they turned—I swear to God—into Satan. They started chewing up my furniture, peeing everywhere. I had to sell 'em both.

"Then we got a pit bull. But then he ate a Brittany. So then we had another dog, sort of like a dingo type of dog. And I just couldn't housebreak that dog for anything. I have not had good luck with dogs," Hatfield concludes.

"Somebody had already worked with T-Bone, though," he adds. "It was obvious. Because he would fetch, and heel, and sit, and all of those things." Hatfield stares out at the glacier of traffic, none of it going anywhere. "He appeared to be a very well-trained dog already, when we got him from the pound."

I remembered the way he used to rage, when he would approach that iron bar in the olden days. What I think might have finally happened within him is that the calm has finally arrived, or almost arrived—that it has come as if from within the iron, leaving it like a fever.

Serenity lay beneath the rage, it seems, but surely it must have been a long way down there, and the iron, the weight, so heavy.

WHALE SONG

UNTIL 1970, WE DIDN'T EVEN KNOW THAT THEY SANG. The military knew it—while listening, ever vigilant, for the approach of Russian submarines during the Cold War, they had been hearing and recording whale song for parts of a couple of decades—but in the world above, we heard nothing, knew nothing. When the first recordings finally emerged into a non-militarized world, the power of the surprise and the beauty of the songs, more than any other factor, gave birth to the modern environmental movement, which was able to clarify an entire generation's angst and desperation into one crystalline response, one simple storyline.

Many already understood that the slaughter going on in the whaling industry was wrong; to know now that such immense and sentient animals made such beautiful, eerie songs, and yet to know nothing of the meaning of the songs, galvanized people into a unified, sacred rage, a green rage for peace. Slowly, they wound down the great grinding bloody gears of the war machine in Vietnam, battled the whaling industry to a near stop.

Rivers in the homeland were aflame with toxic solvents, corporations were honing to the point of gargantuan excess their ability to lie, the government was as corrupted as a washed-up seal carcass seething with maggots, and yet here, suddenly, was this beautiful, haunting sound that pierced the heart—an ancient song from the ancient world, the blue shimmering world in which all life began, but from which we had been cast, or had chosen, perhaps, to abandon.

No scientist in the world will tell you that we know yet why humpback whales sing. A friend of mine, David Rothenberg, has written a fascinating book, *Thousand Mile Song*, which analyzes whales' music, and has found it to be the most complicated music in the world. He and others believe that whale songs can transmit vast distances underwater (hence the title of his book) and is enthralled with the discovery that, each year—after much trial and error, and much jazz-like riffing, with different males all around the hemispheres listening to one another, then answering back, making subtle variations—every humpback whale in the Northern Hemisphere finally and simultaneously and unanimously decides on the perfect arrangement that becomes their one song for the rest of that year. Their collaboration becomes the composition they all sing, the long, complicated underwater orchestra that fills the seas and drives lonely sailors mad with longing and other emotions they—we—cannot even name.

It's a big argument. The prevailing belief appears to be that whale song, coming almost exclusively from males, is all about sexual selection: that the "best" singers—which might sometimes be a measure of creativity or intelligence—get the "best" or most females. The only trouble with this neat and simple theory is that no one has ever observed a female whale paying the least bit of attention to a singing male. (Often when they sing, the males gather in a group and hang upside down, vertically suspended in the blue, with their enormous heads tipped down.)

The fact that no one's ever observed females responding doesn't mean it doesn't happen. Perhaps they go away for a while and think about what they have heard. Perhaps they're making up their enormous and complicated minds.

There is one musician in the world—at least one—who thinks the humpback whales do *not* sing for purposes of sexual selection—or that that is not the primary reason—nor even that all birds do, nor even all insects, but that instead there is something else in the world, something perhaps equally as large; that just as there can be a thrumming desire to procreate—a summons to carry life forward—so too is there a twin and somewhat parallel desire to create beauty, to create art.

As you might imagine, this would be a pretty hard thing to prove.

———————

David Rothenberg is a world-class clarinetist who was educated at Harvard and now teaches philosophy at the New Jersey Institute of Technology. He's recently recorded an album on the famous jazz label, ECM, and is known by many for his avant-garde music. Featured in the BBC documentary *Why Birds Sing*, he's traveled around the world, playing his clarinet to different social animals—lyre birds in Australia, beluga whales in the Arctic—seeking to insinuate, gently, his own notes into their music, participating in creative, jazz-like fashion with whatever sounds they are creating.

His is not quite the pursuit of interspecies communication but more the qualitative exploration of his theory, his belief, that if music is about art, beauty, and emotions, then there might be a place for him to participate with other species, as if treading the invisible high-wire pathways that extend from one species to the next, crossing chasms previously thought to be impassable.

It is very important to him to believe that art exists for its own sake in the world: that it does not need justification or explanation by science. I've come to Hawaii to listen to him play his clarinet to the whales—he's been here once previously, and has one recording of what he believes was a whale picking up on his, David's, blue note—repeating it, improvising and adjusting, then appearing to lose interest and moving on—but with that one note now embedded in the skein of that whale's music, and a part of the collective song that would emerge later that year. David's artistic offering embedded in the one song. Like a sequence of DNA, a fragment of genome, twisting and glittering in the undersea light when sunstruck, illuminating a small portion of the ocean with his own emotion.

And why? Why does DR want art and beauty to have its own stand-alone reason for being, unjustified by anything other than its own existence? He believes this with the certainty of faith—ferocious though not arrogant faith—he *knows* it.

If you can believe in something, doesn't that kind of mean it's there? And if you have faith in it, doesn't it also mean it's there, and surely not just in you, but in others, even if in strands and waves that have not yet been finished being woven?

The important thing, I think, is that the whales are among the largest animals in the world, swimming around right beneath our noses, singing their hearts out. You can be in a little boat out in the ocean and can even hear them below—some of the sound waves rise, spread around the boat, and envelop you, yet there is no written record of the phenomenon, no acknowledgment in any of the world's literature, no record of it in any of the world's oral cultures. *We just didn't know.* Maybe people thought it was just the sound the ocean made, or the beautiful grinding and squealing of an immense earth rotating.

───────────

The island's beautiful, of course, as is the water; it's Hawaii, after all. In February and March the humpbacks gather here to give birth in the warm shallow clear waters before resuming their journey north. They will pass back through in May, bound for Alaska, where they will feed on tons of krill—a tiny shrimp-like creature that blossoms under the winter sun into swarms that stretch a mile wide sometimes. (Humpbacks, like the largest of whales, are baleen feeders; a mature humpback can measure sixty feet and weigh fifty tons.)

Barnacles form along the whales' sides, sometimes thousands of pounds' worth; if the whales don't find a way to shed them, the accrued weight would eventually sink even so powerful a creature as the humpback. It's been theorized by some that the clear and relatively sterile waters around Hawaii starve the barnacles each year so that the scutes and plates of armor fall from the whales' skin like jewelry being shed, the scales glittering where, in places, they line the bottom in the approximate shape of the great and sentient beings that once passed by overhead.

The whales—and the island of Maui, where they linger in March, as if on vacation—attract dreamers, do-gooders, strangeness. Like iron filings drawn to a magnet, they come here, interesting people, and sometimes broken people, seeking a kind of repair, seeking *something*. Interesting people, wherever you throw a rock.

One of the grand dreamers is Dan Opitz, a diver and full-time self-financed filmmaker, who got a loan of two hundred fifty thousand dollars to make his third film, the acclaimed and award-winning *Cracking the Humpback Code*—a work of luminous mystery and reverence. Opitz, who is German, first became interested in diving and cetaceans when, for his fifteenth birthday, a girlfriend bought him a ticket that allowed him to swim with dolphins. These relatively small considered acts of generosity that end up changing lives.

A big man—hulking—he doesn't do anything small. He's not a Buddhist, but says if he were to believe in any kind of religion, that would be it. So when Dan decided to get a tattoo, he had one of the Buddha inked onto his back, life-sized, so that if you see him walking on the beach, it looks like the Buddha is going away from you.

When I say that he is a diver, I mean he doesn't just paddle around in the coral with a snorkel, but goes to the deepest bottom of the ocean and walks around investigating the wrecked hulks of battleships and Japanese and American bombers that were shot down during Pearl Harbor days, with undersea coral frond-forests rising tall around him, waving gently in the ocean floor's currents, as if stirred by a breeze. The propellers on the bombers are motionless, and seemingly little is different between sky and sea, save for the long stream of silver bubbles rising to the surface from Big Dan's lungs.

His girlfriend (a different one) is in Germany, but he can't stay away from the island, and the whales. He has a trim little boat and goes out on the water to watch and listen for the whales as often as he can, whenever he can. Just prior to my arrival, he and David had gone out listening and recording—not clarinet-playing. Dan is a stickler for the law, a tidy precision that seems at odds with his boundlessness. The Marine Mammals Act prohibits the harassment of whales and other mammals. David wouldn't necessarily agree that playing music—certainly not his music!—is a harassment, but it's important to Dan that he not venture whatsoever into any gray areas of the law.

Dan takes David and me upstairs in his suburban home to show us his dream, and it's there that we understand why he has taken the yearly lease on this house, despite the fact that he's absent for half the year. As one might imagine, rental properties in Maui aren't cheap, and lone Dan doesn't need all the extra space, all the extra bedrooms. In essence, he's just paying for air. But when we go upstairs to the top floor, we understand why.

The view is stunning, breathtaking. A wall of light welcomes us, a wall of windows, and because it's the highest house in the burbs, you can see out over all the other rooftops, and over the village of Paia, and over the waving tops of the palms, to the soothing blue rolling waves beyond. Even to a non-sailor it is bewitching—you feel everything that was previously tense within you loosen and dissolve, or realign. It's almost impossible to look away from the vast blue ocean—it is like air—it seems that to look away would be to hold one's breath, to cease breathing—and yet the aesthetics of the room itself, one long room with a gleaming wooden floor and white walls and so brightly lit, with a drafting table and neat desk and bank of sleek computers at the far end, also compete for a visitor's attention, so that there is a confusion of grace, a bounty of the aesthetic, and a perfect, beautiful, delicate balance of the infinite blue sea and the life of the mind. The White Room is how I think of it, spare and elegant, cleansing and pure, and it's up here where Dan does his biggest and deepest dreaming, his life's dreaming.

His dream is to purchase an immense ice-breaking ship and refit it to become a magnificent research vessel, capable of following the whales all around the world, with laboratories and diving and filming capabilities, and fleets of tiny submarines that are able to be disgorged from the mother ship's belly, like little guppies being born as the mother ship motors along in the depths, as the submarine pilots film and study the life aquatic.

He wants to take his footage and convert it to a big screen, but more: he wants to build a vast indoor viewing theater in which the 3D images of humpback whales are projected by light into the dark void just above the theatergoers' heads, so that the whales are singing just above and all around the viewers, with the darkened theater filled with the sound of their singing.

"It would change people's lives," he says. "If they could only see the whales, and hear them, like I have."

His hand trembles as he opens a manila folder that rests on his desk. In it is a mock-up of a brochure advertising the theater—as if the thing is not a dream, but has already been built. He has expensive, detailed blueprints of the whole operation, ship and theater. There in the White Room, he pulls up a web page that shows a couple of ships he's interested in bidding on. There aren't many ships in the world that big, it's a lot easier to buy one used than to contract the building of one from scratch.

Will he get it done? I for one think that he will. I can't remember the price tag—maybe $60 million—and I can see his vision, can see it becoming as big as Disneyland: changing people's lives and consciousness, integrating science and technology with spirit.

He offers to take us out in his little boat later in the week, and we accept his kind offer. We leave him then, and leave the White Room, though even after we have driven away, it seems that I can still feel the dream throbbing, pulsing, from that one house, up in that lofty lookout, from which vantage a person can see so much farther.

———

We each and all have our weaknesses and wounds, our ridiculous flaws. I for one do not want to be the kind of person who makes fun of others about anything, and least of all about what should be the most sacrosanct thing, a person's spirituality.

And yet it's hard to take seriously—at first—that which we encounter the next day. David has lined up a couple of spots for us on what he calls "the hippie boat," a charter outing filled with a ragtag collection of dreamers and do-gooders, among whom David with his clarinet, and me with my questions and doubts, are no more and no less eccentric. In the early morning cool, we're being ferried in a tiny motorboat that sits anchored offshore like a pirate ship.

A green sea turtle treads water next to our boat, watching

us, its eyes surprisingly like a human's. The captain, Christine, is wiry and sun-weathered, maybe sixty-something. We're the first ones on the boat—she gives us a hand up and puts us straight to work storing things, and now others are being ferried the short distance out to our boat, an eclectic mix of islanders who have saved for this one day of whale watching and others who have put it on their calendars and traveled thousands of miles. David made the journey last year and says that there was a naked cellist but that it doesn't look like she's here today.

Some of the passengers, however, are familiar to David. One fellow he remembers is a distant relative of Admiral Peary; he has an ivory narwhal tusk that was bequeathed to the family. The majority of the travelers are middle-aged women, but there are people of all ages. Everyone is white. Captain Christine takes her money from everyone, telling us that she feels there will be "major, major blessings" today. She's a little harried, but who wouldn't be, with forty strangers suddenly on board?

There are musical instruments everywhere: guitars, of course, and chimes, and cymbals, and any number of instruments I have never seen or heard before: crystal bowls with special pestles, which when run around the rim of the bowl will create a wailing, howling, eerie resonance. A young man climbs aboard with a giant golden multistringed instrument that looks like a crossbow, with an intricate lacing of wires: it's a wind harp, which he will hold to the sky and tilt, as if summoning with those angles a music that already exists—that always exists—but which we cannot normally hear. As if he will catch such sound briefly in the net of his wires.

And finally, there is an immense seal of a man, also a repeat customer, known simply as Fish, who, other than carrying a hundred or so extra pounds, is a dead ringer for the late Jerry Garcia, and who is in the company of two attractive young women in small bikinis.

Christine gives us an exuberant pep talk, telling us that we belong to the Cetacean Nation now. As best as I can tell, the prevailing sentiment if not full spirituality on the boat is an earnest amalgamation of Buddhism, Christianity, druidism, paganism, animism, and Zoroastrianism. A not-very-nice part of me—a part that is made uncomfortable by a spirituality that appears to be wholly untempered by doubt, and therefore, to my possibly narrow way of thinking, suspect and of lesser value— wonders if they're so desperate that they're buying it hook, line, and sinker, grabbing at any life raft tossed to them in an extremely turbulent sea.

If I cannot feel unreserved compassion for them, then the least I can do, it would seem, would be to avoid judging them. From time to time I glance over at David as if to say, *These are your people, musicians all*, but David's expression is inscrutable, hidden behind his dark glasses; if anything, he seems to be enjoying himself hugely.

We begin to see whales immediately. Their bull-like heads breach the surface in the distance, their broad black backs gleam and glint like obsidian under the sun, and finally, at the end of each dive, their wide tails, the last thing to disappear from sight, appear to pause, wave, waggle before sliding back down into the mysterious blue. We cheer whenever we see one, and Christine unabashedly steers the boat toward each one, upping the engine's rpm.

But the whales are shy—there are other boats about, too, playing our game. Surely all of these whales have been hunted by tourists before, and they submerge before we can draw close to them, disappearing well before we breach the hundred-yard viewing limit decreed by law.

There is of course a loophole—you can pilot your boat at an angle that might intersect with the whale's path, then shut your motor off and drift, essentially blocking their way—and if the whales choose to continue on with their established trajectory in such a way as to bring them within that hundred-yard buffer, then a boat captain is not likely to be prosecuted, for in theory the final approach is of the whale's choosing.

Slowly, the musicians have been coalescing, repositioning themselves so that they can all see each other, and as if through some unspoken internal communication and consensus they begin warming up, each playing their various instruments; gradually they ease into what sounds like some olden folk tune. For musicians possessing such an odd miscellany of instruments, and to have never played together before, it doesn't sound half bad—other than the lyrics, which are an endless refrain of "We are family . . . We are family . . . We are family."

No, we're not, I think churlishly. But they're happy—literally, rhapsodic—and again the sound, with David climbing in now with his clarinet, is pretty good, especially out there on the water, with the wind washing over us and the boat flying across the waves.

And then something amazing happens.

A pair of whales—a mother and a big yearling—appear off to our right, just within the hundred-yard distance. They're breaching, leaping clear of the water—a formidable launch for such enormous creatures—and though we could be wrong about this, it seems that there is somehow a synchrony or match between their joy and ours: between our music and their willingness to associate with us.

The musicians, delighted with what they have summoned—the most enthusiastic audience ever!—play louder and with more verve. David, who has been laying back and letting the other musicians take the lead, is playing the heck out of his clarinet now, a wild, wailing, joyous sound, improvising and yet accompanying the guitarists and bell ringers and drummers and bowl rubbers and mandolins wonderfully—and with each pulse, each blast, the whales edge closer, alarmingly so, until we can see the joy in their eyes with each leap, the *mirth*. They're right alongside the boat, leaping again and again, spending themselves against the sky and encouraging the musicians to play louder and faster and better, which they are doing—David is playing out of his mind—and with each new ascension of his effort and his talent, the whales leap ever higher, so that even to my skeptical mind there is no doubt whatsoever that it is an accompaniment, a duet of sorts— whales and humans, music and dance—and although our boat is traveling fast, they are staying with us, even surging ahead of us; teasing us, it seems, racing us.

Why should it amuse us so, that they are spirited, and capable of knowing joy, and of communicating? What brutal and perverse shell have we placed around all other forms of life, steadfastly ignoring or stubbornly denying that their cultures and spirits, their days and nights, are meaningless, compared to our lofty own?

Such denial across the generations does not inflate or build up our own importance or position of relevance. Instead, it demeans it.

To swim and soar as the whales are soaring this day—to do that even one day in our lives—would surely alter, transform, our existence—would be a life changer, a great *whoosh* of almost unbearable joy, the experience of a lifetime—and yet their unending days, across the decades, may well be filled with this intensity, joy, sweetness. They may be living at a level we cannot even comprehend enough to know envy, and perhaps for us this is a mercy. All we really know how to do thus far in the relationship is to kill them.

Eventually—soon enough—they tire of us. Rolling over on their sides, they waggle their flippers at us and then roll away, peeling away like fighter jet pilots in a stunt, and submerge, vanishing back into their world—two of the largest creatures in the world becoming invisible again.

But for a long time, what they cast over us lingers.

Later in the day, we stop and anchor for the end-of-cruise swim. Captain Christine attaches a long lateral rope between the anchor rope and the ship. She opens a trunk filled with flippers, masks, and snorkels and invites us all to dive in and "become one with Mother Ocean," but to be sure not to swim beyond the tether of the rope. No small number of the travelers slip out of their swimsuits, though others of us, more chaste, remain suited.

Whales—three of them—appear again, though only briefly. Whether we have summoned them or have coincidentally stopped in one of their resting places, I don't know; they are visible only briefly. Not all of us see them, but Fish does.

With a single wild war cry of "*Whale!*" he goes running half the length of the ship and launches himself as if out into the void, the world's most enthusiastic human cannonball.

He is out there above the ocean for a long time, soaring, improbably huge and round—for just a moment, it seems that he is never going to descend, will instead only keep traveling out and up into the sky, fueled by nothing more than his own exuberance—though finally, the spell of his ascent dissolves, the caul or corona of his magic dust frays and corrodes, and he becomes leaden, collides with the sea like the Fish he is, in a great mushrooming plume of spray.

A few swimmers were in the water already. Some of them, with their masks, will report later that they were close to the whales—were nearly among them, underwater—but that when Fish hit, the whales bolted like minnows.

Again, I'm of two minds: I do not want the whales to want to be among us, I want them to remain isolated and protected, unchanged by the relentlessness and bottomlessness of our needs, our emotional claims: the broth of our damning paradoxes and unpredictabilities. And yet if I could have gotten my mask and flippers on in time, and been one of the first out of the boat, I just as surely would have wanted to be one of the swimmers out there with the whales, even if for the most fleeting of moments: to see the broad streak of black amid the blue, a flash of white belly streaking away.

Everything is connected, but we do not have to embrace every physical thing in the world to know that this is so. If a song—inaudible to us—can travel a thousand miles underwater, then so too surely can there be other connections that we cannot see or hear or otherwise know, between all things. Little wonder that we, such newcomers to this infinite garden, sometimes feel confused, befuddled by the bounty of choices, and other times gridlocked, dead-ended, struggling against the occasionally snug though other times lax embrace of all those other invisible wires and strands.

We swim for a while, the stronger swimmers drifting out away from the safety tether of the rope, while the less confident among us stay very close to that strong central strand, its yellow length anomalous in the dazzling clearwater blue. A discordance, but one to which we cling, like barnacles.

We putter along in our fins and masks, singly and in groups of twos and threes. The cloudless sun bathes the ocean equally, yet radial zodiac spires of blue and green and yellow and white light spin before us at the near surface, falling away to the deepest and most bottomless blue imaginable. I know that at the very bottom it's black, but my eyes can't see the bottom; for me, there is only blue, everywhere.

Other swimmers pass through the bouncing, spinning zodiac of wave-lulled light, their pale naked bodies made graceful as mermaids by the giant extended fins they are wearing.

At first I can only hear the amplified rasps of my own irregular breathing, as I repeatedly blow out gusts and gurgles of wave-sloshed snorkel infill—each breath a struggle, yet there is no option but to keep on going, the ocean is too beautiful. But gradually I become more accustomed to the rhythm of the breath-ing, and in the quiet spaces between my own whale-like puffs, and when I hold my breath and stop struggling, dog-paddling, kicking and stroking, and instead just drift, I hear it, the singing.

It is all around me, beneath me and above me—I am sur-rounded by it, am floating in it. I do not claim to understand what it is saying, nor how many whales are singing, nor how far away they are: but I am in it, and it is beautiful, and—this is the most striking impression—there is very much the feeling that if I hang around just a little longer, I will come to understand it. The dis-tance between their communication and mine is vast, but it feels that the knowledge is near.

Perhaps David is right. Perhaps if their songs are only about beauty, then indeed that is a near thing within us: a thing we may not yet have fully embraced, but which lies within our already-developed range of abilities, or on the near cusp of them.

One more image, one more song, one more kindness. We're close, and as I drift there, listening, I don't want to leave.

One more image. A few days later, David and Dan Opitz and I are out on the water in Dan's clean little boat. His trailer is fixed, and the water is as slick as obsidian. How can this be the ocean? I have never seen such stillness, not even in the sky. We've brought recording equipment and have lowered the microphone over the edge, are sitting there in the flat bright heat sunning ourselves like fishermen, waiting. We each are wearing huge padded earphones, listening to the indecipherable clicks and squeals of humpbacks that are out there somewhere, singing about who knows what. Soon they will be leaving these crystalline waters, making their own slow and steady progress into the future, one foot at a time, one more mile, one more season, one more song.

Cracking the humpback code, Dan Opitz calls his goal. He thinks it will happen, though I can't imagine the science and brain technology that will be required. The magnitude of the effort seems laughably at odds with the three of us lying there in repose, listening and basking, and with the water so glass-slicked smooth, for as far as we can see.

The headphones are uncomfortable and the songs are distant, Dan says; the noisy chatter and clatter, the maddening whine of outboard motors dominates the soundscape, and we take the earphones off and break for lunch, lazy and sleepy and floating as if on a lake of peace. There are some scientists who speculate that whale song travels along precise frequencies of thermoclines in the ocean—mysterious contours where all the water is some certain temperature—following that horizontal plane all the way around the world, preserved within that one thin sandwich of special temperature or even chemistry, like digital light trapped within a fiber-optic cable. *We don't know, we don't know anything.*

I'm up in the bow. Dan and David are crunching potato chips; they can't hear it at first. I can't tell if I'm imagining it, replaying the sounds of earlier recordings in my mind, but it seems to me that I can hear it, a whale singing.

"Listen," I ask them, "do you hear it? Is it a whale?"

They stop chewing for a moment. "It *is* a whale," Dan says, "and it's right beneath the boat."

I'm hard of hearing—too many chainsaws, concerts, lawn mowers, and shotguns in my youth, without ear protection. I'm not used to hearing things others can't hear. But Dan and Davis are scrambling to turn on the recorder again, the hull of the boat is acting like a receiver. The sound is striking the hull and coming up all around me, faint and muted but—even I can tell—close.

A whale breaches, fifty yards out. No one ever tires of the miracle of it. A smaller whale breaches next to the first one, but not a baby, not a calf. Dan Opitz is very excited, says they're two males. He doesn't have any idea what they're doing. Getting ready for their journey, he guesses.

The whales begin swimming toward us slowly, coming straight at our anchored broadside: not with aggression, but with a leisurely luffing. The big one is in front, and the smaller one trails him. Dan is photographing them, eager to see their tails, the white markings on which are as distinct as our own fingerprints. Photographer, moviemaker, cruise ship naturalist, dreamer: will his theater and research vessel ever get built? There is so little time left in any one life, and here we are out on the flat water, kicking back, drifting, listening, instead of him out trying to raise all that money.

The largest whale submerges—the elegant double-yoke white markings look like the whiteness of glaciers—but then he surfaces again, as if he had known that Dan wanted to photograph the tail, and now he keeps coming.

He's not going fast, but he's so much bigger than the little boat that if he even touches it, he'll tip it over. But there is no aggression. I don't know what it is; it's something from the other world, something from the world below.

We watch. There's nothing else to do. It's too beautiful to turn away, too beautiful to protest, too beautiful to be frightened.

When he is within about ten yards, he turns to the right, a perfect ninety-degree right-angle maneuver, and tracks a short distance parallel to our boat, then makes a perfect ninety-degree left turn, as if tracing a cookie-cutter rectangle around us—as if, in a cartoon, we might suddenly fall through a trap door he has cut in the surface of the ocean, following an imaginary or invisible dotted line—and the smaller whale behind him, as if following some chemical or electrical wake, travels precisely the same path, with what seems like mechanical replication.

Both whales are massive, and though they are warm-blooded, the thing I remember is how chilled they were: how coldness emanated from them, radiating as if from a block of ice, as the colder water from the farther deep—the singing deep—slid from their backs, and that temperature difference stirred and washed over us.

They proceeded carefully, delicately, around our boat, showed us their tails—their identities, or the only way our brute species knows to identify them—and then slid back down into their world again.

We just looked at one another. Dan was somewhere between peace and awe, but safely just this side of rapture. There wasn't anything to say, really. We sat there a while longer in the perfect blue and listened for them to begin singing again, but if they did, we couldn't hear it. In a few days they would all be gone, gathering and massing in some secret place—some unknowable place—and leaving on their long journey, while we sat there, anchored in the motionless blue, bathed by beauty, washed by beauty, and tried, as hard as we could, to understand it.

THE BEAUTY THAT WILLS US ON

THE BIRDERS ARE OLD, INTENSELY ALERT. TWENTY OR more of them move through the brush slowly, weaving like dreams. They have risen early to meet their passion. There's a proposed mine threatening that, and much else—another mine in southern Arizona's long history of scraping away the beautiful sky islands of mountains, sucking up all available water to bathe the damaged soil and stone in acid mix to then precipitate out the glitter that we paste and affix and fasten to our wrists and fingers and necks in order to feel beautiful. The Rosemont copper mine, this time.

It's cold—dawn, February, down near the Arizona–Mexico border, south of Tucson—and whenever there is movement back in the brush, the birders all stop and watch, waiting—some keen-eyed with binoculars still hanging from their necks, others with binocs already raised, their eyes gifted suddenly with the sightedness of gods—and no matter how drab or dull the first bird of the day may seem to a non-birder like me, to these veterans of beauty, it seems amazing. They rhapsodize about sparrows. They've been coming here for a long time.

In the midst of a war, one has to write or speak about war, but one has to write or speak about beauty, too. When to do which? No one knows, I think. Perhaps you know only each morning upon awakening.

Some of the elderly birders are couples, who hold hands as

they walk along the birding trail. Others are friends, and as they stand there peering into the brush as if into the great mystery of their lives—hoping and believing that, as it often does, the mystery will in time present itself and will pull them in, as close as they wish or dare—they rest a steadying hand on each other's shoulders. My informal survey indicates that most of them believe the mine cannot be stopped. Every one of them will do what they can do, but they have each been defending beauty and integrity for a long time, and have seen a lot of loss. Just to the south, a great anti-immigration wall has been constructed, physically dividing one county from another—blocking the flow of humans back and forth, sealing each of us further into our own diminishing capsule, but impeding also the natural passage of animals that for hundreds of thousands of years passed across that invisible line of the imagination with the freedom of birds: jaguar, ocelot, coatimundi, Sonoran pronghorn, wolf, bear. Now, all cut off, all isolate. Only the birds can pass over and through now, and where they are coming, there is already often no water. They seem to fly following the old pathways of memory, or perhaps hope.

I will likely never see any of these people again.

Sometimes I get tired of arguing for or against things, yet it seems I always answer the bell, always show up whenever there's a fight, or a need to stand and defend, or attempt to defend. Might I one day feel tired and worn out, with my imagination dimming, so that I might not be able to envision a way to win, a way for beauty to burn brightly, intact and mysterious and powerful in the world, strengthening and building our puny little hearts and the not-insubstantial lives those hearts power, in our comings and goings? Beauty like little oases or wellsprings at which we stop and sit before pushing on in our travels, our migrations.

Ruby-crowned kinglet. Say's phoebe. Some kind of pipit. Vesper sparrow, Lincoln's sparrow, house finch, female cardinal: one by one, the birds are stirring, going about their business, taking little dust baths, feeding, singing, courting. There's a dew and in the rising sun the grass blades ignite, rainbow prisms incandesce, and the birds fly above it as if with no interest in these temporary jewels that will dull quickly as the sun rises higher.

We peer through sunflowers as if into a kaleidoscope. Ladder-backed woodpecker, Gila woodpecker, Savannah sparrow, kestrel. We cross a narrow wooden footbridge where there used to be deep water, but now is only a web of cracked mud plates. A man named Al tells me he used to see mallards, snipe, rail here. Today, nothing, just dust. We move on, searching, or rather looking.

An owl—no one's sure what kind—leaps up from the grass and flies away into the sun. No one, not even here among the experts, is willing to make a guess—they squint after it eagerly, hoping for a second clue, as if it might for some strange reason turn around and come back—but it does not.

The old birders tell me that often on these outings they encounter migrants, following these brushy water courses, or courses where water once ran. Immigrant trails exist everywhere here. Lesser (Lawrence's) goldfinches, the birds far more brilliant than the mineral for which they are named, flash and rise and fall, sparks among the brush, delighting the brief humming life of our brains. The mine will suck millions of gallons of water, far and away the most precious mineral in the aridifying Southwest.

Great horned owl. Bewick's wren singing with a song like an old-time rotary dial telephone. How much change these old people have seen, how much more we will all see. Of course everything is temporal, everything is flux, but surely too at some point to stand quietly in the face of violence and injustice is to condone it with that silence.

We come to a barbed-wire fence and note where the prongs have snagged not only the hair of passing deer, but scraps of faded color from the shirts of humans traveling down this narrow brushy trail: a natural history of collapse and exodus.

Black phoebe, Cooper's hawk. White-crowned sparrow, green-tailed towhee. Later in the spring, flame-colored tanager, elegant trogon, thirty-six species of wood warblers, and an entire planet's worth of hummingbirds.

We must have courage, we must have fire, we must have energy, there is a war and all hearts are tempted to grow numb, to withdraw and tuck in as if to roost for the long night. We must not allow this to happen, we must burn, we must travel on, with morning's fire in our hearts and beauty everywhere we turn, amid the great burning.

ICE FISHING

TO SAY I'M NOT MUCH OF AN ANGLER IS AN UNDER-
statement. I get how fishing is kind of like hunting—particularly
bonefishing, where you literally stalk the animal, as if with a bow
or gun—and I can see how reading trout streams might be a little
like reading a contour map, or a forested cirque, a north-facing
slope, a gentle ridge with aspen—*there*, and *there*, and *there* is
where they might be, let's go see—and yet most of the time, or
so I understand, you don't see the animal. There's an extra layer
of separation, of distancing. I understand there's opportunity for
crossover, but I'm just hardwired for hunting, not so much for
fishing.

So you'd think ice fishing would be way, way down on my list
of things to do, maybe even at the bottom. It does not even hold
for me the curiosity of novelty, for I'd been once before: a not very
good experience up in Fairbanks, in late January, in the reckless-
ness of youth. It was thirty-eight below and there was some beer
involved and a black Lab who played with the fish we caught, the
fish freezing as solid as sticks of wood. I had never seen a dog
retrieve fish before, and I went home as soon as I could.

But my longtime hunting partner, Bill—a Midwesterner, an
Illinoisan—big-hearted, exuberant, generous, sweet, and tough—
wanted to go, was getting northwest Montana cabin fever, which
as far as I can tell runs only a degree or two lower than, say,
Fairbanks cabin fever. He'd had an artificial hip put in the day

before Thanksgiving, and here it was mid-January—Lowry, my eighteen-year-old, was heading back to college and had never been ice fishing before—and so it was a no-brainer. It would be Bill's first postsurgery outing. A ceremony: the new life, the new Bill returning to the old Bill.

He asked if we wanted him to pick us up at eight and we said how about nine or nine-thirty? I could tell by his face that maybe ice fishing was better in the morning, though that made no sense to me. Wasn't it cold down there, and dark? Why would a fish, an ice fish, care what time it was, and wouldn't it be colder at dawn than midday?

Bill's a sweetheart. "All right, nine-thirty, sure."

———————

I love how simple things are in the Yaak. His old 1970 GMC pickup. Two plastic buckets to sit on, and a real folding chair for him: Sue—Bill's wife—insisted. A ladle. Some tiny ice fishing rods, looking like children's toys. A tackle box with a few plastic jigs. A Styrofoam container of fat little worms. An ice chest of cheap beer.

Sue had found some old Yaktrax cleats for him, and we started up the trail slow and easy. It had been a cold year so far, but one of the driest; there was barely any snow down, which was preposterous for northwest Montana in January. It made for good walking, and we were to the lake in no time.

How wonderful it is, that condition of life when things are still new. Bill, in his sixties, with a new hip; me, in my fifties, working an ice auger for the first time, and in my home valley, looking up at the high ridges and mountains where I had hunted and killed deer and elk. Lowry, still in her teens, for whom so much of the world was still new. Not everything, but still, a lot: working that auger herself, and ladling out the floating ice, and dropping a line. Settling in to her bucket perch, and waiting.

Time, then, for stories, from one of the valley's elders; one of the finest storytellers in the valley. For some reason, Bill's got Raymond on his mind—Flamin' Raymond, named for the time his car caught on fire, inexplicably, but he just kept on driving it, right on into town, like the proverbial bat out of hell. Maybe he thought the wind would eventually put the flames out, but more likely, he just didn't give a damn.

Low's laughing. The three of us, out on the smooth ice, mid-January. Nothing, just each other.

Flamin' Raymond was bad to borrow things, Bill said. He had this weird tic or something, where if he didn't return it to you after about six months, he figured he owned it. So you had to go over there and ask if you could borrow it back, whatever it was. Electric drill. Maul. Spark plug wrench. Whatever.

"I went over there to re-collect my sockets one time," Bill says. "He was busy fastening this metal ammo box to the floor of his jeep, to use like a glove box. He was wearing this big old Colt .45. I didn't know if he'd borrowed that from someone or not.

"His toolshed wasn't twenty steps away, but evidently he didn't feel like walking all that way to get a drill, so he just pulled that gun out and shot four big holes in the floorboard of his jeep, *blam blam blam blam*. I thought I'd be deaf forever. He shoved those lag bolts in the bullet holes, screwed the nuts on, and that was that.

"He used to burn tires outside and cook over them, the way you or I would cook on an outdoor barbecue grill," he says, shaking his head. "It wasn't right. I was over there one time, he was grilling a deer leg over those burning tires. He asked me if I wanted any. I said no thank you."

Stories, while we wait—I believe Bill could fill eternity with stories, and none of them ever having to take place outside of this relatively small valley—the million-acre fishbowl of it, with the high snowy mountains helping to separate us from the rest of the world and shape us, over time, into something more akin to the valley. It's a ragged fit, for sure—just ask Flamin' Raymond—but it's a fit, nonetheless, or the start of one, and an amazing thing to realize, to witness, to participate in. I'm so glad Lowry's here, getting to hang out with Bill and listen.

We don't get to listen long, as it turns out. Fish on the line, the sudden and lovely tug and arc that you don't have to be an ice fisherman to understand. What to do about it, I'm not sure, so I sit there watching the rod dance and buck and, not wanting to get Bill too excited, wanting to stay cool and mellow so that he doesn't leap up and blow out or otherwise unstring his new hip, I point to the rod and say, as calmly as possible, as mild as pudding, "I believe something is happening."

My equanimity has the opposite of its desired effect. Bill springs up and toward the rod, in the process unstringing something—a wrench of pain crosses his face, coupled with an *Oh crap I just made a mistake* look—but he makes it to the rod in time, sets the hook, and reels it in, expertly keeping the fish in the center of the ice hole: and what a lot of fish it is, a big bull-headed humpbacked cutthroat, close to two pounds, Bill says—pleased and surprised, even in his pain—and the smile on Lowry's face, the rabbit-being-pulled-from-a-hat disbelief—this one big lake, this one little hole, and a fish, a *big* fish, came up out of it—is one of the sterling images, sterling memories, of a long white winter.

Just before the fish was killed, it rolled and thrashed, writhing and twisting, and was quickly caked in snow like the piling of a fleece jacket, white as cotton—it looked warm, like that, against the great cold, and even bigger, too; furred, almost like a mammal—a husky, a Malamute—and we grinned at one another and settled back into our seats, ready for the next. And, of course, for more stories.

Only one more fish presented itself that morning—an even larger one, from the same hole, and it, too, was reeled out, killed, placed next to its comrade. We would each be able to take one home; the morning was essentially complete. Not that the success of any outing, any journey, can or should be measured by productivity—that damnable word—what is the productivity, for instance, of a story, or a friendship?—but still, there was a nice symmetry to it, the two-ness of the big fish, snow-clad and paired like that.

We drilled a dozen more holes that morning, perforated the ice, Swiss-cheesed it to the point where we joked about falling through ourselves, but we never caught any more fish. Two more bites came, also from that same initial one-hole, but we weren't able to bring them in—one a giant, by the weight on the rod and the look on Bill's face when it slipped the hook—the previous winter, someone had caught a five-pounder in this lake—and soon enough it was early afternoon, time to walk to the edge of the lake and gut the silver fish and pack up and walk back through the woods, meat-laden, and being cautious on the downhill, with Bill's new hip.

In the morning Lowry and I would drive to the airport so she could fly back to college and learn things.

THE HUNTERS

Note: This essay on the Deepwater Horizon spill was first published in July 2010.

I'M NOT WRITING TO OFFER AN APOLOGIA, BUT I HAVE to say, life in the oilfield was wonderful. How much of that wonder was due to my youth—as well as the specific joy of youthfulness in the 1980s—and how much was due to the nature of the work—the joy of the hunt—I cannot be sure. I think it must have been mostly the latter, for there were old guys (there were almost never any women) who pursued the oil and gas with just as much fervor as the younger geologists.

We never called it crude, or black gold, or Texas tea. There were no clever nicknames, there was only the pure thing itself—oil if in the liquid state, or gas if gaseous—and our pure and steady fever, our burning. If we ever referred to it as anything other than oil or gas, we called it pay. Four feet of pay, twenty feet of pay, thirty feet of pay. Sixty feet of pay was a lot, enough to change your life.

I worked for a small independent oil and gas company, which was owned by a wealthy individual who drilled his wells with the aid of a group of a dozen or so investors, rich people who believed in him and in us, but who were also entirely willing to stop believing if we one day ceased to be successful.

Speaking only for myself, I didn't ever worry about that. I

never mapped a prospect, never drilled a well that I didn't believe was going to find pay. Success rates were somewhere in the neighborhood of baseball batting averages—between 10 and 30 percent—but the baseball metaphor does not carry much further than that, other than perhaps the ability to salvage a game—or a career—with one certain swing, a key delivery at the most critical time.

It wasn't like baseball at all. It wasn't like anything. The closest thing was maybe hunting—pursuing, with blind instinct and whetted desire and only a handful of clues, the hint of one's quarry far into the wonderful wilderness of the unknown. Lands no human ever saw, or ever will see, ten thousand feet below the ground. Beaches that received sunlight and warm winds hundreds of millions of years before the strange, momentary experiment of mankind arrived, cold and shivering, with neither fire nor fur. Beaches that were then buried over, still hundreds of millions of years before we first stirred, so anomalous and far from the spine of the main and older tree of life.

You were haunted by dry holes. The nature of the work—the rarity of the treasure—dictates that you're wrong more often than you're right. This rarity is what makes the payoff so spectacular. But despite knowing this, after each dry hole, you couldn't sleep. You couldn't believe your maps were wrong. The earth was wrong, you told yourself. You must have just missed the pay by a few inches. Not by miles, but by inches.

I believe the word for such behavior is *denial*, a noun commonly associated with its closest cousin, *addiction*. We were addicted to the intensity of our hunger—the almost limitless depths of it—and to the certitude that we were needed, that we were vital. Such a feeling is not quite as wonderful as the condition of being loved, but it is similar, with its dependencies, and far more reliable.

Something that's not being reported in the press is how deep the blowing-out formation is, or if British Petroleum even knows from what formation the hydrocarbons are spewing, or how thick the formation is. Typically, the larger reservoirs are deeper, but the fact that this one is blowing black oil (deeper horizons generally contain oil that is greenish in color and, at even greater depths, exist as natural gas rather than oil, due to the pressure at those depths) suggests the reservoir might be a shallower formation than BP was prepared for. Shallower, and yet larger: maybe the biggest in the world. Maybe they punctured, and tapped into, a thinly buried transoceanic pipeline. Is anyone missing a few million barrels of oil—half a day's worth or so?

Why is this formation, this reservoir, behaving so monstrously, with enormous and apparently increasing flow rates? Is an immense salt dome—plumes of salt, ten thousand feet thick—swelling and bulging, flowing like a gel and squeezing this reservoir? Is it belching its gas in erratic hiccups and burps? What makes us so sure, with all the geologic intestinal pressure, that the relief wells won't blow out?

Highly experienced oil rig operators from Norway, the Netherlands, and elsewhere are offering their assistance. So far, it seems, we haven't accepted much more than oil-skimming booms and other bits of equipment. Why aren't we accepting more help? National pride? Strange maritime laws? Film crews, photographers, and reporters are also apparently restricted from entering public airspace near the Deepwater rig, and some journalists say they've been denied access to oil-stained beaches by Coast Guard and BP officials. Who benefits from this secrecy—other than BP?

Has anyone thought about the fact that hurricanes in the Northern Hemisphere rotate counterclockwise? When—not if— one strikes, this will likely drive the oil up onto the Texas coast. I'm sure Texas governor Rick Perry has the oil booms and the National Guard already mobilized, right? We'll see how firmly he'll hold on to his Tea Party secessionist dreams at that point. My guess? He'll be crying for the feds' billions faster than you can say "Bobby Jindal."

―――――――

It's not enough to distrust BP, or any large corporation. These days, you have to know how they work, the ins and outs of each industry, and the secret heart, the secret ethos that governs the spiritless movement of each through our stressed history.

I'm here to tell you, BP doesn't intend to just walk away from this beast, this monster, empty-handed. They will be lured back to it again and again.

What I am wondering is why BP hasn't tried to cap the well yet, now that they have a housing over it—to insert a one-inch tube into the pipe string, the slender mile-long straw they currently have attached to the makeshift cap, and pump concrete down that tube. While BP has tried the so-called top kill maneuver—an unsuccessful attempt to push heavier-than-water drilling fluids down into the well to eventually stop the jet of oil—to my knowledge they haven't yet tried pumping heavier-than-everything concrete.

If oil can go up that pipe string, as is currently happening—tens of thousands of barrels a day—then concrete can probably be pumped down. This seems to me to be BP's best chance to deliver a knockout punch and cap it and kill it before the hurricane season really gets going.

Apparently no one has thought to ask this. The BP folks are sitting on this, and so many other things, like a secret. Their inside knowledge of a not so terribly complex technology is their power. Unlike the formulas for the secret recipes of benzene and toluene that Halliburton pumps downhole into these same wells—their "frac" (short for fracture) fluids that are potent enough to dissolve the interstitial cement of the eons, allowing a little more gas to seep up the wellbore—this knowledge is not a trade secret. If oil can come up the makeshift string, concrete can go down it. I haven't heard one person ask about this. We're just standing by the side, vesting our power and authority in the people who least should have it.

We're all indignant—we, who with every mile driven, every mouthful of food eaten (organic or otherwise), are complicit—but ours is not a righteous indignation, and we know it. Instead, we feel the grief and depression wrought by extreme self-loathing; there is much to loathe, these days. It's extremely hard to imagine a path to rehabilitation. We need a model for changing identity and renouncing addiction, and yet there is none. No wonder we're frightened and angry.

I used to live down on the Gulf and I feel guilty that I am not more depressed—more devastated—by this toxic gush into the heart of the Gulf, or what remains of it, riddled as it already is with massive dead zones and floating islands of plastic three miles long—islands large enough to colonize and build resorts upon.

To possess an ecological awareness, wrote the American ecologist Aldo Leopold seventy years ago, *is to understand that we live in a world of wounds.* The shrimp were on their way toward extinction in the Gulf anyway, due to our channelization of the Mississippi River, the great source of their nutrients. Our flood control of that vast living system is robbing billions of tons of sediment that would otherwise keep building the Louisiana delta and marshes that the shrimp nurseries depend upon, and which serve as a buffer against hurricanes. South Louisiana is sinking fast without this sediment. As this happens, the shrimp populations will blaze out with one final pulse of productivity (toxic productivity now, for as the marshes sink and disintegrate beneath the storms, they will release one last burst of nutrients themselves)—but there is no more capital; the marshes are living on the debt of the past.

That doesn't make what BP did right.

The corporation of BP—possessing now, due to a right-wing Supreme Court, the constitutional rights of an individual, but none of the responsibilities—is buying up ad space on the internet under the phrase "oil spill." They are contributing billions to congresspeople who grovel before them. The oil companies tell us we can't afford to combat global warming, and that we can't afford to not drill in sensitive areas. Such bans will make the cost of oil go up, cry the watchers of Fox News. But what we are not acknowledging in our addiction is that oil and gas are as heavily subsidized as any other American industry. Many of the corporations' costs are externalized to the consumer, so that our energy consumption, energy addiction, is dependent upon such sleight-of-hand accountings as those that attend to any of the other socialized price supports that right-wingers pretend to find so terrifying.

The multinational oil and gas corporations—the biggest companies in the world, which in no way care whether America lives or dies, is free or captive, healthy or poisoned—have long succeeded in manipulating the U.S. Congress to assume many of the costs of production, transport, health care issues, global warming, the cleanup of toxic spills, etc. Part of the secret of "cheap oil," as we are finding out, is that it is not so cheap. Instead, we are paying our giddy debt forward with ferocious momentum.

Even when they drill on U.S.-held properties—public land and government leases owned by the government—they refuse to let the government know what's going on: even when the government is a partner in the drilling, via farm-out and override royalty interests, the oil companies refuse to let the government see certain papers and equations, such as the formulas of the fracture fluid the oil companies inject into the well bores and into those public lands, where the fluids make their way into public drinking supplies. It's a trade secret, the oil companies say.

They could patent the toxic brew, the earth-killing concoction, and protect their trade secret that way. Maybe they don't because they know it's so toxic it would be illegal. But it's illegal to not share it. Our government just lies down, intimidated by the myth of science, and by the power of big oil. Even today, big British oil is telling the media that they'll be around in the Gulf for the long haul. What cheekiness! Isn't it we the people who should be telling them that it's actually we who will be the ones deciding how long they'll be around? The $20 billion "trust fund" Obama negotiated is a drop in the bucket.

This brings us to the matter of the so-called relief wells that BP keeps promising to drill.

In more manageable environments, a relief well is slant-hole drilled, with the new well bore trying to angle in and intercept the existing wellbore of the blown-out well, so that heavy mud or concrete can be pumped into the reservoir, tamping down and ultimately extinguishing the well. New technologies make it easier than it used to be, but still it seems a long-shot proposition— imagine the odds of intercepting the same slender borehole (ten-inch diameter) from a thousand or more feet away and maybe ten thousand feet above—trying to aim two miles of flexible pipe toward such a minuscule target while drilling through ancient stone. Sometimes it works; other times the pipe gets stuck or breaks. The truth is that nothing has worked so far.

My fear—my belief—is that we've gone way too far out into the deep end, to a place where not only are the old-school in-land physics of the oilfield profession irrelevant or misleading, but where the pressure of deep-horizon reservoirs and their behavior is largely unknown. We're drilling on theory, but in the meantime the earth is blowing out its spume in reality.

Sometimes—sometimes—a well blowing out with tremendous vehemence will eventually collapse on itself. The formation will begin to cave in around the borehole, without pipe being set, sealing off the formation like a boulder, or boulders, being rolled in front of a cave. We might eventually get lucky—too little, too late, of course, and despite BP's secrecy and ineptitude. Is this the best we can hope for? But even if it does collapse on itself and we are saved from our own dumbness by dumb luck, then what?

The disparity between what we don't know and the depth of our hunger is a gulf of terrifying size and immediacy. What's going on in these deep-water prospects is reminiscent of gold mining in the 1880s, when crews would turn giant hydraulic hoses on entire mountains and sluice the whole mountain away, washing it downstream, bathing the spoils in acid in order to gather the scant nuggets within. Barbaric, we say of those miners and those times, primitive. But it was all they knew. Their technology was not commensurate with their appetites. Nor will it ever be. Call it the inverse of Moore's Law: human appetites have always been expanding at a rate greater than the rate of technological advance; this disparity is what helps fuel technological advance.

If the first well blew out despite the heavy drilling mud, why on earth does anyone who knows anything about this think the second and third well won't blow, too? No one knows the size and nature of this reservoir that's been discovered—no one. The only way to drill with heavier mud would be to use concrete, which is what you use to plug a well, not a producer, so why bother?

What I suspect the BP executives are thinking is this: We'll try and get some other boreholes into this reservoir and produce it before the government shuts us down. Yes, it's a risk, but maybe we'll get lucky, maybe we can manage to keep the monster in check next time. Maybe it's not as big and strong as we fear it is, and yet as we hope it is.

It's worth the risk, they must be thinking. If the relief wells blow out too, what's more oil on top of oil?

They can't help but do the math. Sixty thousand barrels a day from two wells multiplied by 365 days a year at eighty dollars a barrel with a thirty-year reservoir must be starting to look like real money. Why, that's over $100 billion, from just two wells! It makes the $20 billion relief fund seem but a drop in the bucket. A profit.

———————

In every industry, in every country, our old economic models are falling apart like wet cardboard. The old models held up for a while, but they are not holding up anymore, and hurricane season is upon us.

BP needs to try to put a thinner tube down through their well housing as fast as they can, pump concrete into the formation, and then walk away.

They will never walk away.

Maybe it sounds hypocritical, my nostalgia and support of the small independent oil and gas producers who work not in fragile public wildlands, but in old inland basins in the south and east, where the wilderness has long fled. And maybe I am something of a hypocrite. I have solar panels on my home, I drive an old Subaru—but still, my footprint is huge, and my appetite is huge.

Every time we blink, we are using oil. The food distribution systems that give us our calories to blink, to speak, to laugh and love, to rail against the government, come from petroleum. We are choking and drowning on oil; our affluence is short-lived and unsustainable, and now, with the same sudden panic known perhaps to the brown pelicans whose oil-soaked wings will no longer keep them aloft or afloat on the shining Gulf waters that were their home for the last 40 million years, we are sinking, overburdened, going under.

People are scrambling, trying to rescue us, and we are trying to rescue each other, but we are all going under.

The true price of oil in my estimation is currently somewhere around three hundred dollars a barrel. *Too expensive!* you cry, even as we are shelling out three hundred twenty-five for it right now. Carrying BP's water. Carrying their buckets of oil-soaked sand. Carrying the trillions of dollars of productivity being lost due to global warming. Like children, we ignore the consequences of our choices, day after day, and the full and extended costs. There may not be an industry or a corporation we don't carry on our backs, whether health care or automakers, banking or real estate speculation or home mortgages or mining or logging or farming. It is all imperfectly accounted for; we have all been living too high, hiding the true costs of things.

When I remember my days in the oilfield, there's one image that comes to me most often.

I was in my late twenties, working eighty-hour weeks: burning the candle at both ends. We were drilling a deep well down in the swamps of south Louisiana, in a location so far beyond the end of the road that we had had to construct our own floating road of lashed-together boards—broad planks of cypress—to go out into the swamp another mile or two, extending our reach. It was a big project.

It was dark and I was driving through the swamp and through the forest in the darkness in a heavy rain, going a little too fast. The floating road was slightly underwater in places, so that often I was bluffing, aiming the company vehicle from point A to point C, trusting my route would get me there, and that I would stay on the floating road. As if my will or desire alone was enough to make it so.

I drifted off, however, and the car nosed down into the swamp.

I can barely recall the strength and nonchalance of the young man I was—the hunger I had for the world. It didn't bother me at all that water was now gushing into the car. It wasn't my car, it was the company's. I was on a mission. I picked up the well logs, put them in my briefcase, climbed out through the window, and continued down the slick board road, ankle-deep in swamp.

I walked for a long time. Finally I saw a faint lone light in the woods, an old shack with one lantern. If the light had not been burning I would never have believed anyone inhabited the leaning shanty.

I hated to do it, but I needed to see if they had a phone. I paused, then rapped on the door.

I had assumed the inhabitants were sleeping soundly—my approach had been soundless—but so instantaneous came the reply to my knock that the two events, my knock and the dweller's subsequent inquiry, seemed simultaneous.

The voice of an old woman rang like a shot—"State yo' name!"—and was shouted with such authority that I didn't hesitate in the least, but answered her right back, "Rick Bass!"—as if the name of a twenty-five-year-old white boy from Hinds County meant anything.

Miraculously—as if I had uttered the one correct phrase that would gain entrance—she opened the door, and she welcomed me in. For whatever reason.

She didn't have a phone. I couldn't tell if it was a question of access, or if she simply scorned them. I visited a while, then went on up the muddy road, toward the tiny backwoods village several miles distant, and the cinder block hotel where I could rent an old beater car from the night clerk, a sled that would get me back to Jackson before daylight, so that the glowing lit world, the world of myth—the world we did not yet know enough not to believe in—could continue.

Looking back, everything about my answer amazes me: the unapologetic cheeriness of it, neither arrogant nor insouciant. I knew it explained nothing, but that no explanation was needed. I was on a mission: not quite a hero, but a messenger from the gods. If she wanted to have my name—if that was what was most important—she could have it. The night was young and I would get out of this just fine. I had made it out to the rig all right—the glow of the tower, isolated in that dark forest, looked like the glow that might come from the landing of an extraterrestrial space-craft, and steam rose from the pipe that was being pulled from the hole, the drill string steaming and smoking like something being born, the roar of diesel engines like that from an army, if not a civilization, a town. I had been there, gathered the treasure, and was headed back.

I had the treasure in hand, and was driving the logs back to Jackson, several hours north. It seems impossible that not so long ago there were no cell phones or scanners, no computers or even faxes. We had a crude portable instrument called a telecopier that we carried in a briefcase, like a portable nuclear bomb, but its transmission of the logs was blurry and stuttery; the preferred method was for me to just ferry them to the bosses, as if by pony express, pulling up in front of their mansions at three, four in the morning, knocking on the door.

They answered in their bathrobes. We would spread the paper logs out on the table like biblical documents. The light seemed dif-ferent, back then, and at that hour, in the kitchen—a gold light—while we studied the logs and saw for the first time the fruit of our labors, the degree of our wealth, with exhaustion limning the edges of our vision. Who would not want to live such a life? We kept the world going. We carried the world on our backs while the world slept, and we kept it going; for as long as we kept going forward, so did the world.

I remember those days so well: the power and heady feel-ing of being needed, of possessing a valuable and honored—and honorable—skill. Finding oil is an honorable skill. The independents—who are fast going out of business, like the in-dependents in any industry—still know this. The giant corpora-tions we have entrusted blindly with world power care nothing for words like *honor*.

This is the dangerous truth. The hungers in the men and women who are working the crane lift-gear levers of those blind husks and blind souls of corporations are every bit as hungry as you or I. They are good at what they do and are on fire with their hunger and they will track the oil down to the ends of the earth. But they—unlike the independents—have no limits on their powers.

They will find it and will drill into it, no matter what the depth, no matter what the pressure. If we continue drilling at such absurd depths, this will not be the first such blow-out. It will instead only be the first one, the one that disturbed our blithe innocence.

President Obama says that as a nation we have to grow up now, have to put away childish things, and that our moment is now.

We'll see.

BORDER PATROL

SOMETIMES I'LL BE FLYING SOMEWHERE, LOOKING DOWN on the same snowy mountains where, perhaps forty-eight hours earlier, I was hot on the trail of an elk, or hunkered down in blue dusk, watching a white-tailed buck come creeping in, made curious by the sounds of my grunt tube. On the plane, I'll be dressed up (silent protest against those of my species who wear sweatpants on an airplane or, far worse, shorts—and, worst of all, a wifebeater T-shirt . . . *Why?*)

—I'm not judging them, I'm just saying it's gross—

—And I'll be amazed by how slender the difference between then and now can be, and of the borders that can exist between any two things: the lines almost always invisible, but somehow significant.

Would my seatmate be discomfited to know that, as recently as the day before—yesterday!—I had opened the deer's belly and pulled out the heart, liver, kidneys, stomach—all of it, with bright red fresh blood up to my wrists? Probably.

I might even find myself judged.

Are we not all innocent, are we not all guilty?

I look out the window and down at those same mountains and feel like an imposter, a pretender, because I rarely feel more real than when I am hunting and gathering—no matter whether I'm successful, only that I'm searching—and on the plane, then, it will seem to me that my life above those mountains—at, say, thirty-nine thousand feet—is therefore somehow less real, and tinged with something artificial if not fully fraudulent. Another invisible border.

It's funny, which deer you remember, in those years when you are fortunate enough to secure one. It's fun to hunt the big ones, particularly during the rut. I like very much, appreciate very much, and remember well those deer that have presented themselves to me late in the season, close to or even upon the last day. In such instances, you don't care anything about the antlers, or the weight of the deer—in fact, it's a good feeling to be pleased with so modest a gift—and this had been the case for me this year, with a nice young three-by-four I met way back near the Canadian border, halfway up a long sloping ridge that led to the top of the mountain and the international boundary. A roadless area. I don't know what I was doing back there. I mean, there are other places to find deer, closer to home, down lower in the valley. I think I might have been scouting for next year's elk, seeing if there were any back there, so high, and so late in the season. I'd already been fortunate enough to secure an elk and might have been doing some research for next year.

He was with does, but wasn't really running them, not seriously. The rut was over. The does saw me and ran—I wouldn't see them again—and he followed them.

I followed their tracks in the deep snow, up over a little rise, down an aldered draw, up another rise, and there he was, just looking around, like a present. Winter sunlight on his hardened little basket of antlers.

Blood in the snow.

I had to head back down to Missoula that night. I cleaned him, hung him up, packed out a load, but left the quarters behind—I couldn't fit them in my little daypack. I would come back for him the next weekend. In theory, the bears were already hibernating; it was the first of December. I hoped. I love what Jim Bridger said about such matters, and how long one can let meat, good wild meat, age: "Meat don't spoil in the mountains."

It's a busy life, outside of the slow time spent carefully and quietly following tracks. I was due to entertain a French documentary crew the next weekend, who were filming a special on conservation measures I'm involved with in the valley where I live. They arrived dressed in black—two from France, one from Belgium—and, like some young urban professionals with too many irons in the fire—how to entertain my European guests, and how to be their artistic tour guide?—I asked if they would like to help pack out.

"It won't be very heavy at all," I said—"we can each bring out a quarter—but it's a pretty good ways back there."

Yes, they said. *How far?*

Shit, I can never answer these questions satisfactorily. The only true answer, of course, is *It depends on how fast you walk.*

"A couple of hours," I said. Hell, you could do it in a buck forty-five, or you could lollygag and do it in six or eight; I didn't know. Who ever walks in a straight line, when they're hunting? Or for that matter, when they're walking anywhere, in the woods?

Rather than taking my ragged-ass Subaru, with its license plates three years expired, the windshield shattered from a deer collision (good eating, that one)—we threw the old bloodstained backpacks in the trunk of the shiny new rental car with its out-of-state license plates and motored up valley, turned onto the lonely logging road that led north to the trailhead, and powered through the night before's snow, wheels churning.

On our way up, we passed, improbably, another car coming down the logging road: the county sheriff in his shiny new navy SUV. There wasn't really a lot of room to pull over and our traction wasn't very good anyway, so I advised the Frenchmen to just wave and keep on keeping on.

It wasn't exactly like we ran him off the road, but he did study us pretty hard as we plowed past, and he kind of had that look on his face like the Man does sometimes when he wants to pull you over but knows he really doesn't have any probable cause. You're white. You're home free, innocent until proven guilty.

We waved merrily, berets and all—stylish black mufflers, black leather gloves, designer sunglasses—and motored resolutely forward, appearing for all the world to be in a tear-ass hurry, rather than simply unwilling to stop and lose our momentum.

"I think we'll be hearing from that gentleman again, and I don't mean in a postcard," I said.

We parked at the trailhead and left before he could turn around and come interrogate us. You know how it is: you don't want any-one, particularly a local, knowing precisely where you hunt.

It took longer than I'd expected. They weren't wearing the best footgear for the ankle-deep wet new snow, and they kept stopping to take photographs of the strangest things: a piece of bark, the day-struck crescent moon. A wolf turd. How unusual the world must look to them, I thought, how immense and over-whelming. *They're going to go into a tizzy,* I thought, *when they see the snowed-upon deer carcass; the little prince, the little king, crumpled and hollowed out.* Nature red in tooth and claw.

Except we—I—couldn't find him! So much snow had fallen over the week that my trail was filled in. I knew I was close, very close, but I couldn't quite zero in on it. The good news was that other predators hadn't gotten it—there would have been a busy radial of the tracks of coyote, wolf, bear, marten, lion, etc., con-verging on the sun-center of what I had once and briefly thought of as my meat—but the bad news was that I was tromping in circles, embarrassing myself before my guests. I know I wasn't presenting the American sportsman in the best possible light: *Yeah, I killed this deer, I think it's around here somewhere.* As if I were looking for a set of dropped car keys. So much for the heap-big spirituality of using all of the meat.

Thus motivated by shame, I somehow found the little deer—he was much farther downslope than I'd remembered, and in more of a thicket than I recalled, though if something had dragged him down there, those tracks, too, were covered up—and the camera crew began recording the disassembly with all sorts of lenses and goofy avant-garde angles. They said nothing the whole time, not in French, not in English, not in Dutch.

We loaded the packs and started down, into the bluing dusk. Why is it always dusk, up here, in the winter? There's barely ever time for anything. It was interesting, watching the pleasure the visitors took in executing the ancient act of bringing meat to camp. I could see them changing, almost step by step. There was less banter and more of a quiet pride; a new steadiness. It was interesting, and I imagined they would talk about it a bit, when they got back home.

What I *know* they must have talked about was the reception all four of us received when we got back down to the trailhead. Flashing blue and red lights in the gloom: not just our friend the sheriff, but two different Border Patrol vehicles, and the four of us burdened with packs that were clearly filled with *something*: a veritable packtrain, an entire string of mules.

Oh, you are so busted, the agents had to be thinking, and when they asked us for our identification, they probably couldn't believe their luck: France, France, *Belgium*. Maybe they'd receive a promotion; maybe they'd get a trip to the White House. There was no telling who—or what—they had captured. (I didn't have any ID on me, but claimed to be a local: the oldest story in the book. I was terrified they would run a check on me, find out my various overdue bail bonds, criminal trespass mischief in various state and national capitals, and thought seriously about making up some bogus name.)

We chatted calmly. My foreign visitors could tell this was not quite normal for the hunting experience, but I stayed cool. There were German shepherds in the backs of the Border Patrols—I could see them in there, and could hear them whining—wanting, I guess, fresh meat—and I thought, *Oh, you fuckers, shut* up.

We visited for five minutes or so—it felt like thirty—with the incredible leisure of the just-busted, until finally, one of the agents just *had* to ask, pretending that it was almost an afterthought— *Oh, say, so what's in all the packs?*—and I had to tell them, *Meat, real good meat, man.*

I don't wish to get those kind and affable agents in trouble, but boy were they friendly. They didn't even blink, didn't ask us to show them the meat! Have you ever heard of such a thing? They said they'd been down on the U.S.–Mexico border, in Texas, training for a couple of years, but then had gotten rotated up here.

Oh so carefully, and oh so gradually—I was certain, absolutely certain, that they were baiting me, and that at any second, the cuffs were going to come out—we bid them goodbye. We didn't ask if we were free to leave, but just kind of pretended that we thought, assumed, hoped, took as our due, the God-given fact that in these big mountains, we were.

They didn't try to stop us! Five steps to our car. We heaved the heavy packs into the back. Disbelieving, we got inside. We buckled up. We turned around. We drove down off of the mountain and out of the woods. What alternate reality was this?

How did they know we were telling the truth? There was no blood on our hands. It continued to puzzle me. Part of me wants to believe that they were such skilled observers of the human condition that they were able to tell, with almost 100 percent accuracy, the truth-telling within us—and yet, with so much at stake, wouldn't you just be dying to take even the smallest peek inside the pack?

I thought about this a lot.

And after several months of studying on it, the answer came to me, and I was embarrassed by how long it had taken me to figure it out. They didn't need to look in the packs because they had already seen it all, like the Wicked Witch gazing into her crystal ball: drones, unnoticed by us and silent as harriers, had hovered overhead, filmed all—our innocence, and our captivity, here in the borderlands. Free at last, maybe, but not as much as before.

THE LARCH

FOR AS LONG AS I CAN REMEMBER HAVING KNOWN THEM, I have been wanting to write about larch trees. I've been putting it off for fifteen years, because for one thing, it's like writing about lichens, perhaps, or a clock which, if not broken, moves its hour hand perhaps only a fraction of an inch each year.

They don't speak, not even in the wind, really—resolute, unlike the soughing and clacking limbs and trunks of the limber lodgepole, and the playing-card deck-shuffling clatter of aspen leaves in summer and fall—and even their dying comes slow. Sometimes a big larch will remain upright for a hundred years or longer after it's died—perishing in a huge fire or, occasionally, just dying and finally rotting, having outlived one millennium or another—and even after they fall over, snapping the other trees around them on their way and shaking the earth with their thunder, they remain there, solid and real, for centuries; in many ways, as alive or more so in their earthly slumber and decomposition— possessing, or housing, more writhing life in that rotting than they did even in the upright living days of green and gold.

They are, of course, every bit as glorious in life as in death. While among the green and the living, they possess numerous attributes, one of the most underrated of which is that of water pump: intercepting snowmelt and surface sheet flow that might otherwise drain off to the nearest road and be carried away from the forest, unutilized. But the larches capture and claim and hold within the forest that water which might otherwise be lost, and they convert it to astounding height, and to magnificent girth.

What else is the function of a forest, first and foremost, if not to do this: to capture and filter water, to merge with sunlight, to create intricate being, intricate matter?

The big larches don't just claim and hold that runaway, slide-away water; they circulate it, too, each tree a miniature weather system unto itself, returning hundreds of gallons of water to the ecosystem each day in the form of transpiration, a fine, even invisible mist emanating from the needles, just as lung-damp breath is emitted from a human; on cold and damp mornings, you can see the same clouds of steam rising in plumes from the larch trees, just as you would see them sifting from the mouths and nostrils of a forest of people.

This is not to say that the larch are gluttons, greedsome water scavengers robbing from the poor and the weak, totally out of control. One of the reasons they can get so big is that they can live so damn long, if you let them—if you don't saw them down. Around the age of two or three hundred, they really begin to hit their stride, and, having clearly gained a secure place in the canopy, they can concentrate their efforts almost exclusively thereafter on getting roly-poly big around the middle. In this valley, there are larch that have lived to be six and seven hundred years old.

They can prosper with either seasonal or steady access to water, though they can prosper also on the drier sites, such as those favored by the ponderosa pine. When need be, they can be prim and frugal with water, as in a drought, calibrating their internal balances with exquisite deftness to slow their growth as if almost into dormancy, where they hunker and lurk, giant and calm, awaiting only the freedom, the release, of the next wet cycle.

And they tolerate—flourish in, actually—fire, about which we will see more later. Like any tree, they have certain diseases and pests that can compromise their species—dwarf mistletoe,

which sometimes weakens them through parasitic attrition—
still, the larch keep soldiering on—and larch casebearer beetle,
which is kept in check by the fires, and by the incredible battal-
ions of flickers and woodpeckers (pileated, black-backed, Lewis's,
downy, hairy, American three-toed, and more) that sweep and
swoop through these forests, drilling and ratting and tatting and
pounding, searching and probing and pecking and cleaning and
aerating, almost ceaselessly, during the growing months. But for
the most part, the larch at present are relatively secure in a world
where so many other trees—fir, spruce, dogwood, oak, pine—are
undergoing an epidemic of rot and beetles and blight and gypsy
moths and acid rain.

Who can say for sure why the great larches are—for now—
weathering the howling world so well, in these latter centuries
of such intense environmental degradation? From a purely intu-
itive level, I suspect that the answer has something to do with
the larch's ancient jurisprudence—with the way it has evolved so
carefully, so precisely, so uniquely and specifically, to be safe in
the world.

The larch is two things, not one—a deciduous conifer, bearing its seeds in cones but losing its needles each autumn, like
a hardwood—and has selected the best attributes of each, the
ancient conifers and the more recent deciduous trees, to fit into
the one place on earth that would most have it, the strange dark
cant of the Yaak, tipped perfectly into its magic seam between
the northern Rockies and the Pacific Northwest: as if this land,
possessing such seething diversity in such random, unmappable
mosaics, was nonetheless really created with one perfect species
in mind all along, the larch.

Or perhaps their sturdiness in the world, their calm and elegant forbearance in a world filled with drought and fire and disease,
comes not from their wise evolutionary strategy of keeping one
foot in each world but from the fact that they lie so extraordinarily

low, sleeping or near dormant for the eight or nine months of the
year when they either have no needles at all (the first little spindly paintbrush nubs not sprouting out some years until May), or
when their needles have already shut down production and have
begun to turn bright autumn gold, which can happen as early as
August. Perhaps, by sleeping so much, they age only one year to
other trees' two or three or even four years.

In this regard, they are like a super-aspen, or a super-oak, calibrating their explosive leap of life to reside perfectly within that
tipped thin window of sunlight and moisture in the Yaak, the
three-month growing season, and then shedding their needles,
just as the oak and aspen drop their leaves, once that period of
growth has ended, for there's no need to invest in keeping them
hanging on, dormant or barely alive, through the winter. Better
to shut it all down, and sleep completely.

But the larch are like a super-pine, too, or a super-fir, possessing the eager colonizing tricks of the conifers that have flourished
for the last eon in the huge landscape-altering sweeps of drama
that follow the large fires in the northern Rockies—casting their
seed-sprung cones from high above, down into the fertile ash,
and in that way stretching like a living wave, or like an animal
walking, into new territory.

(In the northern Rockies, some things run from a fire and
other things follow it—elk following the green grass that follows the previous autumn's flames, so that in one sense, and seen
through squinted eyes, the elk can be said to be the grass can be
said to be the fire, with very little difference in the movements
of any of the three of them—all three generated and directed by
the same force. To that series of waves can be added the larch,
colonizing those new burns and then reaching for the sky, rising
slowly into hundred-fifty-foot peaks that can take centuries to
crest.)

So the larch, like the Yaak itself, is two things, not one: fire and rot, shadow and light. And in keeping with another of the stories of the Yaak—the fact that what is rare or even vanished from much of the rest of the world is often still present, sometimes in abundance, here—the larch is the rarest form of old growth in the West, though in the Yaak, it is the most common form.

Biologist Chris Filardi has looked at the maps of distribution for larch, as well as the habitat type found here, and has declared that the Yaak is "the epicenter of larch." This species is the one thing, I think, that is most truly ours. So many of the Yaak's other wonders are down to nearly the thin edge of nothing—five or six wolves, fewer than twenty grizzlies, a handful of lynx, a dozen mated pair of bull trout, one occasional woodland caribou, a handful of wolverines, fourteen little roadless areas, one pure population of inland redband trout.

The larch, however, are at the edge of nothing. This is the center of the center.

Increasingly, I am convinced that the larch trees possess, more than any other one thing, the spirit of the Yaak. The valley is imbued with a multitude of other spirits, but for me it is in the larch that the Yaak's greater collective spirit is so often most tangibly felt.

All of my Yaak life, I have been wanting to make an essay about what larch mean to me. I've been putting it off, though: procrastinating for fifteen years. (During that time, how much girth has one of the old giants put on? Another half inch? And yet, magnified throughout the forest—millions of such inches—surely the power of glaciers has been equaled, in that incrementalism.)

I've been afraid of attempting such an essay, such is the reverence I have for the tree.

Their interior wood, all the way through, is the red-orange color of campfire coals, a darker orange than a pumpkin, darker orange than the fur of an elk, and while I haven't found a scientist yet who can or will dare guess why the inside of the tree, never seen except when the tops snap off, or when the saw bisects the flesh, should be that fiery color, I think you would not be able to disprove the notion that there might be some distant parallel pattern or connection, out at or beyond the edge of our present knowledge, wherein fire likes, and is drawn to, the color of the larch's interior orange fire, for the larch is nothing if not birthed of fire.

And again, not just any fire, but the strangeness here, in the Yaak, of fire sweeping through and across a lush and rainy land that, when it is not burning, is rotting, and which is always, even in the rotting and the burning, growing.

Seething, roiling life, and life's spirits, being released in every moment of every day and every night, upon such a land. A continuous breath of it, upon this land.

I have thought often that the shape of their bodies is like that of a candle flame. Broad at the base, measuring three, four, sometimes even five feet around, they maintain that barrel-thickness for what seems like their entire length before tapering quickly to a tip, not unlike the sharpened end of a pencil.

This phenomenon is even more pronounced when their tapered tips get knocked off by wind or lightning or ice storms, leaving behind what now seems almost a perfect cylinder, and which continues living, even thriving, without its crown—able somehow to continue photosynthesizing and maintaining its vast bulk by the work of the few spindly branches that remain. Sometimes only a couple of such branches survive to nurture that entire pillar, so that one is reminded of the tiny arm stubs of another ancient, *Tyrannosaurus Rex*.

There's some deal the larch have cut with the world, some intricate bargain, part vainglorious gamble and part good old-fashioned ecological common sense.

They've cast their lot with the sun, rather than the shade, and as such have evolved to colonize new open space, such as that which follows a severe fire, or the slashes of light that infiltrate the forest whenever other large trees fall over. Because of this, they race the other sun-loving trees—the pines and, to a lesser extent, the Douglas firs—for that position at the canopy, where they can drink in all of the sun; where they have to suffer no one's shade.

But if they expend too much energy in that race for the sun—if they channel almost all of their nutrients into height at the expense of girth—then they'll run the risk of being too skinny, too limber, and will be prone to tipping over in the wind, or snapping under a load of ice or snow, or burning up like a matchstick in the first little fire that passes through their woods. What good then is it to gain the canopy—to win the race for that coveted position aloft—if only to collapse, scant years later, under the folly, the improvident briskness, of one's success?

───────────

When the two species, larch and lodgepole, are found together, as they often are up here, the larch will have been hanging just behind and beneath the lodgepole, for those first many years, "choosing" to spend just a little more capital on producing thicker bark, both for greater individual strength—greater static strength—as well as to get a jump on the defense against the coming fires.

It's always a question of when, not if.

As the lodgepole begins to reach maturity and then senescence, however, the larch begins to make its move, and as the lodgepole completes the living phase of its earthly cycle and begin blowing over, leaving the larch standing alone now, the wisdom or prudence of the larch becomes evident even to our often unobservant eyes. The glory of the larch is manifested.

By this point—seventy, or ninety, or a hundred years old—the larch will have developed a thick enough bark, particularly down around the first four or five feet above ground level, to withstand many if not most fires.

And now, with the competition for moisture and nutrients removed, and the canopy more fully their own, the larches are free to really head to the races. They didn't have to outcompete the lodgepole, for those first seventy or a hundred years; they just had to stay close enough to tag right along behind, right below.

But now they can "release," as the foresters call it: having the canopy to themselves, they continue to grow slightly taller, but now pour more and more energy into girth and a thickening of their bark: battening down the ecological hatch against all but the most freakish, outrageous fires.

(So deep become the canyons and crevices, the corrugations of that thickened bark, that a species of bird, the brown creeper, has been able to exploit and occupy that specific habitat: creeping up and down those vertical gullies, those crenulated folds a few inches deep, picking and pecking and probing for the little insects that hide beneath the detritus that collects in those canyons, and even building its nest in those miniature hanging gardens.)

Again, fire and rot are equal partners in this marriage, in this one landscape quite unlike any other. Burn or rot, it makes no difference to the larch, really, how the lodgepole dies, for in their close association, the larch is going to feast upon the carcass of the lodgepole, and assimilate those nutrients: either in the turbocharged dumping of rich ash following the fire that consumes the lodgepole but only singes the thick bark of the larch, or in the slower, perhaps sweeter and steadier release of those same nutrients from the same fallen lodgepoles as they occasionally decompose into rot, rather than burning—waiting for a burn that never comes, or rather (for always, the forest will burn again), a fire which does not come again until after that dead and fallen lodgepole has rotted all away, has been sucked back down into the soil and then taken back up into the flesh of the larch, the larch assuming those nutrients in that transfer as if sucking them up through a straw—which, in effect, it does, through the miracles of xylem and phloem.

At this point, of course, it's off to the races for the larch. They just get bigger and bigger, in the manner of the rich getting richer. And they seem to put all of this almost ridiculous bounty—sometimes literally, this windfall—into the production of girth; they pork out, becoming still more resistant to the perils of fire and ice and wind, so that now time is about the only thing that can conquer the giants, and even time's ax seems a dull gnawer, against the great larches' astounding mass and solidity.

———

If the growth of the lodgepole represents reckless imprudence and a nearly unbreakable flexibility, then the larch is surely solidity and moderation. If the larch symbolizes the dense connections of community, and the notion that when one is hurt or bent, all are hurt or bent, then the larch clearly represents the inflexible and the isolate, the loner, the individual, seemingly independent in the world, and as rigid, in his or her great strength, as the lodgepole is limber—the larch standing firm and planted, almost ridiculously so, in even the strongest storms, while all around the larch, the rest of the forest—not just lodgepole, but all species—is swaying and creaking, waving back and forth like a horse's mane.

(Sometimes the force will be so great upon the larch that they'll snap and burst, rather than bending, and their top will go flying off, the top cartwheeling through the sky like a smaller tree itself—the larch shattering, but never bending—and afterward, the hurt larch will set about its healing, sending up a slender new spar or sucker in place of the old top, cautious but determined, and unwilling to cede anything, not even into death—remaining standing for a century or longer, even after the life force has finally drained out of it.)

But the mystery does not go away.

Just across the border into Canada, along the North Fork of the Yaak, grow some of the biggest larches in the world. Grizzlies, wolves, elk, and moose pass through these old-growth forests, and pileated woodpeckers bang like cannons on some of the slowly dying ones. I'm not sure why this region is the epicenter within the epicenter, but it is. Perhaps it's the heart of fire, in this valley, or once was. Or perhaps it is the heart of ice, in winter. Perhaps both. Whatever the reason, the larch along the North Fork are immense and powerful, extraordinarily free of twist or camber or other defects or weaknesses.

And if you wander over into Canada, lured by the old forest's siren majesty, you might stumble across some ancient little metal placards tacked here and there to a giant tree, at the edge of a tiny marsh, which, dated sometime in the 1940s (the trees themselves perhaps five or six hundred years old, and still growing strong), inform you that this indeterminate Canadian forest, unbounded by any other signage or perimeters, is a "natural area," dedicated to the study of larch under natural conditions, and even editorializes that "some places should have value simply by the fact of their graceful existence, and for the lessons they can teach our scientists."

Our artists and community members too, I'd have hoped they'd add to it someday, though still, I can't quibble.

There is no similarly protected larch forest over on the U.S. side of the North Fork, though I wish there were. In fact, I wish we would begin managing a system within this forest now that would commit itself to a hundred-year plan of developing more old-growth larch, and reconnecting the isolated patches of existing old-growth larch, so that someday a hundred years from now a traveler—man, woman, child, or moose; bear, elk, wolf, or caribou—could set out on a warm summer's day and pass through the leafy cool light of an old larch forest, the duff soft underfoot and the air smoky and gauzy with the sun-warmed esters and terpenes emanating from the bark, and the odor of lupine sweet and dense all throughout the grove—and that the traveler could walk and walk, and never leave the old-growth canopy; could walk all day and then into the night, through columns of moonbeam strafing down through the canopy, and still be within the old forest; could pass out of this country and into the next, and still be in the old larch forest.

I'd like for travelers to be able to walk for days in that manner, until perhaps they forgot that this was not the natural condition of the world; until they came to be comfortable with and accustomed to the rhythms of the old larch forest, and knew the world, and this valley, as it had once been.

I know that's a lot to ask for, but I don't think it's too much.

———————

Western larch weighs forty-six pounds per cubic foot, dried, up here; in the Yaak it's the heaviest, densest wood in the forest. It's like a cubic foot of stone, standing or fallen.

Often they're so heavy, so saturated with their uptake of nutrients, that on the big helicopter sales, in places so far back into the mountains, or on slopes so steep that not even the timber industry's pawns in Congress will have been able to appropriate public finances to build roads into those places, the sawyers will have to girdle the big larch trees a year or more in advance of the logging.

This allows the life, the sap, to drain slowly out of the behemoths, so that when the helicopters do come, and the girdled trees are finally felled, their dead or dying weight is considerably less than if they were still green, and the helicopter companies are able to save money on fuel, and there's less strain on their engines.

————————

As powerful and unyielding as the larch is, it often becomes even more so as it ages. Silviculturists speak of certain species that will "release" when their competitors die or blow over or are cut down, or are simply outcompeted, and wither away. You can read the stories of these individual competitors, year by year, in the growth rings sampled by an increment borer, or, in the case of one of the giants being felled, in the cross section made by the saw and sawyer.

The spaces between the growth rings expand and contract through the years, charting the individual's explosive early growth, and then the slowing down, as if for a breath of air, and then, when a fire or wind comes through and cleans out some competitors, an expansion again. To me such tales of thinning and thickening read like the scan of a kind of silent music, not just for larch but for any species being examined—a silent symphony of rise and fall, contraction and expansion, segue and chorus.

When the larch is "released" from its previous competitive constraints, it's a wonderful thing to see, in that tale of the growth rings. It seems while viewing the ever tightening bunching of growth rings in a cross section, one can almost feel the drought, or absence of sun, or cold weather, or depleting soil nutrients that caused the larch's growth to be so labored, in that tight or constricted period.

But the larch endures, bides its time. And even when the internal girth is expanding only slowly, the outer bark is thickening, providing further protection against the wind and disease and fire and ice in the world. The tree is still growing, becoming stronger, without appearing to grow.

(Again, because it is a larch, it is two things: secret, in these periods of hard-to-measure growth, but then ostentatious, the most visible tree in the forest, during October, the best and sweetest time of year, with the forests of larch turning the viewscape of entire mountain ranges upside down, from the soothing lull of blue-green to the hypnotic flames of orange and gold.)

Over time, the weaker trees fall away, as they must. The larch takes a deep breath of air, of sun, and stretches again; releases. It's one of the few words used by industry that I find adequate and fair. Industry views these "releases" simply as an opportunity for the larch to produce more fiber for them, while I view them as powerful expressions of biological glory, and the liberation brought about by the virtues of endurance.

It's like a kind of dramatic, visual music, and I'm always awed by it whenever I see it; whenever I touch the growth rings with my fingers, and count the scores to that music, that rising and falling and rising power, year by year.

What makes the Yaak so magic? What makes the larch so magic? What makes the Yaak the epicenter of larch? Surely it is in large part due to the incredible confluence, here like no place else, of those three elements, fire and wind and ice: those three forces sawing back and forth across a land scraped thin by ice, with the winds then depositing the dust of that retreating ice, and the early forests that crept in over that dust burning and burning and burning.

In many places in the Yaak, the scientists' soil surveys indicate that the soils are poor, with nearly zero growing potential. Tell me then how and why the stumps and carcasses of larch four feet in diameter litter the forest floor in a swath that runs from the summit thirty miles north, up the North Fork, and many miles farther, over into Canada. If the soil is so poor, how did those trees grow and prosper, when they started out a millennium ago, and why did we cut them?

I'm convinced there's a way to represent all this growth as sound—some of it lightning-quick, some centuries-slow—and am convinced too that such music, whether faintly audible or not, lays a balm on any human heart that will stand quietly for a few moments in its presence.

The fire has a sound, too, as does the slow sinking of rot, as does the heavy crashing and clashing of ice storms, their dagger teeth gnawing at and carving this incredible forest.

Fire, ice, and wind: the larches' response to and shaping by the fires are dramatic, as is the flame-like alacrity with which they leap from dormancy each spring, and with which they retire for winter's slumber each fall—but I have to say, I think it is their patience by which I am most impressed, and of which I am most envious.

They possess the power of the wind, in resisting the wind—in battling it to a draw—and they possess the power of fire, in not merely surviving the fire, but prospering from it. They possess too the power of the glaciers, in the profound glory of their steady incremental growth, and the sublime power of creep. Grow a while, then rest, in winter's deep snows. Take a breather, but lose no ground. Leap, then, when energy returns with the sun, and push on.

I love the odor of them, I love the sight and touch of them. I love to lean in against them, to spread my arms against them, to touch the thick laminae of bark, to sit beneath them in storms while all else sways, as branches and streamers of moss whirl through the air.

I love to listen to the pileated woodpeckers drumming on them, and to the scrabble of little clawed animals scrambling up and down the bark of the living, as well as upon the fallen husks of the dead.

I love to see them lying on their sides in the ferns, rotting slowly—resting again, with the rain and sunlight still somehow feeding their magnificent and rotting bodies, even as they continue feeding the forest around them.

They are geological in their immensity, as well as in their natural life span. I want to believe they will be well suited to the coming temperature variations, the dormancy demanded not just by winter's extremes, but by the coming heat and drought of global warming. I know they lack the pines' flexibility; they do not know how to sway. Still, I believe in them, admire them, am in love with them, am grateful to them, dream of them.

And I still dream of someone, one day—not me, other than in my old man's dreams—being able to walk from the summit of the Yaak to the Canadian border, in a swath of uninterrupted old-growth larch, ten miles wide, as once existed, as evidenced by the remnants still present, both standing as well as by their remaining stumps.

The shape and nature and spirit of this land would accommodate such a vision yet: it is only up to our hearts to ask it.

In the Yaak, they are the one thing that is ours. So many of the other elements in our forest are the rich threads of diversity that have arrived here from elsewhere, with those threads then braiding to form our own unique and powerful weave—but with the larch, we are for once not at the edge or in the seam of anything, are not poised tenuously at the edge of anything, nor the fragile margin of any fading distribution, but are instead, for once, the pure epicenter. They are ours, and we are theirs. They have helped shape everything in this valley, and everything in this valley has helped shape them.

———————

Again, they are at least as powerful in their dying and going-away as in the fullness of their life. The long upright residency of a century or longer, even after they have died from a great fire, or old age; the even slower disintegration, once lying back down, earthbound. Even in their yearly death, while losing the gold fire of their needles in autumn, they give back to the soil, particularly if a fire has just passed through, for the myriad wind-tossed casting of their needles acts as a net and helps secure the new bed of ash below, which might otherwise wash downslope and into the creeks and rivers, scouring the watercourse and eroding the soil.

It is a beautiful thing to see in the autumn, after a fire, those gold needles cast down by the millions upon a blackened ground. The two colors, black and gold, seem as balanced and beautiful as gold stars within the darkest night.

Strangely, however, it is perhaps in their absence that they might be most strongly felt. Late October and early November, after they have just gone to sleep, is the time I think of as most being their season. The sky above feels fuller, in the absence of their needles. There is suddenly more space above, in a time when our spirits need that; in the dwindling days of light, with winter's fog and rain and snow creeping in.

One night a damp wind blows hard from the south. In the morning the hills and mountains are covered with gold. It's an incredible banquet, a visual feast, and our eyes take it in all at once, and a thing stirs in our blood, a strengthening and quieting down both; and farther back in the forest, the bears begin to crawl into their dens, seeking sleep also.

If the gold needles had stayed up there against that cerulean October sky forever, surely we would have eventually gotten used to it, and taken it for granted.

Now, however, down on the ground, it's within reach—we're able to simply reach down and scoop up a handful of that incredible gold, and it's all around us.

Hiking down off a mountain from far in the backcountry, I stop at dusk, weary. Without shedding my burdened pack, I take a seat on an old fallen larch, one of those ancient giants from the last century, its heartwood finally rotting but with its outer husk still firm.

The immense log is covered completely with the gold confetti of its descendants all around it, and there is no table or other furniture I have ever seen more elegant or beautiful than that impromptu bench, nor more timely—I was tired, and needed a place to rest, so I sat down, and it was there for me—and I sit there resting for a long time, watching the dusk give itself over to dark.

And just as there is no furniture that could be the equal of a fallen larch, wild in the woods to rot or burn at its own pace, or under the pace of this landscape that is so intensely its partner, surely there can be no gold-lined streets of heaven superior to what awaits the residents of this valley, upon awakening on such a fine October morning, after a night when the wind has blown hard, and when our dreams of a night sky filled with swirling, shimmering gold are exceeded only by the beauty of reality, when we first step outside that next day, with one more season being born into a ceaseless and enduring world.

WOLF PALETTE

THERE IS COLOR IN THE LAND AGAIN. OR PERHAPS IT was always there, like a pigment in the soil, but was simply rendered imperceptible for a while. But not for long. Not all that much separated the land—famous already for the mineral-rich hues of its cliffs and mountains, its gurgling hot springs and bubbling mud pots—in terms of time or space, from the breath of the wolves that would bring the color back like painters.

The wolves, to the best of anyone's knowledge, had been extinguished from Yellowstone for only seven decades: shot, trapped, poisoned, eradicated. In terms of space, only a veil of country had separated them, some seven hundred miles, more or less. Any one of the Yellowstone wolves—any one—could have covered that short distance in a week, rather than taking the better part of a century. There is an increasing wealth of science, and of knowledge, accruing around the recolonization of Yellowstone, but its recolorization will always be wrapped in mystery.

The wolves did not return on their own. It took a massive reversal of public sentiment and 160,000 letters to Congress and the U.S. Fish and Wildlife Service and ceaseless lobbying, public education, and outreach by environmentalists before fourteen wolves were finally captured up in British Columbia and transported to Yellowstone in 1994, where, after dramatic political maneuverings of lawsuit and countersuit, they were released into the snows of Yellowstone. An ocean of elk and bison awaited them.

Maybe they would have eventually recolonized Yellowstone without human intervention. They were already beginning to ease back down across the border, filtering into Montana through places like the Yaak, the Ninemile, and the Flathead valleys, but the American public wanted them sooner. So we went out and got them, brought them here in trucks and helicopters, wrenched from their old homelands, and with significant mortality. Not that a more natural recolonization would have been entirely seamless.

Already, not one of the original recolonizers survives; in the wild, a seven- or eight-year-old wolf is getting old, and a ten-year-old wolf is ancient, and ten years have gone by. Already, the last of those first returning—or returned—wolves have gone under, down into a soil that did not birth them, but which sustained them, and from which they summoned a seemingly miraculous flowering of wildness.

There is color in the land again. How can the crimson blood of elk in the snow release a bluebird? How can black and silver wolves combine, like pigment, to unleash a new surge of yellow warblers and brilliant tanagers back into a landscape long absent such threads, such an abundance of colors?

Upon the wolves' return, so sudden was the transformation, so quick the reparations, that it seemed a marvel that the landscape—brittle and fractured as it had become in the absence of even that one species—had been able to hold together as well as it had for those seventy or so years. Not so much like a person, across a similar span of years, living with some awful dose of toxins within, but perhaps more like that same person living with the absence of some stellar, sparkling, wondrous ingredient: some beautiful, shining, gleaming essence, perhaps read about in old medical texts and hypothesized, but never seen or known, only dreamed or imagined.

In the ten years since the wolves have been back, they have reshaped huge sections of an awkwardly leaning ecosystem, one which in many places we did not even recognize as leaning, as if a homeowner were to summon an ornamental landscaping service only to have the workers discover termites in the house's walls and a crumbling foundation. And also as if the landscapers held the key to renewing the building itself.

Elk, the primary food for wolves, represent a substantial reserve of energy and nutrients on the hoof.

By pruning the wildly excessive elk numbers, and by forcing the elk to be elk again, the Yellowstone wolves kept the elk herds on the move, allowing overgrazed riparian areas to recover. The elk were no longer encamping in any one spot like feedlot animals, and the restored riverbanks served as nesting and feeding habitat for songbirds of different hues. Blink, and a howl equals the color yellow.

Now, the elk are not living as long. Their trophic capacity—vessels of sunlight, vessels of grass-meat—is being redistributed with greater alacrity, greater vitality, throughout the Yellowstone ecosystem; there is greater turnover in the mortality game upon which wild nature, and what we think of as a healthier nature, relies so powerfully.

Where previously the overcrowded and static elk and deer herds conspired to keep stands of aspen from regenerating, browsing with sharp teeth any and all young aspen suckers as soon as they emerged, the beautiful groves of aspen, snow-white bark and quivering gold leaves in the fall, are now prospering, flaring back up on the landscape like so many tens of thousands of autumn-lit candles. Entire mountain ranges are ultimately being painted anew—more color, more vitality, more light—by the arrival of, initially, a mated pair of wolves, an alpha male and female, followed by the next wave of other wolves, new wolves.

Certainly the renewal of the aspen, and of streamside deciduous trees that had previously been repressed by the overabundance of elk—willow, cottonwood, ninebark, chokecherry—is not limited to showcase-only values of painterly aesthetics. As in all of wild nature, there is function everywhere—purpose, meaning, and a sophistication beyond our wildest dreams. Cerulean, sapphire, claret, jade—the return of deciduous saplings to the hoof-cut, denuded riverbanks once abused by too many elk has been good for more than songbirds and artists. Beavers, too, have prospered, able now to access their requisite building and feeding materials without needing to venture so far into dangerous territory. This has resulted in the return of more backwater ponds and pools and eddies, the filtering and life-support systems for so much other river life, and has provided a greater distribution of nutrients in the shallow sloughs that back up and create gentle floods behind the beaver dams. In these shallow areas of submersion young cottonwoods prosper—more flame color, and more beaver habitat.

Circles within circles: with more beavers in the system, the wolves will eat a beaver now and again, every x pounds of beaver meat consumed displacing, I suppose, a similar poundage of what would otherwise have been elk meat, so that in the elk herds' relinquishing their previously uncontested streamside territory, they gain a certain freedom and vitality. While an old way of looking at things might suggest that the elk were serving the wolves, it could be said that the elk were serving themselves as well.

It's all more tangled and wonderful than we may ever know, and the best part is we can't really predict or manage or fully measure it. Much as we'd like to, we can't say that three beavers plus one wolf plus two elk, a songbird, seven aspen trees, and a ten-thousand-acre wildfire equal six beavers, four elk, five wolves, and no birds, any more than we can say that chartreuse equals magenta, or aquamarine, or fuchsia. We can spend centuries trying to chase down and quantify those connections, but in a wild and healthy landscape there will always be vast quantities of unknown relationships, and immeasurable consequences. Even with all of the science and learning available to us in the twenty-first century, we have trouble viewing the land, really seeing it in anything but the broadest and most brilliant strokes of color. I do not think it is coincidental that such discoveries—such illuminations of interconnectedness—are emanating from the tableau of one of our largest and wildest remaining wildernesses. So significant is the degree of our not-yet-knowledge, our unknowingness, that we could make major discoveries—witness major illuminations—in any environment, no matter how fragmented and compromised that system might be. But it is in our last few big wild landscapes, I think, where the potential, the opportunity, for discovery remains strongest, and might be most easily or readily encountered.

Like neither saviors nor infidels but simply (or not so simply) like wolves, they returned to their home, bringing great color and breathing a life force that some, in an upside-down world, view as destructive—as if we have become so estranged that we can no longer really tell one from the other. In this regard, the wolves are instructors, and in this regard, we are watching them with fascination, with our senses as well as our returning knowledge—like hunters ourselves—reengaged and keenly alert.

WHALE SHARK

A GANG OF FRIENDS ON A BOAT IN THE GALÁPAGOS, A tiny stippling of new islands hundreds of miles from any other land. Sometimes it's impossible, here in Darwin's country, not to think of Bible stories: the Garden of Eden, Day One of life's origins, etc.

We are sitting below deck, lunching, when a glistening black fin of a shape and size not known to us from previous days on the water—this is no porpoise, no dolphin—creases the glassy blue and noses along, the fin itself a small sailboat, with the slight turbulence fore and aft promising the existence of something big.

We have no idea how big.

We leap from the table. Though I don't know this quite yet, we're going in with the big fish—the biggest fish in the world, a whale shark: not a whale, not a mammal, just a cold-blooded gilled thing, a giant, weighing up to ten tons.

Our guide Juan is first up on the deck, where he begins passing out fins and masks. He hasn't seen a whale shark in over a year.

It's the closest I ever hope to come to an *Abandon ship!* order, and the adrenaline is as sweet as nectar. There's no time to wriggle into the cumbersome wet suits; the crew is already boarding the Zodiacs: pandemonium, yearning. Was it this way for the whalers? I think that it was.

We pull up alongside the great body. The fin marks the spot.

This is a creature spun into being by nothing more than the whirl of the world, and sun: following the currents of plankton, its mouth gaping.

We can see the shadow now beneath the fin. The whale shark turns—the Zodiacs' motors are turned off, we're drifting toward it—and because of this turning, the shallow raft is drifting right across the whale shark, all it has to do is ease upward a little bit and we will be skyborne, a boatful of whale riders, capsized—but the big fish does not panic, just keeps gliding along, and we pass over it.

We could reach our hands into the water, stick our arms in up to the elbows, and touch the giant fish. Thirty-five feet long.

Touch nothing in the Galápagos. To touch these things is to ruin them.

The fish—the world's largest fish—is a plankton feeder; only that direct intermediary to the sun, phytoplankton, could provide enough steady biomass to fuel such a giant.

We leap-slip into the water as quickly and quietly—respectfully—as possible. I'm the first one in. I don't know what to expect but I imagine that such a moment might not come in my life again soon. I pass from *solid*, raft, through the sky, *air*, and into the cold Humboldt current, *liquid*, in the time it takes to blink, and think half a thought or no thought at all, and then I'm all the way in. There are the silvery bubbles of my exhalation and fin-swirl, and all I can see is whale shark in front of me, as dark as a nightmare; as dark as the end of your life. As if the ocean has gone black. There is nothing anywhere but black, and it takes another half a thought to realize that the ocean has been transformed to one fish.

I'd been afraid that the sound of me, of us, would frighten and flare the fish; that it would plunge, would streak away.

But why should the sound of a pebble frighten anything? Why should a single feather frighten the largest fish in the world?

My heart is going faster than it has ever gone, being still, treading water. The last of the sun's heat is leaving my body.

No other swimmers are yet in the water but the captain said *Go*, and I wanted to go, so I went.

The whale shark is not panicked, but neither is it coming over to introduce itself. It's feeding, and basking—thermoregulating, after its night's slumber in the icy depths—the water here, where the currents come together, is 1,300 meters deep—and I push out to meet it, and join it, and to see what will happen.

Rarely in life can I remember ever having entered anything so unknowingly, one where the complications of all my prior experience is rendered useless.

I join the fish at its right side. I paddle strongly, my flippers the opposite of its grace. The specks glow. They bewitch, a mix of firefly light and the yellow sideboard running lights of a great seagoing vessel.

Somehow, I find myself alongside its gills, and it is here that I encounter the startling intimacy of watching it breathe: the four plates of the gill coverings, each seeming the size of a doorway, the four plates pulsing in, out, in, out, as the whale shark drinks in the invisible broth of the sun. Tiny fish are swimming in and out of those giant gills, which open a few inches, then close. The fish swirl and disappear into the gills on the intake, then come scurrying back out, blown back out, current-swirled.

I'm hyperventilating, and don't realize for a while that the panting sound is me. For a while, it seems to be the world's sound. Sometimes I slow down, to examine the broad caudal fin, which, as it catches up with me, passes beneath me as would the wing of an airplane.

It is exactly like flying.

It is not a whale. It is not a mammal. It is not one of us, though we all came from the same place, long ago.

Something happens—I'm not sure what—and the whale

shark begins pulling away: not in a gust or a surge, but simply another gear, so that I'm having to haul ass to keep up.

I'm acutely aware—swimming alongside her head like that—that she is aware of me; that I am neither her focus nor her concern. She could so easily outdistance me; could descend, could leap and breach, could whack me with fin or tail—could bite me, I suppose, or gum me with her truck-grill of a mouth, which time has shaped to be neither grinning nor frowning, but instead perpetually and perfectly scooped open, perpetually hungry, perpetually satisfied. *Just swim.* Follow the sun-path of plankton.

She pulls slightly past me. I'm back beside the tail, now, which unnerves me.

I do not want to be whacked by the whale shark's tail. I stroke harder, to get back up to my earlier position, up by the head: and she slows, and allows me. And as I pass alongside her great speckled body, the sunlight through the water is refracted in the slight waves made by her and my passage, and creates a dappled effect upon those luminous spots, so that they seem to be moving, rearranging themselves on her body—migrating across her body—and this image floods me with peace.

The eye. With every stroke I'm aware of not wanting to spook the animal, am grateful to and respectful of her for allowing me to dink along beside her, as might a young sea lion or fur seal, playing (the things a giant has to put up with!)—and gradually, with my courage building, I swim up a little farther, to get a good look at the entrance to the cave that is her mouth.

Little blue fish hover in front of that cave, darting like butterflies—fish that are nearly the size of my hand, maybe a dozen of them—and I look slightly down and into the whale shark's eye, which is looking into mine.

It's the size of a marble. It's the smallest thing in the world. It's not much larger than mine—indeed, might be the same size. The eye is connected to the brain through an infinitude of circuits and pathways, but this animal has ten tons or more of other circuits and pathways, radiating from all parts of her body into that immense skull, immense brain, ancient and fishy though it may be.

We were all fish once.

How big is her heart, how big is her brain? Are we communicating; is she thinking, assessing, analyzing?

You can't really know these things with a fish, can you? Hell, it's hard enough to know them with another person, sometimes. The eye is there, the eye is seeing me—but does it know me, does it understand in any way my intent, my brief presence in the world?

I can't say yes. I can't say no.

We swim beside her for a long time. Half an hour? Two days?

At first I found that I was hyperventilating, working to keep up: taking short, choppy strokes, like a man shoveling coal into a furnace, or splitting firewood with an ax, while the whale shark glided, cruised, beautifully.

She was pulling slowly away, like an ocean liner leaving a port, one where you hold your ticket but you are not on the ship. It is going across the ocean on a grand adventure but you are not on it, and you find yourself running up the gangplank, you must not miss it. You might never even have realized, dreamed or intended, that the trip of a lifetime awaited, and yet you find nonetheless that you are holding a ticket, maybe the last of its kind, and the giant ship, its portals illuminated by the glow lamps of all the other travelers, each in their own berth, is pulling away, and you must not miss it.

I stroke harder; I must stay up. I don't know why.

I swim alongside her for a long and delicious time.

How are group decisions made among any species? What unseen electricity exists between birds that swerve in flight as one? It comes to us in pretty much a moment—over the course of maybe thirty seconds—that it is time to let the great fish slide on past, no longer accompanied. Part of it is physical fatigue, but part of it is something else. It may be as simple as our brains having absorbed all the sugar they can hold, but I like to think it is more—that it is each of us knowing when it is time to leave even the finest of parties, and to let the host or hostess return to the dignity of solitude—and one by one and two by two we stop swimming and watch the whale continue on, swimming no faster and no slower than before, while we tread water—and feel deep within us that ancient chagrin of the fisherman whose line has snapped, whose net has broken. We let the big fish go.

The Galápagos are doomed, as was the first Garden of Eden, and as will be the last—the ants are coming, the wasps, the fleas and ticks, the goats and rats and cats, the man, the woman, the dark must arrive, the tribulation must begin—but how amazing to witness it from the other side, the side of before—these things to come. To look essentially at innocence, not in an individual, but in a world.

The eye will be drawn more and more to beauty, as we wreck ever more of it. The heart will be ever hungrier for awe, as it is blitzed and bred and corn-fed out of us.

We may yet, finally, one day learn how truly tiny we are, and in that revelation, know neither agony nor despair, but great peace, and—if we're lucky—maybe even a thing like inexplicable love.

Where is the whale shark now? Is she warm, is she cold? Be assured that she is not thinking of us; that we came and went, in but part of a day.

Afterwards, we will talk about wanting to touch her, but not do-ing so. I'm glad I didn't, but I wanted to.

Afterwards, each of us will have different experiences, which we will share, with near-religious fervor.

Terry, for instance, will tell of how when she slipped out of the Zodiac, she found herself right in front of the white-lipped giant mouth, the always-open mouth, and screamed underwa-ter. Andrea will remember being brushed—not whacked—by the tail. We'll read accounts of how divers have been injured and even killed by a swipe of the tail. "I knew it wasn't somebody's flipper," she says." There was no one else back there."

What I remember is this: in a heated world, how ice cold the fish was: like a glacier. I did not touch her, but didn't have to. There was this shell, this envelope of coldness, all around her, which, when you got too close—two, three, four feet—chilled you to the bone. As if the whale shark was made of ice, ten tons of ice, and was gliding along the surface, waiting to get warm. Which may be pretty much what was happening.

The other thing was also related to size.

If you got too close—two, three, four feet—you got pulled in. The sheer mass of her had its own gravity. I don't mean you got pulled in emotionally; I mean there was a physical pull, a mag-netism, and you could feel the great cold more deeply than ever before, could feel it sucking you in, so that in the next second, the next moment, you would be upon the whale shark, and know more fully the mass of that deep cold; and frightened—not quite terrified, but damn alarmed—you pulled away quickly, kicked back out away from that traveling giant lozenge of cold. A chill not quite like any other previously known.

We know that hard times are coming, in a warming world.

We know that the changes will not be kind to us, nor to so much that is crafted, delicate, rare, and beautiful. I cannot change that. I cannot change that.

What could I do, what could I say, when the captain said *Leap!*, but leap?

And so another day passed, in which I changed nothing.

MOON STORY

THIS IS NOT AN ECLIPSE STORY.

I grew up in Houston in the 1950s, '60s, and early '70s, so yeah, the moon shot was a pretty big deal. One of the Apollo astronauts was from nearby La Grange, where my mother grew up—not a moonwalker, but one of the first ones to get blasted away from this sweet blue planet, out into the unknown darkness, to the moon and around and then back, and returning to tell about it.

My own orbit from those days is widening, casting further and farther toward what someday I suppose will be the territory of old age—outer darkness, with only the cold pinpricks of stars for company, while far below and closer to the warm center run and laugh and play the living, almost scurrying, though also with a leisure that approaches nonchalance, even as intergalactic static crackles and bounces off the dry skin of an old outlander like pellets of stinging hail dimpling the fragile heat shield of a space-craft. Look how *small* they are all becoming below, the young, as one's orbit widens, with the distance between one year and the next becoming smaller, like the growth rings of an old tree bunching up out at the perimeter, too close together now to even count.

From those childhood days, I remember the cool NASA ball caps. I had one as recently as last year, with its whirling proton-loop, atomic orbit emblem—until my pup, a French Brittany with the decidedly un-French name of Otis—chewed it to blue and white shards.

(From what oil well first came the plastic that made the hatband? I mean, what farmer's field? What year, and where was I, and what was I doing when that black-green oil first rushed up the borehole? And what of the days before any of us existed? What dinosaur lay down its sleepy head in the Paleozoic swamp and slept forever, being blanketed then with mud and leaves and the slowly warming rising waters, dissolving to no longer be a dinosaur but instead a soup of carbon and hydrogen, baking and sliding away, up one fault and down another, traveling beneath the surface as it had once in its brief assembly traveled above the surface; ascending, finally, to an anticline with an impermeable cap, like the dome of a cathedral, and pausing there, trapped for eons, and reassembling into oil, before the drill bit—1955? 1958? 1963?—pierced the crypt, released the oil, sent it to the plastics factory, where the hat I wore as a child was birthed?)

Farther. The living are specks. As one ages, time compresses. We perceived, believed, fairly early—in our midtwenties or thirties—that time is circular, like the four seasons, or what used to be the four seasons, before we drilled too many holes in the earth. (It is not the moon that is made of Swiss cheese, but our own sweet earth. There are experimental technologies that can convert carbon dioxide into a chalky solid, and it's theorized we could use this solid—in paste form—to fill in every well we ever drilled: burying the carbon we burned and used, for a while.)

My own belief is that the genie is out of the bottle; it's hard even in the fiction of science fiction to imagine filling every old borehole, sucking CO_2 out of the sky and putting it back in the ground it came from, like putty or cement, repairing or patching a fractured, shifting, quaking substructure with the brittle paste of CO_2 chalk.

And yet I'd like to believe. Where I live now, in northwest Montana, is the site of the world's largest asbestos mine. The ore there contains a certain kind of asbestos, tremolite, the mineralization of which results in its fibers being extraordinarily tiny. Seen under the microscope, they resemble quilled arrows with barbed arrowheads; they lodge in the lungs and stomach lining and then work their way inward, a billion microscopic darts fired by unseen archers. The word *Yaak* is Kootenai for *arrow*, for the way the Yaak River charges down out of the mountains and into the curved bow of the Kootenai River, largest tributary to the Columbia. There used to be porcupines up here but they have vanished in only the last fifteen to twenty years. My dogs, especially Point, were always getting into them; the barbed quills made it hard to pull them from the dogs, resulting always in much blood and tissue trauma as I wrenched them free. Indigenous folklore refers to porcupines as the Old People of the mountains, and prophesies that when porcupines disappear from a landscape, it means the landscape is in deep illness.

Time may indeed be circular, for the centripetal pull of it out here on the farther perimeters is starting to feel pretty enormous. What if we could suck all the asbestos fibers out of the air around the town of Libby and convert it, like that CO_2, to a solid form, able then to be buried deep? Future generations might know this valley, the Treasure Valley, for its beauty without the bittersweetness of such scourge, such price, awaiting all who breathe.

I meant to be writing about the moon but feel compelled to say a few words about Point. He was the sentinel case of mesothelioma in a pet in Lincoln County. Mesothelioma hits hard and quick; you have six weeks, max. It's best to have one's affairs in order. When it hit him, I drained the pinkish cancer-fluid from his stomach with a syringe each night before we went hunting each next day. God, he died hard, swelling like a pumpkin every day, but still tottering on, hunting even on his last day of life, until I realized I was torturing us both and had to let him go, had to release him to that which was pulling at him so hard.

———————

In high school, Einstein's elegant $E = mc^2$ was easily memorized, but the assumption of constancy seems an assumption that gets us in trouble in all other matters. Maybe he meant constancy in the moment, the split second in which the equation was applied, but for a long time the string theory people (not to be confused with the performance artists, the Blue Man Group) have been saying nothing we see is a constant, nor can we, nor they, be 100 percent sure anything is real, instead calling all matter, all *things*, an extreme likelihood of quivering assemblages always in motion, assemblages of smaller things arranged to look like, feel like, etc., the thing that we in turn (also a swirling arrangement of matter at any point in time) are feeling, touching, smelling, hearing, tasting, identify as real.

(I often think too that if Einstein, instead of labeling *space* as being the thing relative to time, had referred to it as *place*, we'd all have done better in school. Place, not space. A positive, tactile thing, mortal. *Place*: the back 40, the Panhandle, Indian territory, Madagascar, what-have-you—rather than an invisible thing, *space*, as in outer space, and the association of nothingness. A little frozen rock dust, ice crystals at the end of comets. A smear of yellow in all-else blackness, all-else emptiness.)

As our landscape, our place or space, becomes more fragmented and poisoned, burned, eroded, flooded, and paved over, and as our relationship with time also explodes—all of us moving faster and faster, dervishes until we can whirl no more, and must lie down upon that broken landscape, the broken space across which our churning altered version of time howls—well, what happens next? Does even our own certainty, or the *likelihood* of us, begin to doubt us, until one by one, we each and all begin to vanish, as if to the Rapture?

Or what if we are eradicating—squandering, even—the possibility for and of a rapture, and an afterlife? For if we destroy the land and wound mortally the concept of *time-here-below*, does not the concept of or likelihood of *beyond-time* also go down with that sinking ship?

———————

No ideas but in things, wrote William Carlos Williams, less than a generation after Einstein, as if not so much resisting but instead modifying his equation. Williams's dictum resounds more with the Texan in me, and the boy I was at ten who, every time my mother drove me across town to the Houston Museum of Natural History, ran straight to the exhibit of moon rocks. In my memory, I recall there being a small handful on a plain white surface, nondescript in every way. The geologist I would one day become might describe them as appearing clastic, dry, friable, with an apparent low level of compaction—mafic, brecciated igneous—possibly alkaline? They looked almost chalky, like the pale carbonates of the Hill Country, though even as a child I noted the obvious lack of fossils. But weren't those tiny vesicles testament to gases, suggesting the possibility of a once-upon-a-time oxygen component? And speaking of air—how did the astronauts do *that*? How could they carry that much air with them, or that much water?

What I remember most, beyond the moon rocks' extraordinarily dull dirt color, was my desire to touch them, and my still dogged if now slightly diminished belief that because they were different, rare, hard-gotten, other, they possessed power. They *had* to be treasure.

And if so, why were they displayed so casually—a typed index card stating MOON ROCKS? There was certainly no need for source or dateline.

Surely they contained such power—radioactive or otherwise—that mere three-eighths-inch plexiglass could not contain them. I hovered; paced, stalked round and round the small handful of squarish buff-colored stones. Was it a joke? Were the sapphires, moon diamonds, amethyst, and beryllium in vaults somewhere else while the astronauts pranked us with these chunks of road rubble they'd picked up on their way home from the airport?

I drifted away. The other things—the living—pulled me. The aquariums, brilliant with tropical fish; the huge-eyed little caiman sunning beneath its heat lamp. No one had a clue then what global warming was. It was upon us but we could not see it. We could see it but we did not notice it. The baby snapping turtle, black as tar, as elegant underwater as a ballet dancer, his long Stegosaurus tail trailing, ruddering, as his oversized feet, with claws like a grizzly's, waved in slow motion. His red eyes were studded with an asterisk for each pupil, leading one to suppose he perceived a different world than the one I beheld; and which of us was to argue the other's reality?

The rocks were an embarrassment. The geologist I would become wished the astronauts had stayed longer, dug deeper, searched farther. Climbed a mountain. Gone around to the back side. To have not returned until they found something better.

The moon. I believed then and guess I still do that the landing really happened. Though I do sometimes wonder, why has no one gone back?

I know NASA wasn't all about the moon—that one little speck of light out there in so much darkness—but it's interesting to me that I grew up in a culture where often the dominant association with any mention of the moon was to "shoot" it, to launch missiles or rockets at it. At the other end of the spectrum, there was plenty of lame poetry about the moon and stars, dewy meadows and so forth.

And yet, other times, it could be so great. The moon in literature.

Walker Percy, from *The Moviegoer*:
"The train has stopped and our car stands high in the air, squarely above a city street. The nearly full moon swims through streaming ragtags of cloud and sheds a brilliant light on the Capitol dome and the spanking new glass-and-steel office buildings and the empty street with its glittering streetcar track. Not a soul is in sight. Far away, beyond the wings of the Capitol building stretch the dark tree-covered hills and the twinkling lights of the town. By some trick of moonlight the city seems white as snow and never-tenanted; it sleeps away on its hilltop like the holy city of Zion."

Amy Hempel:
"'Tell me things I won't mind forgetting,' she said. 'Make it useless stuff or skip it.'

"I began. I told her insects fly through rain, missing every drop, never getting wet. I told her no one in America owned a tape recorder before Bing Crosby did. I told her the shape of the moon is like a banana—you see it looking full, you're seeing it end-on.'"

The poet Jim Harrison, in "Sketch For A Job-Application Blank":
"My left eye is blind and jogs like
a milky sparrow in its socket . . .

... I strain for a lunar arrogance ....
   Light macerates
   the lamp infects
warmth, more warmth, I cry."

And in "Returning At Night":
". . . in the root cellar
the potato sprouts
creeping through the door
glisten white and tubular
in the third phase
of the moon."

Patty Griffin does the best cover of "Moon River." Nanci Griffith's "Once in a Very Blue Moon" is very fine, as is (duh) Creedence Clearwater Revival's "Bad Moon Rising" (I'm told two of the Fogerty brothers lived in the Yaak Valley when they were younger; how I wish to believe that the lyrics to "Run Through the Jungle" were informed by that wild if unprotected landscape.) Oh, yeah—like I'm gonna forget—Neil Young's "Harvest Moon," also covered admirably by the Shook Twins.

It was Emmylou Harris, long ago, whose *Quarter Moon in a Ten Cent Town* first suggested to me that in art, a moon need not always be perfectly round to be noticed or appreciated.

My dad—a geophysicist and a hunter—and my mother, a schoolteacher, before I was born—saw to it I had a taste for nature, not just in the museums, but in the woods. We would go deer hunting every fall up in the Hill Country, at a place we called the deer pasture. A wild, feral land of incredible stargazing. Gillespie County. One night when my cousin Randy and I were outside gathering firewood, a meteor tore through the curtain of black sky like a rock thrown through the thinnest pane of creek ice. We looked up and saw it go sizzling past, scorching and sparking, then nothing but gray smoke with the stench of burned stone. Its velocity might have carried it another five or ten miles past us. Still, I look for that stone yearly, and like to imagine I might yet come across it and will, when I do, somehow recognize it when I see it. That it will be so much superior to the moon rocks of my youth.

My youngest brother, BJ, and I were dinking around at the deer pasture one summer when I decided to pursue a goal that had long intrigued me: to climb nearby X Mountain, even thought it was on someone else's property. In Texas, the feudal notion of private property, the sanctity of personal territory and ownership, is deeply entrenched, ridiculous as it might seem from a biological perspective. The gridwork of fenceposts and barbed-wire lattices the entire state as if dicing it as if into so many croutons. Every strand holds tufts of hair or fur or feathers from all the other passers-through but our own kind.

I had been living in Montana long enough by that point to have become more than comfortable with the concept of the commons.

A little about X Mountain: a little about the rumpled Hill Country, the ragged land updip from the Balcones Escarpment. Geology's cuts and cleavings are almost always beautiful, made slowly more sinuous by time and wandering like a beach's strand-line of before and after. We rip with saws, we bulldoze straight lines through the forest, we dig trenches for pipelines, our rail-road lines and interstates fire through the forest and across the prairies and even beneath the seas like arrows fired or like missiles disgorged from silos tilted onto their sides, so that they now face us and only us directly, rather than pointed with a trajectory toward Siberia, the Irkutsk, Iceland, Moscow. Nature is rarely if ever linear, or even geometric.

I digress. I've exceeded the orbital pull of the subject. The Texas Hill Country contains some of the oldest stone in the world that can be found at the surface—Cambrian sandstone, what was once the floor of the new-made world, the dawn of all life, simple one- and then multi-celled organisms spinning in the sunlit seas, being drawn forward and backward with the tide—organisms so tiny they can't even be seen in the stone in which they now exist forever—though I like to think sometimes that when I'm building a stone wall or flagstone driveway with those rocks, and I drop one, releasing a wisp of arid dust, what I see and smell in that plume is the ground-up ephemera of what life was like a billion years ago: the first scent of us and our kind approaching that long, slow on-ramp.

It is a pleasing smell, and while it arouses no memories in me other than the here and now—hot summer days working in the rock fields with my family, making slow order out of disorder, the disassembled and broken becoming beautiful and whole once more, scent of bluebonnets with solitary bumblebees feasting on their nectar, and grasshoppers rattle-clacking away with wings spread, gliding, the most primitive of flying machines, and yet the most enduring—Ah, shit. Where was I? *Contact.*

The deer pasture where we hunt also possesses some of the world's oldest granite—rock that's younger than the Cambrian sandstone it pierced from below with its once-upon-a-time tongues of flame, the mineral-rich magma surging upward along any vertical fissure it could find, any thinness or weakness in the overlying Cambrian strata—and, where there was no weakness, creating one: the thing which had never seen sunlight before, the minerals that have existed in the great furnaces near earth's dense center demanding their time in the sun.

Some made it out and cooled rapidly; others made it almost all the way out, but not quite—though cooling now, far from the maddening heat and resting just beneath the surface, the minerals in that magma had all the time in the world to rearrange themselves according to their polarities and chemical charges and valences, spinning and rotating as if governed by magnets or twin poles, their earth-center miles below, and the strange moon-rock in the sky, which was maybe related to them or maybe not: and it was in this slow cooling, just beneath the surface, that great beauty was achieved. The crystals began adhering to one another, blossoming into fantastic spires and cathedrals, with each elemental mineral, and each assemblage of elements, having all the time in the world to form and grow. These are the crystals—the slow crystals—I wanted to believe comprised the heart and soul, the inner being, of the moon. *Dig deeper.*

What is the sound of the psychic stall horn, the command to point the nose back down now or be lost forever, when one lives so far from humanity in a place like the Yaak Valley, talking only to one's dogs and even then not much, using hand signals— drifting, keeping the crazed world, the lunatic world, at arm's distance, or beyond? It's a hermit existence that fits some of us better than others. It's the way some are meant to be. Moon-like, in that regard, I guess you'd have to say. "We loved the earth but could not stay"—Wallace Stevens.

At the deer pasture, BJ and I prepared to climb over the barbed-wire fence and set out toward the previously mythic *X* Mountain. Because it was on the other side of fences, it seemed far away. In reality, it was ludicrously close; we were there in a blink.

But before we got there—in that first fence crossing—I snagged my leg on the taut and newly strung barbed wire.

The difference between old rusted barbed wire and the moon-bright silver knife-blade of the taut unblemished product, so ratcheted to its full tensile stretch that the wind passing over it causes it to hum a faint dog-whistle keen—is like the difference between, I don't know, cooked and uncooked spaghetti.

I stood on the firm lowermost strand and lifted my other foot toward the top strand, which is what one can do when they're stretched that tight. But even then, there's usually a little stretch or sag beneath one's full weight. I was expecting it, and when there wasn't, I wobbled for a moment, and in so doing raked my calf across one of the fence's twisted teeth, the tip of a single barb sharper than the point of a knife.

It was the kind of wound that cuts so cleanly there is no pain, only the sudden tickle of blood's wetness on skin. It was not cool enough for the blood to steam but it went from warm to cold quickly as it trickled down my leg and into my sock. In John Prine's great song, "Lake Marie," he pauses in the song to query the listener, "You know what blood looks like in a black-and-white video? *Shadows!* That's what it looks like. *Shadows.*"

I'd never quite understood the leap in allusion there, but looking at my leg in that hyperbrilliant silver-blue light, I was reminded immediately of the song—the blood had the gleaming quality to it of the scorch of old-time flashbulbs. And it was definitely the darkest thing in that mercuric, floodlit world: the only dark thing, I realized, which might have been what Prine was seeing and describing.

The tear—the slice, slash, gash—was right in the balled-up meat of the calf muscle. *That one's gonna leave a scar*, I thought— *who needs tattoos?*—and as we proceeded on toward the hill, it grew smaller the closer we got—the mythic mesa we had seen all our lives but never visited, due to the vagaries of private property—land the colonists took from Mexico, who had taken it, if in name only, from the Comanches, who may or may not have taken it from someone before them—the Athabaskans?

There were shadows now. We passed through a grove of small oaks, the shadows as dark as the trunks of the trees themselves, and I left a smear of blood on blades of grass and on the silver-fire leaves of agarita and shin oak.

We started up the admittedly steep slope, but with every step, the mountain before us shrank until it could not even really be called a hill. It was a flat-topped bump—a little neck of caliche, limestone, remnant of older sea times, compressed to chalk; not as ancient as sat atop, and with many of its onetime contemporary chalk-strata eroded, ghost-whispered tumbling downstream back toward the new ocean, the Gulf.

We stood on it, looked out. I felt like a child. I was, what, maybe forty? Perhaps not even.

The moonlight bathed us as we strolled around the hill's flat top and through its scrubby wind-blasted juniper. I know this is a wretched cliché, moonlight *bathing*, but it's true, it poured down and over us as if molten silver. Sometimes a cliché is a cliché for a reason. It was brighter than most daylight, yet there was no danger of moonburn.

The reversal in scale—the grand becoming almost minute—made me dizzy, as did the moonlight itself. Back when photographs were taken with cameras, not phones, and you took the film to a print shop for developing, you had to look at the strip of negatives to decide which reprints you wanted, if any, from those sepia strips. Dark became ghostly bright, and light became unseeable dark, and I felt that I was getting a glimpse of the way the world really was, if not to me, then to someone—someone else's reality—and whether that was raccoon or scorpion, bumblebee or night-blooming cereus, hummingbird or swan, I could not say, only that we were in it.

The top of this great mountain—visible from thirty miles away—was not much larger than some of the shoulder-to-shoulder suburban lawns where I had grown up in middle-class Houston. It was about the size of a burger joint's gravel parking lot.

And yet: it was so level, in a land where nothing else was. We walked around on top, feeling much closer to the moon now—hundreds of miles closer, rather than a hundred feet—a jack-rabbit, pale as bone, looking like a snowshoe hare in winter, or the white rabbit in a magic trick, leaped from hiding and dashed away—and at the southern end of the mesa, just as I was about to turn around and go back to the other end, I noticed something I might not have seen in daylight: smooth white round river stones, atypical for that country, and spaced evenly in an arc.

They were grown over with grass and lichens, but the moon-light brought them out in bony relief. Now I could see more of them, each no larger than a skull, but enough of them, I realized, to form a circle. The circle was grown over with grass and low juniper. But it was by God a real teepee ring, which made sense to me, though I'd never seen one around here, only in Montana.

What was a hundred or a hundred and twenty-five years to a stone, or even the placement of a stone?

I didn't really mind being up there, uninvited by the absentee landowner, who simply had his cattle grazing below, but I was a little rattled by having stumbled into a ceremonial spot uninvited. It had long been unused, of course, but still: the incredible light made me feel superilluminated in a way I did not want to be, and I apologized for barging in, and we made our way back down, with my leg still painting bright red the low vegetation through which we passed. Indian paintbrush, it's called, *Castilleja indivisa*; one of the perhaps hundred thousand or so microaggressions with which we bruise our way through the world daily.

We made our way down the steep slope following a trail worn not by humans but by the hooves of deer—too steep for cattle, which was likely why the ring was still intact—and walked back toward the glimmering silver fence.

We had not gone far at all when we encountered an immense white-tailed buck, his velveted antlers glowing, as if he carried above him a silver nest of fire.

Big bucks like that are always nocturnal. This one looked uncomfortable, however—as if he were being called upon to swim through that silver light. It was so strange and thick it seemed like a chunk of light, elemental, like a mineral, rather than reflected waves of light. After watching us for a few seconds, the buck turned and ran and vaulted high over the fence, arching like a rainbow, with not even the tip of a hoof touching the top strand.

He landed lightly and continued on into the thick juniper beyond, bobbing like a spark: the living, taking refuge in the living.

We approached the same illuminated fence, touched it first, as if it might be hot, and then climbed carefully over it; there could be no squeezing through or under it. Easier perhaps for a fat man to get through the eye of a needle.

The Old Ones who had sat up on that little hill—who were they, how long had they sat there, what thoughts had they considered? Where were they now, and will each of us one day become just as invisible? It seemed impossible, yet I knew it was so. Still, it seemed to me that if one lived, burned brightly enough, one might exist always as a kind of echo, or shadow: in the way that, in beholding the mirror of the moon, we are seeing an echo of the sunlight that was cast many years ago—light-years—and which, reflected, falls down upon us, the echo of an echo, encasing us as if in amber.

A suspect theorem, and yet, what is the downside in believing it, or even hoping?

It was hard to imagine, however, there could be much downside in the just enduring, in the hanging on—the extension or attenuation of a once-bright burning by echo or reflection. Come what may when darkness falls, I find it difficult to believe we are not sometimes already in some sort of betranced afterlife, walking around on petrified ocean floors that are a billion years old, following caliche roads white as summer clouds, all of us bathed—sometimes—in silver.

It seems important to live as if this is all there is, and if something remains or carries forward for a while after we dive back down into the soil, then so be it. But now! On a good day—on the best days—who would want anything more?

Much is made of the moon's pull on tides, and of the way it scrambles our soft brains, pulls them this way and that. D. H. Lawrence might believe such tugging reveals who we really are—the raw soup of us still so newly emerged in the world that, evolutionarily speaking, we are but jellyfish, still being shaped, molded, rolled around; an experiment, a farther braiding off the ancient tree of all other life. Not the trunk, by any means.

Lawrence wrote:

> "Blood knowledge . . . Oh, what a catastrophe for man when he cut himself off from the rhythm of the year, from his unison with the sun and the earth. What a catastrophe, what a maiming of love when it was made a personal, merely personal feeling, taken away from the rising and setting of the sun, and cut off from the magical connection of the solstice and equinox. This is what is wrong with us. We are bleeding at the roots."

He announced also, more famously:

> "The essential American soul is hard, isolate, stoic, and a killer. It has never yet melted."

Also this: Cormac McCarthy, from his novel, *No Country for Old Men*:

"It was cold and there was snow on the ground and he rode past me and kept on goin. Never said nothin. He just rode on past and he had his blanket wrapped around him and he had his head down and when he rode past I seen he was carryin fire in a horn the way people used to do and I could see the horn from the light inside of it. About the color of the moon."

As with the previous pondering, about the half-life of any echo of our physical selves remaining after we've moved on (fill in the blank: Elysian fields, greener pastures, better things, just rewards), I don't presume to wax about what comes next, not even tomorrow.

As one of the last or next to last generations before the heavily cloned or the lightly modified begin to walk among us, it can often seem as much like game over for *Homo sapiens* as it must have, at some point, for Neanderthals, or Cro-Magnon. That the fire in the horn is flickering.

Maybe there is a further and farther realm out there, to which we are all headed, at which some of us are reserving a booking in the penthouse suite while others are destined, this go-round at least, for the mansion's basement. I think my own aspirations in this regard might be to be the groundskeeper, outside as much as possible. I'm remembering now the end of Jim Harrison's 1978 novella, *Legends of the Fall*:

"If you are up near Choteau and drive down Ramshorn Road by the ranch, now owned by Alfred's son by his second marriage, you won't get permission to enter. It's a modern efficient operation, but back there in the canyon there are graves that mean something to a few people left on earth: Samuel, Two, Susannah and a little apart Ludlow buried between his true friends, One Stab and Isabel; and a small distance away Decker and Pet. Always alone, apart, somehow solitary, Tristan is buried up in Alberta."

We are not the only ones who are directed this way and that by the swing and pull of neap and full, by the release of first quarter and third quarter, attentive and perhaps addicted to the solace of distance and, less frequently but with greater intensity, to the intimacy and passion of proximity. On full moons, zooplankton rise to the surface as if in the rapture; oysters spread wider their limestone lips; deer, bedded down, rise as if in a trance no matter the hour of day or night when the moon (which is always full, we must remember) is either directly overhead or, curiously, on the other side of this small earth, directly underfoot.

Preceding the full solar eclipse of 2018, there was a frenzy of billboards throughout the West, with every lucky farmer whose land fell beneath the dashed line of the eclipse's path across the country—not from east to west, in the style of Manifest Destiny, but reversing the curse, many hoped, from west to east. It's gone now, as forgotten as KC and the Sunshine Band, a one-hit wonder that people of a certain age will remember briefly. The arc fell on the just and the unjust, on the rich and the poor alike. Jackson Hole, south Bozeman; Gooding, Idaho. At the perimeters, on overgrazed pastures of dirt, looking like something from Steinbeck's America, wooden towers were erected to serve as billboards a year, even eighteen months in advance, advertising parking spots and viewing locations. Such was their anticipation that the hand-painted sheets of plywood became sun-faded long before the event, giving the appearance that the eclipse had come and gone many years previous; or that the eclipse itself had aged the signs, delaminated and dilapidated now after having dared profit from such a holy phenomenon. The red spray paint— PARKING, $5.00—blurring now, wavering like old bloodstains. As the months melted and we were all pulled closer to the day of reckoning, a sweet kind of unification seemed to be happening: the mass of us becoming increasingly aware of the time, date, location—the countdown—with our minds adjusting like crystals in cooling magma, or iron filings attentive to the movement of a powerful magnet, aligning in parallel and then converging from all directions to behold the approaching singularity.

As will be understood by now, bearing a few pagan tendencies if not quite a willingness to commit fully to the requisite ceremonies and customs of such a sect, I was torn between wanting to take off work and hie down toward the Bitterroot or Gallatin country—only about eight hours, each way (by car; on foot, days, even weeks)—and wanting to behold the phenomenon in my own home valley, reduced or partial though the show would be.

I wanted to feel what my valley felt: wanted to take note of the wind, or breeze—if there was any shift in current, in direction, when the partial darkness fell, as is reported in the Bible for such events, "over the land." I wanted to take note of any possible skip or stutter in the pull of gravity beneath my feet, in my home; wanted to hear if the calls of ravens became different in that darkened hour, and whether the hermit and varied thrushes— crepuscular singers, lovers of the gloom and gloaming—began to sing.

I also—like almost everyone, I think—did not want to experience it alone. As if only by witnessing it with another of our kind could it be said to be certain, or 99.9999 percent certain.

For weeks and months beforehand, community service organizations—libraries, notably, and other leftist do-gooders— had been passing out free solar eclipse sunglasses, distributing them with the same fervor with which school nurses gave children sugar cubes infused with a dose of polio vaccine back in the 1960s. Imagining—fearing—an entire population blinded simultaneously by a single skyward glance, accidental or otherwise, or turned into pillars of salt, or maybe both at the same time, for having dared gaze upon that which they had been warned not to behold directly.

Having procrastinated until the day before, I called around only to discover all supplies had run out weeks earlier. The next best thing, I imagined, might be a welder's helmet, so I drove down to town, to the hardware store, arriving an hour before closing. There was one helmet left, but it was so expensive! I wanted the free green plastic eyeshades that were given out at the optometrist's offices of my youth. To pay for protecting one's vision? It seemed somehow un-American.

Inspired by necessity, however, I found replacement glass sheets for welder's masks. The internet had actually said that welder's masks were not sufficient—I found this difficult to believe—but to be safe, I bought three sheets, each a little smaller than an index card. And when I peered through them, it was hard to see anything. I guessed that was why welders didn't use three at a time.

The day of, I drove down valley to the office of the conservation nonprofit I work with. I'd read it was also safer to watch the eclipse reflected in a body of water, rather than staring birdlike directly at the change, so I found a child's blue plastic swimming pool out back and filled it with water.

The staff and I went out into the backyard to wait. There was no morning traffic on the road that runs past our office. We stared at the pool as if awaiting the emergence of the Loch Ness monster; glanced sidelong now and again, up at the same old sun up in the same old sky. Same old birdsong. The in-between time, in the north country: summer winding down, autumn not yet arrived. Torpor.

It came slowly. There was a blurring, a wavering that was, to be honest, a little unsettling: more so, I think, than the coming shadow. To have seen a thing one way all one's life, for sixty years, then to see it, the previously immutable, waver and sprawl a bit—well, what if everything else contained such waver, such wobble?

As if our very existence—once loosened—could then unravel further, back down into the nothing from which we arose.

The edges shimmered in the way that waves of heat rise from highway pavement in deep summer. *Holy shit*, I remember thinking, *it's happening, and on its own time.*

I liked that we all had to be attentive, sitting like schoolchildren, waiting for the teacher to enter the room.

I liked that our office is in an old schoolhouse, back in the woods. A fairy tale.

It didn't get so dark so much as fuzzy. There appeared to be a kind of static in the sky, in the air—the visual equivalent of the itchiness or scratchiness of a wool jacket, as if there were a coarser weave of pixels registering on our hungry brains. We glanced again and again up at the sun—once, I saw the black silhouette of a witch on a broom riding the crescent black moon across the face of the sun, from west to east—but the hive mind was right once again: the image was much more distinct when viewed in the children's bathing pool, and in that reflection, the witch disappeared.

I heard a single car approaching. I saw it was the mail lady, in her white jeep, with her silent flashing wide-load strobe light atop—and I got up and walked out to the mailbox to ask if she wanted to come look into the pool, as if into a wishing well. It was hard for me not to think of Sally Swanger's dark water well in the novel and then movie *Cold Mountain*, where Nicole Kidman, playing Ada Monroe, stares down into its depths and, seeing a swarm of crows, faints. It takes every bit of discipline for me not to tell you what happens subsequently, but it's dark. It's only for your reading and viewing pleasure that I refrain.

The postal lady, amazingly, had not heard about the eclipse. Our valley is surrounded by high mountain walls with relatively little contact to the world beyond those walls.

"Sure," she said. She turned her jeep off and walked with me to the backyard. I can imagine driving the same route decade after decade can get a little numbing, even though the scenery is amazing. Always driving, never walking. A hundred mailboxes in a 150-mile round trip, six days a week. I handed her the magic panes of dark green glass, told her not to look up without them. Told her to look into the pool first, to prepare herself for what she would see above her.

The day was not exceptionally dark, not the pitch-blackness I had envisioned. Instead, its dominant characteristic was stillness—the stillness of hesitation. As if not only the humans were betranced, but everything with a heart that beat or a spirit within, an essence, that pulsed and throbbed.

The mail lady held the loose little strips of welder's facemask glass carefully—daintily—her smoker's stained fingertips suddenly elegant, with pinkies lifted, all delicate.

(Back home, I would put the green glass strips in the kitchen drawer, where I knew they would sift to the bottom, never to be seen or used again. I was only mildly tempted to return them for a refund, and wondered briefly at their provenance—from what beach or ocean floor or mountaintop had the sand been dredged—did it require a special grade of sand grain?—and had an extraordinary furnace of heat been required to process the silica, in order to assist it in blocking, rejecting, one of the most natural and penetrating things in the world, waves of light traveling in a straight line, relentless and pure, falling—again—on the just and the unjust, with equal democratic vigor, so many years after the initial launch of those waves?)

She stared down into the pool, while above us, earth, moon, and sun continued to separate. You could feel it. We were all being returned to our old ways, and it felt—good. Not just familiar, but good.

She liked it. She studied the pool, then—carefully, but also boldly—as if it were for this she had been driving, searching, driving, searching, all her long life—looked upward, through the green glass.

In the forest, the birds were making their little late-morning sounds, but—and I acknowledge fully this may be only my interpretation—they seemed to be a little tentative, indecisive.

I stood beneath the static, the strange dim light that was in no way darkness. I felt cleansed, somehow, lighter. Not so much forgiven as—cleaner. Childlike.

The mail lady stared into the pool for so long that I started to wonder if a spell had been cast; if she might have decided to deliver the mail no more forever. That the little glass plates, unused, would fall loosely from her hands; that she would sit down beside the swimming pool, like the disabled woman in Andrew Wyeth's portrait of *Christina's World* staring up the hill at the big house, and—content now—she would lead a life of such monastic dedication to the baby pool as to forego food—a hunger strike—and, thirsty, would not yet dare to sip from the pool's sun-black water . . .

I wanted to offer to drive the rest of the mail route for her, that day. I wondered if we had saved her vision: if, driving upriver, listening to music, she might have noticed the black witch on the black broom riding the black moon across the sun, and, staring at it, had her eyesight so damaged that she could no longer drive the jeep, her freedom from the office, nor would she even be able to sort mail with much accuracy, her demotion to the dreaded desk job resulting in the misdelivery of hundreds and then, over time, thousands of pieces of mail, usually with nondramatic effects, though occasionally with such devastating and life-changing consequences that—

I inquired meekly what she thought of it all. She looked up, surprised to see me, I think. The witch was on the back side of the sun now, then free and clear, somewhere invisible out there in all that blue sky. Birdsong did not exactly erupt, but I felt, we all felt, the gears—our gears, as well as the world's—begin to move again. Our office staff began drifting back into the office, back to their work of saving the forests, the mountains that are, for now, our home. Or so we believe; so we perceive.

"That was something," the mail lady said, looking back down into the water as if waiting for it to reappear. A more crafty entrepreneur than I might have saved the water from the pool, bottled and marketed it, or served it in the local bar after midnight, a Whiskey Ditch, or Witch Whiskey, Maker's with a splash of witch water.

She, too, was returning to her old self, but more slowly than the rest of us: not as if she, like Ada Monroe, had seen the future so much, but had been taken back, way back, to some point earlier in her life: young adulthood, or even more distant—back to a time whereupon setting out into each day, one not only expected to see such trippy phenomena, but sought them out, on every path, and was often, maybe even usually, thus rewarded.

She walked—shakily, I thought—back to her little white jeep, got in on what always has seemed to me to definitely be the wrong side, turned on her flashing lights—the amber orbit of them whirling so much more slowly than the strobes of police or ambulance or fire—and continued on up the road, changed, lightened, leavened, undone, remade, like every thing, and every one of us, 99.9999 percent certain about almost anything, and diminished, I think, for that excessive belief, that confidence and security, that assurance and trust. Blinded, even.

I was not quite done. I sat by the side of the road like a way-farer, not so much waiting as simply decompressing from all I had seen, and the distance I had traveled. The earth to which I had returned.

I felt extraordinarily becalmed. I felt ready to start again. Felt my old self—isolate, but seeking to assemble, unify; to find beauty, as Terry Tempest Williams says, in a broken world.

And to disassemble: to seek to stretch wider, if not fully pull apart or unravel the vertical, humming strings of matter—I picture them as being like the bead curtains favored by hippies in the 1970s—that physicists tell us represent the percentages and probabilities of reality; to test the almost-certain quality of it, and in so doing, maybe sometimes getting a sniff if not an actual peek at what might be beyond that veil.

I heard a car approaching: other than the mail lady's jeep, the first one all morning on this strange and bestilled day. It occurred to me that other than our staff and the postmistress, I'd not seen another human, and that for whomever was driving the approaching vehicle, it had likely been the same for him or her.

This world is beautiful but it is never quite finished. One can always push against, sand or polish—or prune or shave—its furthest edges. Without even really knowing what I was doing, I stood up, stretched both arms out in front of me in the classic zombie pose, and began walking away from the road, stiff-legged, Frankenstein-like, headed for the woods, trapped by the light, as the car and driver zoomed past and, hopefully, if for even just but a moment, did a double-take, and wondered at what they were seeing or thought they were seeing, before being sucked on farther up the road, as if being drawn toward wherever they were going rather than navigating by free will, desire, hunger: all the shimmering vertical curtains that identify us, get us out of bed in the morning, and keep us moving, moving forward, relentless, if confused.

Horoscopes had promised that everything would be better, after the eclipse. And, for a little while, they were.

The savvy ones did not stay at home like me, but went deep into the wilderness, on their own, to nestle on a promontory and wait to be bathed in momentary darkness, with only the edges of all things limned with a corona of fire.

Do they know the answer now, if even only subconsciously, while I still search? When we see, are we really seeing? We know of the 99.9999 percent predictability that whatever we are looking at is "real," is true—is a highly probable likelihood of reality—but what does 100 percent look like? Does it even exist? Does it exist in the moon's shadow, as it occasionally falls upon us?

Does the strange planet of us, in those ninety or so minutes of a total eclipse, sag and begin to disassemble or unravel—down to 99.99998 percent, or 97.63 percent—still real, still true, but with stuttering, shuttered images of either a further reality or a further unreality ahead, depending on whether one is looking forward or backward?

I think it feels like the latter—that the past contains a rubbled foundation of fragments and segments of reality, by virtue of their having endured. That in the old darkness, we feel most strongly the calling of our species—the experiment of us. That if we are not yet fully real, we might yet one day make ourselves real. I have to believe the fire in the horn we carry is the will to adhere, will to cohere, amid the shimmering unpredictable. That even when we rage and destroy or disassemble, it is to some degree so that we may then be employed, so to speak, reassembling that which we have pulled apart.

Much of what we behold—that which we have made and woven—is as but a dream, surreal and even unreal. As if we have lost our way in the darkness. As if where we began—on the platform of the old stone, at the edge of an old sea, craving light, craving shelter and protection, craving food from the garden, craving craving craving—was the thing, the first moment, that came just after we stepped up from out of the stone. That the old implacable stone is the truth and the light, and that the quivering, shimmering likelihood of us, as we exist or mostly exist right now, but an extreme probability. That those things, the events we call coincidence, wax and wane in almost orderly if not predictable fashion—cascading over one another sometimes like dominoes falling, with such pattern or near-pattern that we are disturbed—and other times with such a wildness, a lack of connection on our movements and our days that we feel, once again, alarmed, startled, bereft.

Always without knowing why. Always without being able to see the reason.

We move around in the light, but we cannot yet see. But how we crave, more than ever, those five points of attachment: touch, taste, scent, sight, sound. Come back, rock. Come back, moon.

THE STAMP OF THE AFRICAN ELEPHANT

WE'VE BEEN SEEING ELEPHANT TRACKS FOR SO LONG, and in so many places, that it's almost as if we've stopped thinking about the animals that made them, and have become accustomed instead to perceiving the animal only through its tracks.

I'm not saying an elephant is a deity, but it is surely an Other. You can look so hard for clues to the nature of a thing's existence that you forget how to see.

Thus it is that we barely recognize the animals standing motionless in the trees before us: hulking silhouettes in the shady grove of an island in the middle of the river of bright burning sand. Our Namibian driver, Andreas, points them out. "Elephants," he says, and a part of me wants to correct him, or my own eyes, and say "No, mountains." The elephants, or silhouettes of elephants, are all staring, watching us, and Andreas stops the jeep at a respectful distance to let them become accustomed to our rude intrusion. They remain motionless, though something about the unity and stolidity suggests that there is a communication going on between them, in that perfect immobility. Finally, as if a consensus has been reached, the broad flap of one ear stirs, fans the stillness of the heated shade-air in which they are all standing shoulder to shoulder, and the muscle of them shifts and seems to relax a notch or three; though still, defensibility and unity remain the potent message projected.

We stop again when we draw even with the elephants, about

fifty yards distant. Andreas is jumpy, utterly tense—just this side of frightened. He still has the clutch depressed with his left foot, and is keeping his right foot on the accelerator, ready to pop the clutch and bolt.

There is something almost overwhelmingly attractive about them, something that makes a person want to trust them, know them, admire them. There is something that we are drawn toward, something we see in them that I think we want to see or pretend is in ourselves: a presumed camaraderie, so that we are tempted to assume what I suspect feels to the elephants like a forced bonhomie.

We are awed by their obvious power and strength, and by their intelligence, and by the presence of their more tender emotions, even within animals so strong and fierce—and yet I think there is a part of us that empathizes with what we perceive, mistakenly, as the physical clumsiness or psychic isolation of elephants. We perceive that they have baggy, wrinkled skin, and that they shuffle with heads lowered, trunks hoovering the ground for scent, and we think, *Here is a fellow traveler for whom the world is still a riddle*—and we are tempted to seek them out.

We observe how there is no other animal in the world even remotely like them, and we misperceive that in that solitude there is loneliness. We move toward them with patronizing gestures, offering them positions in our circuses, and in our labor camps, and in our zoos, and are surprised somehow when things do not work out according to our plans. We shoot them and saw their tusks off to make into jewelry, in an attempt to make our own selves appear more beautiful and less shambling, and then are surprised and disappointed when they "turn on us."

Across that distance, we behold each other. With the elephants as well as ourselves repositioned, we can see now that there is a baby among them, an infant by comparison to all the others around him—and that it is heart-meltingly cute. The baby, alone among them, possesses no reserve, and appears to be trying to scamper out of the herd and come over to where we are, to investigate or even play, but the adults, the old aunts and uncles, matriarch and patriarch and older brother and sisters, have it surrounded in a corral made by their thick legs, and every time it tries to scooch through, one of them pushes it back gently and shifts a leg in such a manner as to refortify the prison, the containment, the safehouse; finally, exasperated, the baby elephant contents itself with peering out from between two of those gigantic legs, its head squeezed between the column of them, with its little trunk twisting and twirling, trying to take in our curious scent.

Frustrated, the baby begins making odd little chirping sounds and fans his ears energetically, but the bars of his prison squeeze together more tightly, and with an audible sigh he plops down to nap, lying down in the sand like a man on a couch. Andreas eases out the clutch, tests the forward motion of the jeep to make sure everything is still working—that we haven't somehow become bogged down in the sun-softened sand—and feels compelled to tell us finally that a friend of his was guiding some tourists on a similar elephant-watching journey, where everything was going fine until the guide discovered that their Land Cruiser had gotten stuck. When the elephants likewise came to understand that the truck was stuck, they charged, as if thinking, *All right, fish in a barrel.*

The guide had a gun and was barely able to turn the elephants by firing at them, striking the lead female in the ear, drilling a hole in it that did no more damage than if one were to fire a shot through the frond of a palm leaf. Dennis and I listen to this and then look back at "our" herd of elephants, trying to discern any such capacity for betrayal, or what we would perceive as betrayal, but can find none; all seems to be only indolence, utter sunstruck lassitude.

Through Dennis's binoculars, we study the intricate striations of thick skin, with those myriad wrinklings (which increase the surface area exponentially, allowing even greater mass to aid in the dumping of excess body heat) matching exactly the striations and planes and laminas of cross-bedding in the sandstone bluffs behind them: as if the elephants have literally arisen from the sand, stepped out of it and into the land of the living, but still possessing the mark of their origin and the stamp of their maker.

The driftwood piles of spars next to the resting elephants appear identical to their tusks—appear to be constructed of their ivory tusks—and yet we pay no mind to the driftwood, desire only the ivory, and I do not, cannot, understand why. Did some opportunity for choice exist within our own minds, our own path, not so long ago—six of one, half dozen of another— wherein we chose an attraction to one over the other? And if so, *why*, and how might things have been different if we had somehow chosen an attraction to beauty that did not involve killing?

It seems these days that one might as well be imagining a different species, and a different outcome to things, if not a different world. I for one hope that as a species we can find our way back to a course that more properly celebrates the crafted, intricate, fitted beauty that is the underpinning of an older world, and am glad that there are still some creatures, such as elephants, that are so large we cannot miss seeing such beauty.

HEARTS AND BONES

WE FLY NORTH TOWARD THE BIG MOUNTAINS, THE Brooks Range, and then through rather than above them. Sitting up front with the pilot, I hold a paper map in my lap like an old-school navigator. The names of the lakes and narrow valleys scroll past and melt away like our days themselves. What we do in this world matters; what can we leave behind that is beautiful? A filigree of Dall sheep trails across the windswept snow of the night before—one of the season's first—looking like delicate fringed necklaces on the mountain. We see a few sheep bounding away from us: smart sheep. Our pilot is Dirk, a third-generation bush pilot. His eyes take in all the mountains at once; if a stone is overturned, he will know it. He sees everything from up here. Wolverine, often. Bears, sheep, mountain goats, and always caribou. He can spot a lone bull when it is still just a speck. His job, his life, depends on seeing everything, and for the time being, we are in his care. He is making decisions that affect us profoundly.

It's the best time of year: the clear light from above spilling, shifting gold, pouring, washing in sheets down the red and tallow-faced tundra, ribbons of yellow-colored willows like lace fringing the white froth of the hard-charging creeks, and all the rivers suddenly flowing north. So close to the top of the world now.

Dirk points out fresh digs in the mountainside, where the grizzlies have been chasing ground squirrels. It's serene up above like this, and the day is extraordinarily clean and bright. There's so much life! So much activity, even in the broad midday light, which, in September, still lasts plenty long. All the daytime movements, animals busying themselves for migration or hibernation, give the strange impression of passing over a suburban neighborhood on a fine autumn weekend. Oh, look, the grizzlies are out tending their garden. A flock of white-fronted geese, a wide triangle of them, slides past below us in that way birds do when you're going one direction and they're going the other—a pulse of white being pulled away like a tablecloth trick. Gone.

We're almost through the mountains. We're flying through the last valley, the little plane buzzing—coming out of the mouth of the last canyon, heading north, the tundra sprawling flat before us as if to eternity—and as we pass the last ridge, we're astonished by what we see: a polar bear up in the mountains, striding bow-legged like Colossus straight up that steep slope, going up into the Brooks Range, heading south.

Because we're coming out of the mountains, flying between the two flanks that form the mouth of the canyon—being disgorged from the canyon—we're really, really close to the white bear. We can see his eyes—I want to call it a him, and if it were a grizzly, I'd identify it as a male. We're not that far above it. We can see the afternoon westerning sunlight in its eyes. Unlike a grizzly, he doesn't turn and run as the plane passes, but instead bows his legs in even tighter and pauses, as if wishing we'd come just a tad closer so he could stand up and swat us from the sky. You don't have to be an animal behaviorist to know he's pissed.

He is twice the size of the biggest bear I have ever seen.

We fly past him, and he continues up the mountain, not in a hurry but steadily, as if he knows precisely where he is going. Because we have a photographer with us—one who has come like a hunter looking for that unique shot that might help turn the tide of madness that has us considering oil development in the Arctic, and in the Arctic Ocean, and in the Arctic National Wildlife Refuge—Dirk lands the plane on the tundra, on a meandering riverside gravel bar, and we pile out, hoping to hurry up the slope and see the great animal again.

There is no way we are going to catch up with that animal on foot. I would have little compunction about following a grizzly—a gentle, sensitive animal so long as it's not protecting cubs, and usually able to broker a deal of peace, able to negotiate—but about this gigantic white bear, who, the last time we saw him, was pissed, I'll be honest, I have qualms.

We have no rifles. We don't even have bear spray. All we have are camera lenses. There's a tiny emergency flare gun in the back of the plane; that's all. We hadn't planned on stopping—we were going to fly straight to the coast, to Kaktovik, another thirty miles or so farther on, to the place where the land ends and the sea begins. The country gets big quickly down on foot. Just us, weaponless, and a thousand-pound bear that we're hurrying after.

Dirk ties the plane down, drives stakes into the time-packed gravel outwash as if setting up a tent. The wind lifts the wings of the little plane and rocks it, thus buckled, so that it seems it is straining to lift off again. Dirk is professional, nonchalant, as if seeing a polar bear up in the mountains instead of down in the plains is, though unusual, an ordinary occurrence. As if chasing after the bear on foot is normal.

We do not catch up with the migrating, or wandering, polar bear. He's had a half hour and a mile head start. His (or her) stride outpaces ours with every step. He and his kind may be disappearing from the earth, but he is leaving us behind. We do not see him again.

I love the airplane culture of the Alaska bush, and am not unaware of the dark irony of using a plane or a car in order to celebrate the far north. Landing on gravel bars from which sometimes protrude the tips of mastodon trunks, and the stone or carved-wood points of awls and spears. The tinkling spray and clatter of sun glinting on beach sand and gem shards, prop-washed upon our landing. The plane bouncing, skittering like dice rolled hard.

We fly over the conflict zone, a much-contested 1.5-million-acre section of land known, unimaginatively, as the 1002. That's government-speak, all these decades later, for the crypt of tundra beneath which oil is believed to lurk. It's an obvious misnomer, that geometrical, straight-line, mechanical signature of mankind in a landscape that is curved, sinuous, organic, unmanipulated, seething with life, and doing so very fine without us. Doing better than fine.

I do not want the drilling to proceed here. I want the oil to stay beneath the snow forever.

Snow geese graze below us like, well, a field of snow; there are so many of them. As we pass over, some of them—a few at first and then a lot—stir and scatter, the white block of them kaleidoscoping into a mosaic of autumn, blood-red and butter-gold tundra, and the soft brown of melting earth. The white fragments of their flock disperse in mesmerizing, swirling currents, all directions at once—like an ice floe falling apart, except that after we are gone, they will reassemble.

In the curious way of our species, I try not to look at it, the blurring ghost of the 1002's artificial line—the signature of old politicians who are dust and bones now—and instead look past it, pretending not to see it, focusing on the beauty, not the wound. Not the mistake.

————————

After waiting one's life to see it, of course one should discover that the Arctic Ocean is guarded at its gates by a white bear. Just as there should be a place in our minds where time and events move differently, and where old rules and routines fall away—a place of vibrant imagination—so, too, must there be a physical correlative somewhere in this world, even if only at the top of the world. The alternative, I think, would be too lonely to withstand.

The flight over the last remaining tundra almost goes too fast—another fifteen minutes? We spy a grizzly galloping through willows in the flat mosaic of vegetation—from the sky, the subtle wrinkles of old river channels vanish, as if here the land is ironed smooth by the severity of time—and already, we've reached the place we're bound for. It's as if the world and its distances are suddenly getting smaller up here; the ocean is ahead of us before I know it. Is this what the end of life is like, I wonder?

It does not feel like the end. It is the top of things, the top of the world, but it does not yet feel like the end.

The water's bluer than I had imagined. I had been envisioning slate-gray waters so cold that they would be entirely void of color. But on this day in early September, the cloudless blue sky is reflected in the Beaufort Sea to present a surprisingly placid deep blue, a great and tranquil beauty.

I try to imagine these waters stippled to the horizon with drilling rigs—the last place in the world where we have not yet pierced and paved and torn and sucked—but that is the future, and right now, here in this moment, there is only beauty.

"Look," Dirk says, angling the plane's wings—we're coming in on the tiny village of Kaktovik. Out here, in all this space, the settlement looks like a child's sandbox play area. Only that, and then everything else, the great world beyond, the great world surrounding the one hammered-together, storm-tossed little village.

"They've already got a whale," Dirk says.

We're flying low, coming in for a landing—low enough and slow enough, it seems, that we could parachute safely with nothing more than bedsheets gripped in our hands, ballooning upward—and again the scene appears to be as right and natural as it is surreal and never known. This is not metaphorical beauty.

More than any place I've ever been, this is the abstraction, beauty, made physical.

There are different kinds of beauty. Ideas can be beautiful—but so, too, are things that are yet unattached to our ideas and are instead living under their own lights. A stone, this sky. A bear, a narwhal. Beautiful beyond us and our idea of beauty. Beautiful whether they are seen or not: a bear moving through the willows, curling up for a nap in the sun beneath a willow. A different kind of beauty up here.

Twenty or more Iñupiat villagers surround the upturned carcass of a bowhead whale, its belly white, the meat of its body bright red in the clean, yellow September sun. The lighting below us is luminous—the blue water, red meat, snow-white belly, sun-struck orange beach sand, wet black rocks here and there by the jetty—and the villagers are swarming the whale, hungry animals feeding themselves. Their bare arms are coated to their elbows with bright blood, and we float past, above them, on toward the runway, though I want to linger, to hover. But time will not have it. Time will not stop.

Of course everything should be different at the top of the world. Suddenly the airstrip before us is disturbingly militaristic, preposterously large—broader, it seems, than many Arctic airstrips are long—and our little plane lands like a helicopter; it feels lost, out on all that tarmac, taxiing past all the old hangars and warehouses large enough to house dirigibles. These are the ghosts of war, remnants of Russia-as-enemy. Now the actual foe, the ocean that separated us, is lapping at our feet, soon to claim so much of what we once sought with such ferocity to defend.

The first whale of the year: what a feast. We hurry to the scene as it's winding down in that beautiful, slow, softening, equinox-approaching light. Such clarity of the primary colors, the blood so red. The young men are cutting off double-armful chunks of whale steaks, whale roasts, with cleavers and machetes, handing them out on gaff hooks as if passing out cotton candy at a carnival.

Everyone gets their meat.

One young woman wears a Gap hoodie; an older woman wears a *kuspuk*, a traditional coat with a wolverine ruff. Blood-stained hands are working steadily. The ball joint of the whale's fin—vestigial legs and feet—gleams as white as our own, white as a buoy. Propane fryers roar, hissing fry bread burbles in the hot grease, and the cooks pass some to the meat cutters, who take it with their bloody hands and eat with one hand while cutting with the other. The red blood is beautiful in that light. When they are not holding the meat hooks, they smoke a quick cigarette; the smoke rises from their lungs as if winter has already arrived. There is a sense of urgency now, because the bears have learned that they can scavenge the giant carcasses once night falls, and the bears are impatient. The workers need to be done by dark, which, at this time of year, has finally started coming around again.

It's time. Dusk is here, the hour of bears.

The sound of the young men sawing on the carcass is like that of carpentry or, strangely, the rhythmic scoop and lift of a shovel lifting frozen snow. Sometimes they set down their fry bread and share a quick cigarette, but they're working steadily, quickly. Night, the opposite of white. There are no lights on in any of the village's bright little clapboard houses—blue, red, yellow, white—but that's only because everyone's down at the water. Impossibly big bear tracks—cartoon big—are everywhere along the shore. A land of giants, with us, tiny, along shore's edge.

A young man in sweatpants comes riding up on a four-wheeler, not in much of a hurry but not leisurely either, and says, "He's in the water."

A bear, swimming toward shore: nose up, head up, coming for what's his, now.

The villagers are finished with the carcass. They know; the bears know. They load the carcass unceremoniously (as if there could be a ceremony for this next part) into the bucket of a giant backhoe and wheel away, rumbling and oil smoke straining, to drive the carcass out to the edge of town, where a structure surely like no other on earth has been built.

The only thing remotely like it is Stonehenge. But there are no stones here, only bones—the skulls and ribs and flukes of whales, a skyscraper of whale bones. There are so many skeletons, so tangled together by time—geological strata of giant bones, heaped in a vast tower—that form and order has begun to emerge from the dumping, and I have to wonder if the backhoe driver, over the years, does seek to arrange the great carcasses with some respect, some sense of order reestablished. Ribs stand vertical like the framed studs for a house to come, or a house that once was. The bears themselves—after gnawing ligaments and cartilage and drying red flesh—have shoved flukes into positions that look like the sills and jambs of windows and doors.

It's an edifice of tangled bones, and yet it seems that some of the skeletons, as they lean into and against one another, are supporting and caring for the others. With the immense skulls, particularly, there is a festive quality: some are almost upright, giving the appearance of dancing, or spry hopping, rising from the earth as they did from the sea.

Within minutes, half a dozen white bears are swimming through the bay, making landfall on this little sandbar in the blue dusk, shaking off like seawater dogs, then striding into the sprawling building of bones. They pass through the white ribs, the white skulls, giants among giants. They approach the new carcass, the red one, and begin chewing on it.

From a distance, we watch from our trucks. Again, as when we landed on the tundra, I'm tingling with awareness. What if our truck won't start when it's time to leave? What if the soft sand under our tires becomes slick from a rising tide and we become stuck? I am acutely aware of being protein, only protein, so far north, and it is a strange sensation: In some ways it's as if I have renounced my old citizenship, as if I am perhaps being granted entrance into a much older kingdom. A phrase from the poet Mary Oliver—"announcing your place in the family of things"—comes to mind.

How to describe seeing a polar bear for the first time? What mosaic of words, and in what arrangement, what order? White, huge feet, long neck, shape of head, length of head, shoulders, forearms, fur, flank, eyes? Eyes. Time has spent forever making these animals, these beings, time and circumstance. Time, at the top of the world, and life, the fire of life, the belly-breath ingot of it, blossoming its tongue of fire even from beneath so much snow and ice. A magnificent yawp, magnificent demand, to live.

I find myself thinking of that one thin surgical scar, the line of the 1002. A thin scalpel across the belly.

Other bears are swimming to the beach, which is now becoming an island. The tide is coming in, and a tiny bridge of water separates us from them, at perhaps a hundred yards' distance. Maybe less. I'm dizzy. They look like white beavers as they swim. Pleistocene beavers. How many times can I use the word giant? We've seen YouTube videos of polar bears swimming—an underwater ballet, as if riding a bicycle, and gracefully, with their giant paws displacing vast currents of cold blue water.

It's quite touching, watching them swim. The thing to not think about is that we are asking them to swim almost all the time now. Their land, their firmament, over which we hold stewardship, is vaporizing.

———————

Over time, predator and prey shape each other to be near-perfect mirrors of one another—muscularly and skeletally—and the white bears are in this regard seal-like, with their long sloping necks. Over time, predator and prey shape each other to the same destinies.

How can they make it? How can there be a white bear without a white land? I do not think there can be. The snow is why they are here, only here. The task of remaining forever alive in such a hard land is expensive, extravagant, bold, as is their commitment to all-whiteness, all the time. Without the snow, what was once an asset for the bears becomes a liability. Without the ice, the white bears will go away.

Their arms and shoulders are so large—what any of us used to looking at black or grizzly bears would think of as overproportioned—as to be mesmerizing. So too is their long, easy gait, once they make landfall after having swum so far.

The first bear on the island is the largest, and when it bites into the side of the whale, I feel further diminished; this is an animal that should be eating entire seals like appetizers, not chewing the red rind off bones already carved. This is an animal made for eating seal steaks, not cold bone broth.

The bear crawls inside the rib cage—its muzzle is bright red now, like a mask, one of the last things we'll see in the fading light—and as the bear strains upward for some tiny delicacy (the equivalent of you or me straining to eat half of a split peanut) the ribs of the whale shake and quiver, and I'm reminded strangely of summer up in the mountains, of a blossom shuddering as the bumblebee within pollinates it. The entire whale is moving again, as if reanimated, re-inspirited, as if this far north, at the top of the world, the rules of the world are different. How important it is for our culture of narcissism and unaccountability to believe those childish myths—as if our every wish, our every desire, will always come true. As if nothing will ever go away, and if it does, it will come right back. As if we can do no harm. As if we are not beautiful monsters.

It's true dark now. The lights of the little whaling village—no more than four whales per year, then the long winter—glimmer. In the night, perhaps, they will pad silently, huge-footed, white ghosts, through the little town where no dogs bark, sniffing each house, each yard, to see if someone might have mistakenly left their whale steak out on a picnic table. The bears walking right up to the doors of the houses, perhaps, and sniffing, looking for anything. A smear of blood on the door, perhaps, from where a villager pushed it open. Licking the doorknobs, then passing on.

FIFTEEN DOGS

RIP, BUCK, JERRY, JOE, RED ISSIE. POINT, SUPERMAN, Callie. Linus, Otis, Homer, Ann. Hondo, Sam, Auna. The temptation is to talk endlessly about them—their breeds and dispositions, the great hunts we made together, how they lived and loved, how they died, where they're buried, what I buried them with—so many home movies. How many man-hours, how many days, weeks, months—what percentage of a life—passed by in which I was cleaning up after them in their first year of life, and again in their fading last years? How many hours spent warming water to add to the kibble? Sweeping the hardwood floors of the daily shedding? Lifting the crates in and out of the Subaru, fumbling with leash clips in the snow. How many trips to the vet, how many hours and years spent training them, and learning to read them. Waiting for them to pee, waiting for them to poop. Gloved with a plastic bag, picking it up steaming, looking for the distant trash receptacle. The sweet irony being, of course, that we serve them far more than they serve us. Service animals, we all are.

SAM, DOG ONE, was a basset hound. I don't remember reaching through the wooden lacquered bars of the playpen, grabbing his velvet ears, and gnawing on them while he whined but submitted to the indignity—yet because the story was told to me so often, I believe I remember.

Dog two, another basset, was named Hondo, after an old man my parents knew who docked dogs' tails. *Hondo*, the Spanish word for "deep." We had a backyard in suburban Houston, a new neighborhood out on the oak prairie that was barely a suburb, with so many of the forested lots not yet built on—little refuges of what I thought of back then as wildness. Some of the houses were a bit older than others, but all of them were made of brick. It seemed natural to me to live shoulder to shoulder with tall wooden fences separating one lot from another, and on the dozens of times each week a tennis ball or football went over one of the fences, I simply climbed over and retrieved it rather than going around to the neighbor's door and ringing the bell. Back in my own yard, it was a source of great entertainment for me to give Hondo an empty gallon-sized ice cream carton. He would snuffle his long head into it, sometimes getting it stuck over his head, while he galloped about the yard in suddenly sightless ecstasy. Hondo's half a century gone now. He was sweet, but I was racing past him. He was the first dog I remember dying.

Fast-forward through my adolescence. I grew up amid a stable of my father's bird dogs, impossibly high-strung English pointers, Rip, Buck, Joe, Jerry. Dogs three, four, five, and six: I was moving too fast to bother much with them. I didn't yet know one of the world's great truths, that there are few places a good dog cannot go with you.

My next two dogs, Homer and Ann, numbers seven and eight, were twin black-and-tan hounds, picked up roadside in Mississippi so long ago it was before I became a writer—back when I was just a picker-upper of stray dogs. The first dogs I owned as an adult. I was working as a geologist in Mississippi, living in an old farmhouse out in the country. One morning I was driving back home from my girlfriend's when I passed two tiny pups sitting knock-kneed on the road, outside a crumbling wooden shack, kudzu swarmed and sapling sprung. There was a Gothic wrought-iron fence with impaling spikes, the gate tilted permanently open, a weedy brick walkway leading up to the collapsing porch. Not an unbroken windowpane left in any of the frames.

The pups, little black-and-tans, were patchy as if with mange, disconsolate. Refugees, outcasts. I drove on past, thinking of love, and adventure. My blood back then was carbonated all the time, the blood of an alien. When I walked beneath streetlamps, the lamps sizzled and sparked. I had no time for dogs.

It was green dusk, springtime. Fireflies were just about to start blinking along the Natchez Trace. I could be home just after twilight, settle in, cook my meal. Read, listen to crickets. Maybe call Elizabeth before bed. I kept on driving. Immediately, there was a voice in each ear. I had seen such things in cartoons—not exactly angel and devil whispering in each ear but definitely a back-and-forth conversation between two people who seemed to know me so well they could have been masquerading as me. The two voices only wanted what was best for me, and as I drove the black-ribboned road, I listened. *You really should go back and pick up those little pups. / Ah, they're feral, they wouldn't make good pets, they're irredeemable. / At least go back and try to get the other one, you ought not to split them up like that. / They're wild, goners already.*

A thing I often forget—because I did make a U-turn and go back for them—was that there was a third one, pavement fodder, dead beside where the other two were seated, as if they were in mourning, or awaiting its resurrection.

When I stopped in front of the old abandoned shack, one of them charged me, yipping—at five or six weeks already a defender of the family crest—while the other rolled over on her back and began peeing, a golden arc of a fountain.

The barking pup danced away from me—I was almost able to grab her—and dashed off through the gate, up the weedy brick walkway, puppy-stumbled up the sagging steps, and disappeared into the depths of the haunted house.

I picked up the remaining pup. Improbably, she began to pee again, and I aimed her up high at the evening's first star as if in a ritual. When she was done, I carried her up the walkway to search for her sibling.

I went from room to deserted room. There was no furniture, though in one room there was an old wheelchair constructed of wood, like a miniature covered wagon. All the house's doors had been stripped from their frames decades earlier, possibly for firewood, though the chinks and gaps in the splintered walls were insulated with old yellowed newspapers not as ancient as one might have presumed—some were from the 1940s and '50s, but others from the '60s and not-at-all-distant early '70s. And though there were numerous dried twists of puppy turds stippling every room, the wild little runaway pup was nowhere to be found. There was a back porch even more rotted than the front—trees large enough to be sawlogs pushed up through the floor as well as the roof, their branches seeming to hold up the house—and the forest beyond rolled right up to the back porch like rising floodwater: greenbrier, poison ivy, yaupon, loblolly, cedar. The wild pup had leaped off the porch, I deduced, and hurled herself into the jungle.

Too wild, anyway, I told myself again, as I walked out of the spooky house with my prize, which I did not yet recognize as a prize. I got into my truck and set the pup on the floorboard, should she pee again. I took off down the road. She watched me with doe eyes, and there was no mistaking the message. *Where's my sister?* I turned around and went back.

I didn't have to look very hard. The other pup had already returned to the road and was waiting there like a passenger who'd missed her bus. But as I approached, she whirled again and dashed back into the collapsing house. I hurried through the gate after her, but she was nowhere to be seen. She must have launched herself into the dark forest out back, where I imagined her living in a burrow, like an armadillo or a gopher.

Back in the truck, I told the pup, "I tried, girl." We headed up the road.

I could still barely see the shapes of things: the dark road darker still than the evening itself. I could still see birds fluttering to roost, and bats beginning to hunt.

I went back a third time, and in the darkness, the wild pup was sitting beside the road again. I leaped from the truck and ran hard up the walkway, just behind her. I raced through the house, to that back room with its doorless threshold opening to the jungle, thinking, *There's no way that tiny pup can keep hurling itself out into all those thorns.* I went from room to room, looking harder, and finally found her, cowering under some newspapers. I picked her up, held her to me, and walked back out into the spring night.

THEY TRAIN US too, as writers, I mean. As writers, how many hours do we spend in a lifetime, working to please—what—the page? Why do we do it? For love, surely, is the only answer—love, and companionship. "Why do you write?" someone once asked Flannery O'Connor. "Because I'm good at it," she said. By which she also meant, "So I'm not quite so lonely."

Novels are like dogs, and writing years are like dog years, or worse—they fly past. Some novels you get done in ninety days, others twenty-five years. Dogs fill our art, and it would be easy for future anthropologists to believe we worshipped them. We bury them with their trinkets and toys, and we dream about them decades after they have gone on.

Jack London's *Call of the Wild*: a book about dogs, it seems, was once an author's rite of passage. The great Eudora Welty wrote the best simile ever, about a panting bird dog's tongue being the color of a faded pink rose.

A long time ago, I slammed a car door on the thumb of the writer Terry Tempest Williams. She looked down at the blood spurting from her thumb, trapped like a coyote in her own car door, said nothing, just watched as if from thirty thousand miles away while I tried to open the door to release her.

Ten years later, on a sidewalk in Livingston, Montana, her and Brooke's dog, Rio, a Chihuahua to whom I was giving a taste of elk gristle, leaped into the air like one of Oz's winged monkeys and latched onto my hand, blood slinging everywhere as I sought to shake him free.

On days when the world is moving too fast, the dogs I've had—all fifteen—can blur and compress. I begin to have trouble remembering exactly which dog did what, particularly when the heroics of bird dogs are involved. Hunter and dog become a continuum, combining over time to serve as the distillation of the Spanish philosopher José Ortega y Gasset's advice about shooting (which works for writers as well)—that one should attempt "to seize the bird, venomously."

Some dog memories do not blur, however, and are etched into the spirit that remains unaltered long after the contours of memory have eroded. Dog number nine, Point, a speckled German shorthaired pointer, contracted the sentinel case of mesothelioma for a pet in Lincoln County, courtesy of the W. R. Grace asbestos mine. On the day I had to put him down, I carried him out into the field—he was too swollen with fluid to walk well, and I had been draining him every day, a hideous, poisonous, pinkish admixture of blood and water—whereupon he lifted his head and, tottering, made his way deeper into the swaying grass that towered over him, the tall grass waving in the wind like sea fronds and making a murmuring, shushing sound.

After only a short distance of tiptoeing, he locked up on point, with a rooster pheasant just ahead of him. Point raised his front left paw carefully, as if taking an oath. I stepped forward, and the bird flushed straight up, cackling, and mercifully, mercifully, I was able to hit it for him or I would have been haunted forever after.

His liver-colored brother, Superman, dog number ten, from the same litter, and all but joined at the hip to Point, somehow avoided that fate: Why is one chosen, or not chosen?

Once, on the prairie with Superman—who was not named by me but by the girls for the white V on his chest, and also for their pleasure of imagining me, out in the field, shouting to the sky, *Superman! Superman!*—I jumped a flock of mallards, drakes, and hens tangled together, so that I couldn't shoot right away. By the time they got themselves sorted out and I shot, I missed clean the greenhead drake I desired and watched them all disappear over a low hill.

Superman, as was his unbreakable custom in the days of his youth, followed them anyway, and at a sprint. I whistled and shouted his name to no avail; after several minutes, he returned, cresting that low hill and dragging a white swan that was as large as he was. I could not have been more surprised had he been toting a baby elephant.

The bird was only recently dead, and it saddened me to know there was someone who would shoot such a bird. Had it died earlier that morning, or had it flown nonstop from the Arctic, headed to New Mexico, carrying with it the lethal wounds from some savage Canadian?

It's a sin to waste meat, whether gotten by one's own hand or another's, and so I carried the immense bird, cradled in both arms like a sleeping queen, across the prairie, and placed it in the back of my car. A few weeks later, for Thanksgiving, I brined it and cooked it as if it were a goose and served it to the guests, who commented favorably on its flavor.

All dogs shape us by giving us the opportunity daily to become better versions of ourselves. They were here long before we were, and without question it is they who showed up at our campfires uninvited and who have sculpted us into who we are, and into who we are yet becoming.

They certainly do not need to be our dogs in order to shape us. Many of us have experienced at least once the profound responsibility of caring for a beloved other's beloved dog. Which brings me to dog number eleven, Red Isabelle, an Irish setter.

She had the longest legs, a long red mane, the elegant, feathery red tail, and soulful brown eyes. As she lunged and sailed over the snows of northwest Montana, I would write to her owners, Bob and Catfish, who were living in Italy for six months and had entrusted me with her. I was trying to gradually wean them to the idea that Issie was as willful and headstrong as she was beautiful and—well, how to say this elegantly, indirectly, nonjudgmentally, tactfully?—possessed at certain times a depth of vacuity so pure as to be perhaps the elemental distillation of innocence. I do not mean she was dizzy, disoriented, or inattentive, nor would I in any way use the word *dumb*. It was instead something deeper and impossible to touch or understand. A beautiful red dog permanently, eternally simple.

She ran away at pretty much every opportunity, and it was my great fear that a mountain lion or wolf would get her while she was in my care. During a call to Italy, when I tried to explain what a runaway she was being, and the part about that vacuousness, Bob or Catfish would make little cooing sounds and hypothesize that she was just missing them inconsolably and was trying to find them. Trying to get to Italy. "Have you read *The Incredible Journey*?" Bob asked. Not quite insinuating that it was my fault Issie was unhappy.

I'd never had a dog that needed a leash before. Red Isabelle disappeared for days at a time—and once, for weeks. It's a terrible way to spend one's days, staring out the window at nothing, waiting for the big red dog to come bounding up the driveway. And waiting. And waiting. And considering too how to break the heartbreaking news to her owners.

Her disposition toward chaos was mythic. I reread the works of Jim Kjelgaard—*Big Red* and *Irish Red*—curious about the deeper qualities of the breed. She slept in the daytime as if entombed in a glacier but awakened whining at all hours of the night.

Things she loved: butterflies, birds, clouds, breezes, particularly the self-generated kind achieved when she topped twenty-five, then thirty miles an hour. I am not speaking of when she stuck her goofy, grinning head out the truck window but rather of when she was running along behind it, then ahead of it. The most runaway dog ever. All I had to do was blink, and she was gone.

The disparity between her speed and the seemingly slow-motion reach-and-stretch of those long legs conspired to mesmerize a viewer into believing he or she was witnessing nonchalance rather than pandemonium. Grace, and elegance: in no way did she need intelligence. I think she used the lack of it as a weapon. Of course she tormented me. She was my penance. Bob and I could not be more different; he loved to argue and usually thought he won. I began to believe he'd left her with me on purpose, hoping to wear me down, so that the next time we got into an argument, he would win.

This was back in the days when there was no phone service in the Yaak Valley. I don't mean no cell service—I mean no landlines. No electricity. No nothing, just bliss, and wolves. To make a phone call—to check in with parents back in Texas, just to let them know all was well, or to go over some stuff with an editor or agent, or, for that matter, to talk to someone in Italy—you had to drive seven snowy miles to the pay phone out in front of the tavern, the one with a stump for a chair inside the little glass booth with the folding front door broken off. The pay phone was out of order about half the time, so you never knew until you got there if it was going to be working and if the line was going to be busy—there was not yet the technology of call waiting—or if, maybe worst of all, there was somebody already sitting on that stump, leaning against the glass, head down, an Edward Hopperesque pool of incandescent light pluming down on them.

The night that made me crack, the night in the six-month psychic prison of holding such a carefree spirit hostage, under house arrest, came in lonely February, when I fired up the truck to make the fourteen-mile roundtrip on the long shot of catching my editor. I left Issie in the cabin, lounging in front of her element, the fire, and drove purposefully though not quickly, admiring the winter stars and being a little glad to be out of the house and on an errand.

I pulled into the empty parking lot—no socializers, no talkers that night—and just as I got out of the truck, the great red racehorse of a dog, seeming so much larger, galloping up from out of the night and into that pool of light, leaped upon me just an instant before I realized it was her and not some savage woods creature.

There was no escaping her; she had run behind my car the entire way, and a mercy it was for Bob and Catfish that I had not been driving to Troy, fifty-four miles distant—though I had little doubt that there too she would have greeted me as I stepped out of the truck.

I didn't know how she had escaped. Her will to ramble was as great as were the dark woods dangerous for so blithe an innocent.

It was way too much pressure. I pictured a compass, with its 360 radial degrees emanating from the house. She could just as easily have ended up at Lost Horse Mountain or Lost Girl Creek. Lost Soul Mountain, Lost My Friends Bob and Catfish Creek.

Bob, Catfish, I said, later that week from the pay phone—ten years before email—*y'all gotta come home early.*

It was harder than I let on. Only now, thirty years later, am I exorcising those red demons. They shaped me. They made me cautious, a troubleshooter. If there was a way, a seam, a fissure through which chaos could travel, I could see it first. It governed my days, for years afterward. I've been a long time in recovery, and it has taken much work for me to relearn how to be reckless, carefree.

And she wasn't even my dog, is the hell of it. She was my six-month dog. But how she carved me. She helped move me toward a greater valuing of my privacy, my *time*; the incredible glory of being free.

Auna, number twelve, yet another German shorthair, I had but four years. She had seizures. She sat behind me in the chair while I worked, her chin resting on my shoulder. The basement in Missoula, the year of the Great Recession, gray inversions all winter long, me working on travel brochures and album liner notes, and grateful for the work. She made it to the Yaak, a good little bird dog, skinny as a knife. The day before she disappeared she assembled a strange hieroglyph of little sticks and branches, shaman-like—something she had never done before—on the front porch, then dashed off the next day into the marsh. Elizabeth whistled for her but she only accelerated. And she never came back.

We, as well as neighbors, searched the marsh, and the old forest, for miles in all directions. No blood, no hair, no bones, no collar or dog tags; no eagles, no raven shouts.

Callie, dog thirteen, is six now, a German shorthaired pointer whose full name is Caledonia, not quite eponymous, from the song "Caldonia (What Makes Your Big Head So Hard?)." She is the result of an artificial insemination between her mother, a Westminster Best of Show dog, an extremely social, inveterate crowd-pleaser who trotted in metronomic figure eights between each of the judges' legs, and a hard-charging sire who was a three-time world field trial champion. In other words, Callie is a dog I could never have afforded. Her litter was presold to rich folk who were flying in from Italy, England, and France to choose their various slots in the anticipated litter of six, but—sweet mystery!—her mother, Dixie Dancer, gave birth to thirteen so that the breeder had a crisis of abundance on his hands. I was awarded one of the pups in exchange for agreeing to write about her: a Maserati of a dog, gotten for a song.

She is sweet and hunts like a fiend but gets a little cross-wired sometimes. She points the setting sun, staring across the prairie at the end of each day, frozen, until, after the distant little ball of it slips beneath the wheat fields, she slinks forward, tiptoeing, believing the golden bird is attempting to get away from her.

When I drive, Callie sits beside me and rests her paw on my shoulder.

I remember a friend teasing about her husband, who described their dog as "a little boy dressed up in a dog suit." *Damn.*

Linus, dog fourteen, and his half-brother, Otis, number fifteen, are frilly French Brittany spaniels, dashing little caballeros, who spring and prance like Jack Black in *Nacho Libre*. They jump straight up, above the wheat—a quick airborne glimpse out at the sea of grass in which they and I thrash—and then crash back down. Linus, pointing his first pheasant beneath the snow at 25 below, blue sky, butter-yellow stubble sticking up through the snow, the rooster tumbling, then running, Linus chasing it, catching it, his first lock-solid point and his first retrieve, brilliant feathers falling from the sky.

My daughters love my new dogs, the two Brittanies, and the lost soul, test-tube Callie, at least as much as they did all the previous generations of puppies, then dogs, with whom they tumbled and wrestled in their childhood. They insist on sleeping with all three of them, and also that I bring the dogs with me whenever I pick the girls up at one airport or another on their journeys back home: so much so that no matter which airport we're going to, the spaniels get excited as soon as they see or hear a jet overhead, and once we're parked by baggage claim, they watch the sliding-glass doors intently, their docked tails twitching every time someone comes out, waiting for it to be one girl or the other.

I used to drive through Starbucks with the dogs and request a Puppuccino. The girls delighted in my having to say the word and in filming the Brittanies' frantic strivings for the tiny paper Dixie cup filled with whipped cream, the dogs' tongues lapping at the cup with tongues like those of the specialized nectar-feeding pollinators one sees on nature specials. As the dogs slurped their Puppuccinos, their eyes burned with the same ingot light that ignited when they gazed unblinkingly at the spot in the brush or cattails where a hidden bird was nestled deep, unseen by anyone's eyes but illuminated just as surely by their scent: a billion or ten billion neural firings of ecstasy blossoming in slow-motion starbursts of bliss that then reattached to their fevered, even incandescent brainpan, in the shape of a neon pheasant. Colors not able to be seen by the eye or tasted or touched, but scented, deliriously. A catatonic intoxication.

How will I survive my affections? writes Terry Tempest Williams. To the dogs, the wolves, who saw our campfire, feeble in the all-else blackness, and first wandered up to us, it must seem like but an eyeblink ago.

Not long after Issie, Elizabeth and I had children—Mary Katherine and, three years later, Lowry, and it was with great delight that I gave them my full attention, in my thirties, forties, and then into my fifties. It was what I wanted to do. I'd had enough freedom. We had dogs, lots of dogs: shoeboxes full of photographs. Little girls and puppies? Please. We took film down to Libby at least twice a week to send it off to be developed. Hardly anyone lives up here, as I think I've mentioned. We had all the time and space we could hope for or imagine. It was, I think, a pretty good place to be a dog, and—I want to believe this—a good place to be a child too.

In those photos—dogs-and-children—it's amazing to see how quickly the dogs grow old, as do the parents, in the photos. Only the children remain young, as if suspended in time: in a valley where time touches only parents and dogs.

And yet, not suddenly—it was not sudden at all—I'm in my sixties, living in a big, old, empty house. One tamale for break-fast, a grilled cheese for lunch, an elk-ginger burger with no bread and a kale salad for dinner—with two glasses of Côtes du Rhône, and my Fitbit's 10,000 steps a day, my thirty-minute stretching routine. A week might go without my starting the car. Shovel-ing snow, splitting firewood, fixing things, or trying to fix them, keeping the floors swept and the windows washed so they let in the bright winter sun—everyone has been gone now for, depend-ing on how one thinks of *gone*, about five years.

I take photos of the dogs and email and text them to the girls—Mary Katherine in California, Lowry in New York—and film short clips of the spaniels roughhousing, or of test-tube Callie, bedazzled, nirvana-bound, by the swirling vortices of snow crystals that slide from pine boughs high above jet on a blue sky, a sunny day after a heavy snow the night before. The sun shoots through the ghost-glitter twisting shapes of them—is it smoke, is it sunlit spirit?—and she leaps and lunges through chest-deep snow, trying to point each individual flashing frost crystal, a snap-bulb of ecstasy going off in her mind in every second of every minute of every hour of every day: or when the sun is out.

The rest of the time, she lies by the fire, staring into it, warm-ing herself like a cat, and waiting. Waiting for the next snowfall, or for hunting season, when her genius roars: the best pheasant dog I've ever seen.

The ticking of the old windup clock—my great-grandparents' wedding gift to my grandmother—echoes throughout the house. I putter, I wait for them to come back home. I love my freedom, my space, and the thing that is perhaps second rarest, all the time in the world. Or so it seems.

The spaniels dive into the snow. "Hey, sugarbutts," I call to them. I take pictures of us romping and send them to the girls. It seems a long time ago that I was so psychologically undone by Issie trying to run away, and by Issie galloping alongside me everywhere I went, serving her whims and wills rather than my own.

In the evenings, I go to bed pretty early. I drink a cup of tea and read for half an hour, never a full hour, before falling asleep. (The next day, after writing, I will take a nap.) The dogs, though young, adjust themselves to my schedule. They sleep on the bed with me and nap beside me in the mornings, all of us stretched out on the wooden floor, no pillows, no padding, just wood.

They ski with me, and power through the deep drifts, porpoising, while I glide in circles around the marsh, watching the light change slowly on the mountain—around and around, as if raveling tight the coil of time, then unraveling it. No one is taking my picture, so I am not getting any older. It's good to have something to take care of besides oneself.

Fifteen dogs is not enough. Thirty feels like a good number. Too many dogs have I buried with Jim Harrison's advice, giving them a pound of ground meat to be gulping down just as the needle's administration hits the bloodstream. The late great John Graves wrote of his dog Blue—how the shape of his head, more than any other, fit the shape of John's hand, the palm of it.

I remember when the coyotes got Ann, gutted her, and she came crawling home with thirty feet of entrails trailing pink in the dust from where the coyotes caught her. I shoved them back in, held her together, raced to the vet, an hour away; he cleaned her and sewed her back up, and in less than a week she was her old self again.

We know the heart of a dog is a powerhouse of an organ, capable of compressing seven years of passion into but a single year. When I walk through my yard and out into the forest, it's hard to navigate a path that does not pass by or across the burial site of a dog or dogs, each residing at a different level in the geological strata, the foundation of which I, in my four hundred and twentieth dog year, am becoming. Anyone who has ever loved a dog and been loved by one knows, with the humility of the experience, that they love us even though they know us so well. It's breathtaking.

SWANS

RARELY DO ARTISTS MEET AN OBJECT IN NATURE AND examine it from so many perspectives that it becomes transcendent metaphor. More often, a shortcut is taken wherein the natural object becomes but mere symbol. The rose is love, the old oak tree wisdom or endurance. The dog is loyal, the cat fickle, the wolf ferocious, the fox cunning. And so forth. In this simplistic representation, the object—usually from the natural world—is trapped, static. It can never mean more than that one thing. It is no longer free to move, to travel, to surprise, to change.

The poet Mary Oliver's swans are an exception, and I think of them often, when watching the real thing, the swans of Yellowstone. There's no telling how many times they appear in Oliver's poetry, and never in quite the same way. A poppy-colored beak, an elegant webbed foot the color of charcoal; a white ship bearing happiness, floating across the wide waters. The swans in her poetry are always free.

Like most large animals, swans need a lot of space. That's why they're in Yellowstone. They need entire mountain ranges—multiplicities of mountain ranges.

I have crept up on them in Alaska in early autumn, at dusk—mesmerized as if by a candle flame at their reflection upon the black waters, at the edge of the tundra, the black spruce ever darker against nightfall.

Did these same birds pass through Yellowstone? Possibly;

probably. They follow the spine north. The air they stir with their enormous wings falls down upon us, whether we are looking up at them or looking down at the ground, thinking nothing about them.

They live in Yellowstone as if in a bowl of old fire in no way yet done cooling. A lake of fire. They cast north, radiating like shards and slivers of ice cast from that ring of fire. They follow river veins, like fish; other valleys in the West receive Yellowstone's swans, waters that might never before have had these white ships sail them. I have been watching and waiting and hoping for their slow advance to the Yaak, moving ever closer. The Clark Fork. The Bull River. Finally, this year, the Yaak.

I have seen them following the rivers of mountains, too, flying along the Rocky Mountain Front. One day while pheasant hunting my pointer retrieved one from a pond; a hunter had shot it, it had recently died, and I was able to examine it at length. You might not believe how dense they are, how heavy—how mammalian. How white. Whiter in the hand than even in the blue sky, or upon blue waters.

On several occasions I have been high in the mountains, above a forested pass or saddle, and have seen Canada geese go flying below me, braying, their wings seeming to clip the tops of trees at seven, eight, nine thousand feet.

Some day—in Yellowstone country, or anywhere—I would like to look down onto a pass and see swans likewise passing below, just above the forest's top, so that it is like staring down into a reflection of swans. As if in viewing them, we might acknowledge or activate something very similar in ourselves. Something we cannot always feel within us, until we see them. Until we look at them, and commit to seeing them a little differently, each time we look at them. As we ourselves might wish to be viewed.

WITH EVERY GREAT BREATH

Living and Dying in Lincoln County

Editor's note (from The Whitefish Review*): Vermiculite, an ore found in the Libby, Montana, area in 1881, had been mined in the area since 1919. Vermiculite, a mineral similar to mica, expands when heated into featherweight pieces that have been used commercially for decades in attic and wall insulation, wallboard, fireproofing, and plant nursery and forestry products. It was also used in scores of consumer products, such as lawn and garden supplies and cat litter.*

IN 1919, E. N. ALLEY BOUGHT THE RAINY CREEK CLAIMS and started the Zonolite Company. W. R. Grace and Company bought the Zonolite mine in 1963 and closed it in 1990. Federal government investigators subsequently found that air samples from the area had elevated levels of fibrous tremolite asbestos, which causes asbestos-related illnesses.

More than 274 area deaths in the past 60 years are suspected to have been caused by asbestos-contaminated vermiculite, and approximately 1,200 residents of the Libby area have been identified as suffering from some kind of asbestos-related abnormality. It has been called the worst environmental disaster in our nation's history.

In 2005, the U.S. Department of Justice indicted W. R. Grace and seven current and former Grace executives for knowingly endangering residents of Libby and concealing information about the health effects of its asbestos mining operation. According to the indictment, W. R. Grace and its executives, as far back as the 1970s, attempted to conceal information about the adverse health effects of the company's vermiculite mining operations and distribution of vermiculite. The defendants were also accused of obstructing the government's cleanup efforts and of wire fraud.

The criminal trial began in February 2009 after years of pre-trial proceedings that reached the United States Supreme Court. On Friday, May 8, 2009, W. R. Grace was acquitted of "knowingly" harming the people of Libby, Montana.

Fred Festa, chairman, president, and CEO of W. R. Grace and Company, said in a statement that did not specifically deny knowing of harm that instead "the company worked hard to keep the operations in compliance with the laws and standards of the day."

David Uhlmann, a former top environmental crimes prosecutor, has been quoted as saying about W. R. Grace: "There's never been a case where so many people were sickened or killed by environmental crime."

I'm dressed in my orange county-issued pajamas with some new friends in the holding facility of the Helena jail, having been arrested for criminal trespass in the state capital, the result of overstaying my welcome during a protest against the State Land Board's plans to lease 1.5 billion tons of toxic coal in Otter Creek, Montana. The Otter Creek coal is too dirty to burn in this country; the plans therefore are to build a rail line to ship it to China, via ports in the Pacific Northwest. This isn't the Montana way, nor the American way, transferring our harm to others, not for profit and not for loss, and if global warming is not the moral issue of our times, then none exists.

Handcuffs, then, and a short ride through Helena in the paddy wagon. My youngest daughter, Lowry, tried to bail me out, but cell phones don't work, so to relay messages my jailer has to go back and forth to the sidewalk where Lowry is standing outside the jail in the long summer twilight, waiting. My incarceration has been complicated further by a piece of poor judgment on my part—a single tiny pellet of zolpidem, the generic name for Ambien, which I brought in with me, not thinking the searchers would find it, though they did.

This, I'm told, constitutes a felony in Montana—to carry prescription medicine outside of the container in which it was initially dispensed—and so in an effort to convince the authorities that I simply wanted to be assured of a good night's sleep, should I be overstaying the night in stir, Lowry has had to rummage through my suitcase for all of my various medications. (I've just picked up half a dozen various prescriptions in preparation for a medical procedure in Libby the next day.) Ever the good daughter, Lowry has carried the double-armful of these loose plastic bottles up the steps, spilling some as she goes, to show my captors that her medicated father means no harm, is not a trafficker. (Should I get out, we'll drive through the night to be back in Libby for the morning appointment.)

This story has nothing to do with coal mining but everything to do with a big pit. The coal lies in the future, just waiting beneath the skin of the earth in extreme southeastern Montana's Tongue River country—a land as dry and dusty as my home in the northwest corner of the state is lush and green—while the other mineral that I want to talk about, asbestos, lies somewhat in the past, though it too inhabits the present and the future, having been exhumed and shipped all around the world.

It came from my home.

This story has in it heroes and villains and ordinary people, beautiful country, a corrupt government, a dead dog, several dead friends, and dozens of cardboard boxes of files and records and old newspaper clippings and health records, up in the dusty attic (probably asbestos-laden) of one social activist in the northwest corner of Montana, in the town of Libby, named long ago for a miner's daughter.

It's a big story composed of millions of tiny parts. It defies structure. It drifts along on the breezes, settles and lands where it may.

About the proposed coal mine: you can't make this shit up. The world's richest man is investing in a company that wants to build a railroad through the most southwesterly corner of Montana—the bucolic Tongue River Valley, ancestral home to the Northern Cheyenne and, more recently, cattle ranchers. The power brokers wish to surface mine, from the upper transgressive reaches of a buried old swamp, millennia's worth of low-grade sub-bituminous coal to send, in open boxcars, all the way across Montana and the Pacific Northwest, to ship to China, under a huge subsidy by Montana and U.S. taxpayers, so that developing countries and investors will build new coal-fired plants and get those countries hooked on coal. At that point, we, the United States—or those investors—can then convert the world to a coal economy.

Ironically, the emissions from this toxic coal with its low energy content will be back on our shores within two weeks. But at least we didn't burn it here. *We didn't break any U.S. laws*, the investors can say.

The citizens of China can't protest this, and the billions of impoverished environmental refugees of the future can't protest it, because it is still some short distance into the future, while the trains are carrying their toxic swirling bounty now, broadcasting a brown-black scrim of sulfur, selenium, cadmium, uranium, arsenic along the rail lines, and the windswept communities through which these boxcars—miles long, coming and going all the time—pass, uncontested, unprotected, unreported, the innocuous growl of commerce and liquidation.

There's no science in this, no data is being collected. The Otter Creek coal story of today reminds me, in my jail cell, of that other story from the opposite end of the state, a story that is also still largely underground, and of another rail line, one that spans the entire northern tier of the U.S. It's a story that originates in that other far corner of this huge and beautiful state that is sometimes ferociously independent and yet other times willing to roll over for corporations like a submissive little roly-poly speckled puppy.

———————

All right, time to descend into the pit. The illnesses here are not for the faint of heart, but even in the midst of a silent war there is hope, up here near the international border, almost but not quite out of sight of everything and everyone. Due largely to the work of a fairly small number of politicians and activists, there are still slivers of hope up here somehow, somewhere, even if they are not at first visible, or barely visible: as slender, perhaps, as silvery frost needles shimmering in the air in winter.

How do we live?

How do we die?

Surely the answers are the same.

And yet, before I describe how we die, let me testify—as if presenting a breath of clean cool air—how we live, and where we live.

———————

There was (and still partially is) one certain mountain, Vermiculite Mountain, up in the Purcell Mountains of northwest Montana's Yaak Valley, north of the broad deep Kootenai River, which separates the rock and ice crags of the Cabinet Mountains to the south from the softer, more heavily forested, lower elevation mountains of the Yaak Valley, to the north, where I have lived and spent the most powerful moments of my life. Those Purcell Mountains appear more like the Appalachians than the Rockies.

Along the ribbon of the Kootenai River, lying in the narrow valley between these two mountain ranges, is a slender winding trough that runs with the river east-west toward Idaho and, ultimately, the Pacific. This is the Kootenai Valley, and it contains the little towns of Libby (pop. 2,900) and Troy (pop. 900). It is a landscape of stunning beauty—sylvan forests on steep mountain flanks, ice- and snow-capped peaks. Bald eagles drift up and down the river. Moose wade the river's shallows. There are relatively few people. There is extreme poverty, sometimes as high as 20 to 30 percent.

For whatever reason, the volcanic-cone-shaped mountain—Vermiculite Mountain—up in the Yaak, about ten miles northeast of Libby, contained—and still contains—an extraordinary concentration of vermiculite ore. There are asbestos fibers in this ore. Asbestos historically has been an insulator against extreme heat. It can absorb up to 1,022 degrees Fahrenheit before burning—and this one mountain back in the middle of nowhere, up near the Canadian border, at one time produced nearly all of the world's asbestos.

The reason the vermiculite (a glittering gold mineral, reminding one of mica or even fool's gold) absorbs heat so well is that it swells dramatically during the heating process, expanding with a popping noise as the heat gets trapped between tight structural laminae, exfoliating each layer in the expansion. For fun, children would heat chunks of the mineral with matches and lighters to hear it *pop!* The spent ore was heaped in giant piles all around the county, after the machines had sawed off the top of the mountain, and—for decade after decade—continued clawing out the insides.

The vermiculite was poured into people's attics like kitty litter, to provide cheap insulation, and poured into the spaces between walls, likewise. It was mixed into children's sandboxes, stirred into people's gardens, used as filler for running tracks and skating rinks. It has no nutritional value but there were even recipes that used it in the baking of muffins. Made the muffins real puffy, people said. Asked for seconds.

The asbestos from this one mountain is incredibly toxic. It's killed hundreds of people in Libby and sickened thousands, with the kind of illness where you don't ever get better. For some reason, the asbestos fibers in the vermiculite in Libby are a smaller variety, called tremolite, rather than the more common amphibole asbestos fiber. Either one is incredibly toxic but the smaller tremolite is particularly so in that it is less likely to be filtered by the body's traditional lines of defense. As well, the fibers are barbed, like porcupine quills, so that once they attach—to the lining of the lungs, the alveoli, the lining of the stomach—they are unable to be ejected and burrow ever deeper, bioaccumulating, and ticking, waiting patiently to trigger the end game, the incurable and fast-acting cancer of mesothelioma.

I think of tiny things being dug up out of the earth and broadcast over a town, and the invisible and irrevocable damage that something so small can do. The miners, of course, working at ground zero—driving the stuff around in dump trucks, and descending into the giant pit where ceaseless dust storms whirled—fell like flies—even in the 1940s and '50s, they were dying, it was common local knowledge that the mine was a hard place to work, and hard on a man's health—but what mine wasn't?

There wasn't any hard science showing the *how* or *why*; dying was just what miners eventually did. The times were hard, and you died if you worked in the mine, or you and your family starved if you didn't.

The dust kept billowing up out of the pit and being hauled off down the mountain in trucks, poured into railcars, and sent down the line, east and west, to Seattle and St. Paul, swirling. People were getting sick from working in the mines, and when the workers came home dusty from work, their families got sick from the dust that was on their clothes. There was primary exposure, secondary exposure, tertiary exposure. The fibers blew through the valleys, hung suspended for long periods. I would assume that the frequent mountain valley inversions might aid in trapping these invisible curtains of poison. I can imagine that the fog and river moisture and other particulates—woodsmoke, in that cold damp country, so that the bowls of the valleys themselves seem to smolder—acted as anchors on the upward drift and dispersal of those microfibers, bringing them back down to the lung-level of humans.

To the best of my knowledge, I don't think anyone else understands the dispersal mechanisms and routes, the distribution and density of the tiny fibers, nor how many there are, nor what can be done to clean them from the system, nor what constitutes *safe*, what constitutes *hazardous*, or what might constitute the midrange safe space for the daily living in between. And, understandably, after sixty years of government and corporate and industrial denials, obstructions, and even plain old-fashioned human error, even if there were studies and reports purporting to fully understand such things, I can't think of many of us who would be inclined to trust those answers.

When I think of the country around the mine—the rivers like veins and arteries, the forests, mountains, lakes like internal organs in the body whole—the ridges in the Yaak, particularly, rolling one after another, like the crenellations of a deep and complex brain—the images of treasure that come to me are not of underground petrified rivers of silver or gold, nor lode veins of asbestos, coal, oil, gas, but instead, the treasures at the surface, particularly up on the high ridges, where the winds scrub and scour the stone and blow steadily—places where the forests filter out to a stunted filigree of blue-green, like the outer fringes of alveoli, and where, to a traveler, a pilgrim, there is very much the feeling that you have left one special place, *the forest*—a place of deep sanctuary and security—and have ascended to another special place, a place where illumination exists.

How we die. Slowest first: asbestosis. Under the relentless accumulation of those tiny barbed fibers, the lungs—cut daily by a hundred thousand knives—build up a scabrous, inflexible scar tissue. The lungs strain increasingly to suck in air. Heard through a stethoscope, lungs—no longer supple or even as moist—produce in their respiration a dry, crinkling sound, like brittle plastic being crumpled. The body soon strains harder to deliver to the rest of itself that which was once free but is now costly and rare, and there is never quite enough.

An asbestos survivor moves more slowly than he or she used to, conserving energy and oxygen. No matter that as young people they were once active in one of the most beautiful places on earth—running up and down the mountains in pursuit of deer and elk, or hiking to favorite fishing lakes, or picking huckleberries, gathering mushrooms; hiking, camping, skiing, playing. Never mind all that. Now the most vigorous thing many of them attempt is to walk out and get the morning paper.

Rarely if ever is age kind to the human body, but here the disparity strikes me as torturous: to become slowly captive in one's body, while still looking out at those beautiful mountains that were so much a part of youth and health.

They're not going to get better. It's not like a broken bone that bends nor a surgery that strengthens. Maybe someday in the future there'll be replacement lungs, a way to change out the old, crackly, stiff, impermeable-as-waxed-cardboard ones and throw in a new pair; but no such technology exists.

Slowly—year by year—the biology of the affliction meta-morphoses the body, transforms the vessel that houses the afflic-tion, in the way that the passage of time modifies and sculpts the rounded mountains themselves.

The sufferers—the survivors—develop great barrel chests, with every muscle in the body—diaphragm, intercostal muscles, pectorals, *everything*—clenching and pulling and squeezing, try-ing to pull more air deeper into the lungs.

The heart works harder, too—one day, it will work itself to death—trying to pump oxygen to all the farthest reaches. Ex-tremities grow cold easily. In the early stages, fingernails begin to exhibit the telltale marks of hypoxia: they bulge and bunch up, and take on a clubbed appearance. Sometimes I look at mine, examining them in the light like a prima donna. The nail on the middle finger of my right hand was the first to begin bulging slightly, a couple of years ago; recently, a couple more have begun to swell.

Other symptoms proceed: dizziness, weakness, lightheaded-ness, reduced oxygen flow. The survivor fights for each breath, negotiates for even a fraction of a breath, while outside, the snow-clad mountains shine as if waiting patiently for the survivor to return to them—to hike the quiet soft trails through the shadowy forest, and to ascend those steep slopes with the same vigor that the survivor possessed in the days before things began to add up.

It's not like everyone in Lincoln County has it. Far from it. The majority don't. Only one-third of those examined—whether miners or general air-breathers—show signs of pleural thickening in chest X-rays, a leading indicator of exposure.

In a county of 19,000 residents—an immense land mass mea-suring 3,675 square miles—there are currently "only" about 2,000 survivors being treated for various asbestos-related diseases.

So the asbestosis is the first way to get sick. You don't neces-sarily die from asbestosis, or at least not in a hurry; instead, it can just wear you down, over the space of thirty or forty years. There's time to think about things. During that same time, of course, you might get hit by a truck.

The second way to get sick is quite different. There's a presently incurable cancer, mesothelioma—a cancer of the lining of the lungs or the stomach—that is caused only by exposure to asbestos, nothing else. It's an incredibly rare cancer, and once you get it, it's lights out. It roars through the body, sometimes within short weeks. It occurs in the general population with a frequency of about one in 100,000, so that from actuarial tables, there should have been between zero and one cases in Libby, ever.

To date, thirty-two at the very least are known or diagnosed. Or rather, thirty-two-plus-one. My dog, a sweet speckled German shorthaired pointer named Point—as strong as a little ox—was the first animal in Lincoln County diagnosed with it, in 2005. He was ten. The mill had been closed for over ten years. He was what the vet called the sentinel case for Lincoln County.

Usually the meso, as it's called locally, manifests itself in the lungs, but Point's was in the stomach. It wasn't painful for Point but it wasn't pretty, particularly not for such a once graceful athlete. I went out to his kennel one morning in late July to find him swollen like a melon. He was as prancy and frisky as ever, but he was huge and round, a completely different version of the dog he had been the day before.

I hurried him down to Libby, where the vet, Doug, X-rayed him, found nothing, and then drew some fluid to look at.

The fluid was blood, or a blood-water mixture, and was bright red, like dark black cherry Kool-Aid. It took about an hour to drain it all off. I can't remember how many cc's we got, that first time—maybe half a liter—and slowly, Point deflated, like a pufferfish going down, no longer alarmed.

He wriggled and writhed on the table. Just when Doug thought he had all the mystery fluid drained, he would stick the needle somewhere else in his abdominal cavity, probing, and a new surge of that bright black-red tarwater would come jetting out, filling the hypodermic's chamber.

"I don't know what it is," Doug said. "It could be a bad cancer. You might want to take him over to the specialists at Washington State."

So passed a summer, and about seven thousand dollars. We didn't know what he had. We kept thinking he could get better. We kept searching for an answer, as I went further and further down the slippery slope of dog medical care. If I'd known what it was, I wouldn't have attempted to fix it, would have taken him out in the field as if going on one last early season hunt and then let him die.

But one small thing—a blood test, an X-ray—led to another, and because he was otherwise so healthy—other than those lengthy drainings each day—I kept following hope, the way he and I would follow the scent or possibility or tracks of birds.

An MRI came next—maybe it was just some soft tissue blockage, something easily removed—he still seemed so damned healthy!—but when it showed nothing, there was something else, I can't even remember what. That in turn was followed by the last-gasp effort—he was healthy, and he was dying—of opening him up, full body exploratory surgery—and that's when they found out what they found out. No cure, and the first diagnosis of meso in a pet in Lincoln County. How, why, where, what?

I wanted to bill W. R. Grace for the expenses, but didn't. There were and are people still unserved, underserved, standing in line, or buried six feet under, waiting. We sewed him up and took him back to the Yaak. He lived long enough to hunt the first month of the season, September, and a couple of weeks into October.

I kept draining him, and watching him closely, for the day that he didn't want to hunt, and when it came—a cold, snowy, rainy, foggy day—I fed him well and drove him down to see Doug for the last time, and then when that was over I went on to the gym to watch a volleyball game. The same gym, I wondered, where countless miner-fathers had come straight in from work to watch their sons and daughters play volleyball, basketball, wrestle, or to graduate? Dusting their jeans, wiping their boots on the mat, then coming on inside, the invisible fibers swirling around them like an unseen corona, and with the gym filling up, in that manner—for once the fibers were inside, how to get them outside?

The thing about Point was that he had not been an indoor dog—he had stayed out in his kennel, in a fenced area—and our home was new anyway, had been built well after the vermiculite insulation era. After burying him I went down to the EPA office in Libby and told them about it, asked if they could come up and check things out, but was told with a surprising degree of hostility and irritation that they didn't cover the Yaak, that they were just focusing on Libby and Troy.

The mine was technically in the lower Yaak, just south of Gold Hill, in the Purcells, and there was an old abandoned vermiculite mine, hand-dug, right above the center of Yaak—but they said they didn't have to check it out and that they wouldn't, or couldn't.

I've thought about that for a while. For a while, it seemed to me to be an either-or situation. In an era of new limited government resources, I understood that the population centers should receive treatment and remediation first. But to stick our heads in the sand and not follow leads—to not pursue science—seems utterly foolhardy.

I felt that way then, but wanted to believe the Yaak was safe. If it wasn't, we would have heard about it, right? How could anyone live in the ground-zero center of imminent danger and not know it, or—stranger still—know it or even suspect it, but then kind of look the other way and keep on going, one foot in front of another, one day at a time, hoping that the government and the corporations would keep us all safe and well and sound?

Still, I believed what I wanted to believe. I felt bad for the folks down in Libby and Troy. I had lost a great bird dog, but he was still just a dog. Down in Libby and Troy, at slightly lower elevations, there was real misery going on. I felt like a sentimental fool, having followed the medicine so far down the rathole. I didn't regret having had those last few September hunts with him, but I don't think I would call them $7,000 hunts—though who can really say, until the end of a life?

I was glad Point's illness was diagnosed—that he didn't just fade away in mystery and grief—that his death held some not-insignificant service to humanity, in addition to the pleasure he brought us as a family pet, and the meals we procured from his talents afield—but I didn't have the heart to pursue redress against Grace. I just wanted to stay away from the invisible thing—Grace itself, which was seeking to become untouchably vaporous, if not toxic—and I also didn't want to appear as if I thought a dog's illness was anything like a person's.

W. R. Grace was filing for bankruptcy, negotiating with judges and plaintiffs and mediators—plotting, in that peculiarly American way, their brief vanishing, while at the same time plotting and planning and staging their own taxpayer-subsidized resurrection.

I buried him and moved on. We were renting a house in Troy so the girls could go to school, and the year after that, we rented a house in Missoula, to take advantage of a wider degree of course selection. We kept our home in the Yaak—every day I missed, and still miss, being there for every hour that I can—but I also had to wonder: Did I do an unwitting good thing, getting us out, just as any survivor might also ask him- or herself, *Did I do an unwitting bad thing, coming here?*

The key word is *unwitting*. The volume of all that is unknown just keeps getting larger, like an immense pit being dug.

————————

Illness is a private thing; mortality, all the more so. It's a delicate business, asking folks how they feel about what's happened, and is still happening, and asking them for anecdotes from the days back when they were young and strong.

The defense attorney's attacks on the sick and the dying were grotesque and repulsive, and wrong in every direction imaginable. I felt as if I had seen it all before. It wasn't that the amorality in the courtroom was directionless, drifting, like the whims of dust in a gale; it was that the amorality—or, if you choose to call it something else, such as evil—went in every direction. I don't know what the word for that is: radial, perhaps. It emanated from one source and then went everywhere.

W. R. Grace, sheltered under bankruptcy ruling, was playing with house money; they were able to spend however much they wanted to spend, hiring a dozen or more lawyers, and taxpayers would pick up the tab. The sky was the limit. That court bill ended up being $160 million for a little town of 2,900 in northwest Montana. (The EPA just committed $126 million to try to clean up the Grace toxins—another taxpayer bill for us to foot.)

A hundred and thirty million here, a hundred and forty million there—pretty soon we're talking about real money. A billion would allow us to fight another year in Iraq, where I hear they have some serious chemical exposure problems as well.

Montana's two U.S. senators were pissed. From a press release by Senator Jon Tester, dated October 12, 2012, doing the unthinkable, taking on a corporation:

(Washington, D.C.)—Montana's U.S. Senators Jon Tester and Max Baucus are asking the Environmental

Protection Agency to finalize tough standards on asbestos cleanup in Libby. Specifically, they are calling
on the EPA to honor the findings of its Science Advisory Board in establishing science-based standards
for the toxicity of asbestos in Libby. In a letter to EPA
Administrator Lisa Jackson, Baucus and Tester also
hammered W. R. Grace for resisting more rigorous
standards.

"[W]e were acutely troubled by the response of
W. R. Grace to the Science Advisory Board's review.
In our opinion, Grace lost the privilege to opine on
the science of asbestos when it knowingly—and for
decades—traded profits for lives in Lincoln County,"
they wrote. "We are not surprised to find Grace trying
to cloud the science or hide behind the speculative liability of other property owners. But we take this opportunity to call a spade a spade, and a snake a snake."

W. R. Grace and Company is fighting tougher standards being
reviewed by the EPA's Science Advisory Board. The science behind the proposal addresses a fundamental challenge to answering the question of how clean is "clean enough" with regard to
asbestos contamination.

Tester and Baucus are pressing the EPA to honor the findings of
the Science Advisory Board, arguing that residents of Lincoln
County have waited for more than a decade for justice.

———

I should point out that I am not speaking for Libby, or my part
of Lincoln County, but instead only myself. This is just my observation and experience. I think it's fair to say, however, that when
the mine came in, there was no examination. In exchange for

jobs, the forefathers allowed a self-regulating entity to enter the valley, coming in over those high mountain walls, and carrying the railcars away, hundreds at a time, with the glimmering dust swirling in the high mountain sunlight every mile along the way.

I neither criticize nor judge the decision. Who among us these days does not make similar choices and decisions—what to eat, what to drink, what to buy—with a similar absence of knowledge or analysis?

My point is that on the surface—independent, resourceful, God-fearing, etc.—Libby appears to be a model community. As does the Tongue River country, and Otter Creek, at the other end of the state. But you can't have these world-changing extraction projects come in without expecting to lose all that existed before. You can't. The transformation must occur for the industrial equation to balance. The exchange for the short-term profits. The so-called profits. The liquidation. You give up the land you live on, or the thing beneath the surface.

A little about the geology: while the Cabinet Mountains' stony peaks were being shaved and scoured by the Ice Age's retreat, roughly 10,000 years ago, the Purcells—just across the river, in the Yaak, to the north—hibernated almost entirely beneath several thousand feet of blue ice, with only the tiniest knobs and nubs piercing that glistening, gleaming ice-world.

In essence, the Yaak slept for a few thousand years longer, getting a later start at life than the rest of the region. In this regard then it's almost an utterly new place, having had to start from scratch with bedrock, with the business of the ages: waiting for seed-drift, establishing a bed of primary vegetation and forest, and the beginnings of the patient erosion that would aid in establishing soil upon that late-in-coming bare new foundation of ice-peeled stone.

The surrounding mountains—the Cabinets and Selkirks— would have already had thousand-year cycles of forest growth and rot, fire and rot, with giant carcasses nurturing seedlings, while the bowl of the Purcells would have still been new in the world: glowing, I like to think, in the midst of that forest like a blue brain, ready-made and even inspirited, but still waiting for the first stimulus, first electrical pathways, of life to inhabit those folds and ridges and hills.

How can the most beautiful place on earth be one of the most toxic?

The daily beauty has polished something in people, I think, as nacreous as the sheen of the inner shell of conch or nautilus.

No ice can scour it, the beauty is elemental. Only the dissolution of memory, I imagine, can strip the beauty, though perhaps not even that.

Maybe the identity of this place comes back to its newness. It seems that when I walk here, the air that stirs around my ankles is still original, is first-stirred.

———————

And yet, as simple as it sounds, where, in this country—not just Lincoln County, but in the United States—has that story ever occurred? Where has any one of the fifty states—which hold, through the power of charter, the ability to dictate the conditions under which a corporation will or will not be allowed to operate in their state—successfully challenged this current monstrous hybrid in which the corporations—nothing more than a bundle of words, or a latticework of numbers—possess all the rights of an individual, possess certain inalienable rights, and yet, being monstrous half-human and half-god hybrids, possess none of the responsibilities by which the rest of us hold our own brief charters?

———————

This is important, and it's coming your way: not just on the rail lines that trucked the pixie dust out in boxcar-loads by the hundreds of thousands, maybe even millions, strung all along the northern tier like the glowing blue circuitry of the brain's neural pathways, nor is it coming your way in the Otter Creek and Tongue River trains and the swirling random winds that encircle and wreathe the world.

Instead, it is coming more totally, in the breathtaking wave of a new form of corporate intelligence, one which with its mass and span all but promises to overwhelm the little fires of goodness within us. It's been so insidious that it has operated out in the open. We've seen it and talked about it for so long—the dangers of corporate soullessness—that it's as if we've stopped seeing it, long ago, even when it's right in front of us.

This gives the impression that it's gone away. Now that we are more accustomed to it, we are no longer so afraid.

This new and evolving thing is an approaching shadow, like the one thrown by a spot on the lungs in a chest X-ray as the growth of pleural plaque begins, not just on the surface of the pleural walls, but interstitially, between the cells, and then into the cells, as if in the process of lithification—as if the body, even in the still-living, is being converted totally to an upright column of shimmering, glittering amphibole asbestos fiber—fireproof, perhaps, but lifeless.

The corporations have endured, have weathered the tiny storms of such protests, and are now operating with such impunity that there's no need to hide. They have been granted—foolishly—by the state of Montana the right of eminent domain if such taking serves commerce. The plan is no longer and perhaps never was so much to destroy the little fires within us as to instead just isolate and overwhelm them—to encase them, as if beneath a giant earthen dam, a cap of impermeable clay: a buried civilization, or the outpost of civilization, where such little fires still glimmer and sputter in that all-else darkness, no more powerful than candles, though now with but a fixed and finite amount of oxygen.

———————

Gayla Benefield—a dagger, not a thorn, in the side of W. R. Grace—grew up hunting and fishing and hiking and picking berries in the Yaak. A creek up here is named for her family. She might be the one person you would most want on your side in a fight, and the one person you'd least want to see fighting against you. That she has spent her adult life battling invisible things—unseen fibers, and the spiritless irresponsibility of corporations—has in no way diminished her vigor for such defense and social and environmental justice.

Gayla's father worked at the mine, beginning in the 1950s, got sick in the 1960s, and died. The company gave his widow, Margaret, $37 a week to support her and her five children. Then Margaret died of the same disease. Gayla tended to her over the long years of the slow suffocating death, with her rage building—and her sister Eva's husband, also a mine employee, died, weakened for five years by asbestosis, until the meso kicked in, spreading quickly from his lungs into his brain and heart—the latter an extremely rare medical condition, with the smooth workhorse muscle of the heart almost never accepting cancerous growths.

He died a particularly painful death—essentially a six-week long heart attack—that no morphine could ease, as he sat up in his bed and screamed *No, no, no!*

Gayla was diagnosed with asbestosis—her siblings were too—and now, one by one, many of her children are: a daughter, Jenan, who smoked, and, this year, her forty-four-year-old daughter, Julie, who is not a smoker. Strangely, Gayla's two sons, who work as rock drillers, laboring in the Lincoln County dust and silica, are thus far unaffected. Grasping for straws in completely unscientific fashion, I wonder if this is not somehow an important clue: if the coarser silica they've inhaled acts as a prophylactic, or like an immunization, a stimulant, that serves them in good stead while the finer asbestos fibers assault them.

The two men you would think most likely to have it are the two who don't.

I don't mean to be disrespectful in this thumbnail sketch of the tragedies long suffered by the Benefields. It's simply that I'm not comfortable wading down into the personal stories of betrayal, and the long dying: the miners in their family carrying the poison home, spreading it across the generations. Andrea Peacock, in particular, has recorded these intricacies in great and loving detail in her book, *Libby, Montana.* It's hard to read, and harder still when the names and people are known to the author. It's there, now, a matter of historical record, even in the still-living—the struggle of Gayla and her friend Les Skramsted to hold Grace accountable for their decades of homicide and to drive underground the corporation—this invisible barbed and latticed, vertically integrated accounting structure designed to avoid culpability, and to instead gather and redistribute wealth—or rather, *money.* Andrew Schneider and David McCumber first broke the story of the Libby illnesses and Grace's resistance to responsibility in the *Seattle Post-Intelligencer* in 2000, then published a masterful book on it, *An Air That Kills.*

Rarely do physicians and scientists have the opportunity to study an illness—an epidemic—so rare and new, in which so many of the pages lie blank and open and white, waiting for the accrual of knowledge.

There are days, while out on a walk, thinking about my home, and my good fortune in having drifted into *this place*, parts of four decades ago, when I cannot help but think of this little postage-stamp place on earth as a kind of do-over for the creation story.

It feels to me sometimes also that although the first Garden of Eden story might have taken billions of years to play out—the first simple life appearing on the third or fourth day as the algal stromatolites that helped create oxygen, and then further on into the week, the fishes of the Devonian, and still later in the week, the gradual appearance of mankind into a garden of incredible bounty and beauty, followed by the apple seed of corruption, the arrival of the serpent, etc.—this second go-round, in this new place, is proceeding much faster than the original. As if, rather than stretching out those seven metaphysical days of creation to span four billion years, the same story, with its oh-so-slight variations, has been compressed to less than a century.

If there is a third do-over, might it, finally, require but those seven brief days?

———

We need a registry of how and where things went wrong. We need to begin filling in the pit.

A website should be created as a repository for testimonies from this era. Personal and family health histories, anecdotes, vignettes of growing up and working in Lincoln County—then or now, pre- or post-Grace. Testimonies about outdoor activities, quality of life: it all matters. Don't let W. R. Grace take that away, too. Who knows what data will be important in the future. We need to be gathering it now.

We need to get as much data—scientifically as well as anecdotally—as quickly as we can.

And whether the stories are dauntingly similar, repeating themselves one after another—stories like Gayla's—or possess perhaps bright strange clues of uniqueness, clues that might help scientists of the future form new ideas, experiments, and cures— no matter, it all has value.

I suspect there is value also to those who present their testimonies and fashion their narratives about what it's like here under siege from an invisible enemy in a land of sylvan beauty. Call it an artsy-fartsy hope, but I wouldn't be surprised if scientists and physicists of the future discover that there is an advantage for patients who feel they have greater control, or if not control, participation, in their illness; that they might respond a few percentage points more favorably to treatment, and resist by a greater degree various associated secondary debilitations.

That's just theory. One thing I believe is that they will feel better emotionally by writing it down—controlling the story, and examining the shape of the interior landscape and their personal histories, caught here in a strange point in time, between a very natural and very unnatural history.

This is one of the three main takeaways I have from living this story. The first is control your corporations: rule them with an iron fist, rather than being a simpering lapdog. Rewrite charters to govern their existence; the corporations should not possess constitutional rights. And by God, whatever you do, *don't* let them start voting in our elections.

The second thing has been impressed upon me by Gayla as well as others. It's important to Gayla that the media not use the word "victims," but rather "survivors." Even the ones who have died and gone on were, for a long while, survivors.

It's a vital distinction. The first step in asserting some control over the story as well as over the actions of industry and government is to not think of yourself as a victim.

For a long time, people had been noticing the death and the dying that was going on up on the hill. Former U.S. Representative Pat Williams tells of how when he visited Libby, the union leader, Don Wilkins, took him aside in the early 1980s and said there was something bad happening up there, and gestured toward the mountains. Ten years later, Don himself was dead from what used to be called "miner's disease." No one knows how many other hundreds died of asbestosis or meso in the old days, or how many contracted it. Most death certificates listed "cardiopulmonary failure," or something similar. During that time—in 1985—Williams introduced a landmark piece of health legislation, which would have created a national workers' compensation system to help people with occupational diseases, but the House never passed it, and the Gingrich Revolution and the "Contract on America" killed it, in the deregulatory fervor to provide ever more favorable conditions for corporate power, the cultural acceptance of which was spreading over the land like unseen fog.

So much political pussyfooting went on in those years. The corporation planned to shut the mine down almost the instant the EPA passed the Clean Air Act. The Reagan and Bush administrations fought to keep Libby from being declared a Superfund site. The state of Montana initially resisted it too, and there were predictable polarizations, even at the local level: a split between boosters who didn't want the stigma, versus those who were frightened or sick.

It was like shoving a huge boulder up a steep mountain, but it got done, against powerful odds. It took relentless pressure, ceaselessly applied. Down at ground zero, there were Gayla and Les, and others I haven't met, but whose testimony and record-ledgering is needed; within the EPA, there were a few whistleblowers and champions, like the much-revered Paul Peronard. There was the Kalispell attorney, Roger Sullivan, of McGarvey, Heberling, Sullivan and McGarvey, and there was U.S. Senator Max Baucus, who at last count has visited Libby well over twenty times. It is not an easy place to reach, is on the way to nowhere. Baucus, by enduring year after year, ascended to seniority where so many others did not, until finally he became chair of the Senate Finance Committee, at which point he found himself in a position where he was, ironically, interviewing and approving nominations for leadership of the EPA.

The attorneys operating within the giant crane-like structure of W. R. Grace threw everything they had at defending themselves against criminal charges. The $160 million Grace borrowed from taxpayers for their own defense against the very taxpayers who were suing them was but a drop in the bucket compared to what was at stake.

Had Grace lost the trial—had a corporation actually been held criminally responsible and accountable for its products and their effects—the entire free world would have been remade. Instead, Grace was acquitted of criminal charges. The corporation was allowed to proceed with virtual immunity, and case law precedent was set for all other corporations. You can bet all the other major corporations in the world were watching the Libby case with interest.

The Libby asbestos story isn't just about asbestosis and meso. Gayla has been saying that for a long time. But one story that's not getting out into the public as much as it should be is the prevalence of asbestos-related autoimmune diseases.

So Gayla's working on this, too, agitating for the scientific and political communities to catch up. Specifically, she points out five autoimmune disorders that are showing up in Lincoln County: lupus, rheumatoid arthritis, multiple sclerosis, scleroderma, and fibromyalgia. There are other illnesses, too—one-in-a-million rarities that are showing up in multiples. Gayla is pretty much the keeper of such knowledge. She has files in cardboard boxes, data stacked upon data, cross-linked and connected vertically across generations as well as horizontally across circumstances and time and locations, within the inimitable workings of her brain.

When she dies—and she will one day, almost surely from this disease, this legacy—more will be lost than can ever be gotten back.

She says that the years of fighting the issue and fighting the ever-elusive corporation of W. R. Grace, as well as her and her family's declining health, have ground her down; that she's trying to step away. But what Gayla calls stepping away would be pretty much still be front-and-center for anyone else.

There currently is no systematic wide-ranging analysis of the consequences of asbestos exposure in Lincoln County. In the post-Iraq invasion economy, there are limited financial resources to pick up the pieces of Grace's legacy—caring for the sick and dying should come first, with remediation—if such a thing is even possible. In a finite economic system, that leaves epidemiology, as well as research, a too-distant third and fourth priority.

We don't even know what we don't know.

A billion dollars wouldn't begin to cover it. It takes about half a million dollars to provide oxygen for each asbestosis patient over the course of a long and increasingly physically compromised life.

The cost of cleanup—chasing down tiny invisible fibers—could be bottomless. But that's just the asbestosis and mesothelioma. What about the other illnesses?

I get the sense Lincoln County is being Agent Oranged on this. Sometimes the political community accepts a medical condition that has symptoms but no internal marker, while other times it ignores or denies that problems exist.

The medical community, led by longtime Libby physician Dr. Brad Black, is treating anyone who is sick, and Congress, under the urging of Montana's two senators, Baucus and Tester, is trying to clean up the fibers. I wish some giant electron lint-scraper could be dragged through the air, sucking up with static electricity every last fiber—a cleansing—and that residents could then return for another chance at inhabiting paradise. As well, all people with asbestos-related diseases (ARD) in Libby have been enrolled in Medicare and/or Medicaid (the program should, in my opinion, be extended to the other residents in the county).

But I perceive there's a dangerous lag in reporting and acting upon the as yet undefinable miasma of what might be called secondary illnesses: the hard-to-diagnose and sometimes hard-to-treat conditions of general autoimmune breakdown, which is the result of bodies beleaguered, it seems, by phantoms.

This, too, is one of the reasons we need more testimonies.

Multiple sclerosis, in particular, can be like chasing a ghost. Unlike asbestosis—easily diagnosed, a definable shadow on an X-ray—diseases such as multiple sclerosis and other autoimmune disorders can be hard to pin down. They can come and go, ranging from mild to fatal. Multiple sclerosis—where the immune system begins attacking the body's own myelin sheaths, eroding the protective fatty coating that shields and insulates the wiring of the central nervous system—has been studied for decades, but scientists still don't understand why it appears. Theories include exposure to various environmental substances, or genetics, or bacteria, or viruses, or lack of Vitamin D. Nobody knows.

There are general trends in the prevalence of multiple sclerosis—people close to the equator have less—but there are clusters, too, all over the world, and Gayla says that Spokane, Washington, has the highest reported incidence on earth, just as Lincoln County has the highest incidence of mesothelioma.

What do the two communities have in common? W. R. Grace. The asbestos was mined outside of Libby, but then it was dumped into open boxcars and transported to Spokane. Only when the boxcars reached Spokane was the asbestos poured into sacks for shipping and distribution around the world. Gayla and others say Spokane is sitting on another story like Libby's, and that there, too, people have built their homes on top of toxic foundations.

She also says that if the studies were done, she thinks Libby would usurp Spokane for the greatest incidence of MS in the world.

———————

Who's lucky, and who's not? I'm lucky. Not only have I gotten to live in one of the most beautiful places on earth, doing what I want to do for a living—I also got to experience deeply the last of the last, a dying piece of Americana; an old-school small-town newspaper editor, a community-minded do-gooder who could always be found in his office.

I got to witness, and participate in, the whole journalistic experience, back when newspapers were a big deal, back when they were the voice of the news and the voice of a community. They were a conduit between history and change. Every issue, every day, could be as powerful as a small-scale revolution.

Roger Morris moved to Libby to edit the *Western News* after having worked for a newspaper in a ski town in Colorado. He'd seen the cultural wreckage wrought by gentrification and was enamored with Libby's less-polished edges. The bitter local battles—intense small-town dramas over weed ordinances, for instance—amused him. He was not condescending or patronizing, he understood that the things closest to home are what most consume our hours—but he was stimulated too by the almost mythic propensity that Lincoln County has for so often being ground zero for events of wider historical significance.

In Lincoln County, there was always one federal lawsuit or another going on about a proposed mine in a protected wilderness, or a proposed ski resort, or endangered species violations. There were domestic terrorists at large in the area (and I don't mean the Grace executives, despoiling the homeland killing hundreds, sickening thousands, but less sophisticated terrorists and anti-government zealots, hoarding ammunition and shooting up federal agents, and trying to rob banks, and tinkering with homemade bombs).

There were international water issues, conflicts with our neighbors to the north, and drug trafficking, as well as the trafficking of humans across the border. There was always something, and he was always on the job, working usually with just one reporter, going to county commissioner meetings, school board meetings, congressional staff meetings: interviewing, writing, typing.

The lights would be on in the little newsroom on California Street at almost any hour of day or night, and he loved his community, loved the always messy and usually irreconcilable differences within this little snapshot of ultra-white and ultra-conservative America, isolated hard and poor against the end of the twentieth century. He loved the small-town football games where fans of the Libby Loggers revved their chainsaws after each touchdown by the home team, and he loved hiking in the surrounding mountains, best of all in early summer, in the high alpine country where wildflowers bloomed briefly and wildly right at the edges of retreating snowbanks.

Then came Andrew Schneider and David McCumber's big series in the *Seattle Post-Intelligencer*, and Roger—lucky Roger, you could say, having gotten out of the retrace of hyper-rich ski town life—found himself in the heart of a huge story, one he sure didn't want to be in.

He reported diligently, daily, yearly, as the civil damages trials and bankruptcy proceedings unfolded; he harangued the state, under the administration of Governor Marc Racicot and then Governor Judy Martz, as well as the feds. He was a relentless fly in the ointment, sending out tiny oscillations into the universe. He would have traded his luck for anything, would have given anything for the invisible air to be clean, but it wasn't.

And while it would be an oversimplification to say he was born for battle—more accurate, perhaps, to say that he was born for justice—he found, in the words of Abraham Lincoln, that "In a larger sense, we cannot dedicate . . . we cannot consecrate . . . we cannot hallow . . . this ground. The brave men, living and dead, who struggled here, have consecrated it far above our poor power to add or detract. The world will little note nor long remember what we say here, but it can never forget what they did here. It is for us, the living, rather, to be dedicated here to the unfinished work which they who fought here have thus far so nobly advanced."

Ground zero, hallowed ground; it was his chance to be of use, of service, to his home, his community, and the greater good of man, and he took it.

Roger died quickly. He, like many, had moved here after the mine had closed, but he contracted an extremely fast-moving form of lung cancer, and it was lights out before he could barely even register what was happening.

He did live long enough to report on one more scoop. As a young man, he had worked construction in his home state of New York. He had been on one of the crews involved in erecting the Twin Towers in Manhattan, pouring in W. R. Grace's vermiculite, asbestos insulation that had been mined from the mountain just above Libby, put on the train and sent east, following that railway corridor like a long fuse burning, where it found him, two thousand miles away, and took root.

It took thirty years for the powder keg to explode—to blossom to fire—but it did.

It speaks volumes about Roger's instincts as a journalist that there was a wounded part in him that didn't even yet know he was wounded, but which somehow led him to the source of his illness to come.

Sometimes you can't help but dwell on it. *We need a registry.* A young man, Mark Schmidt, dying of colon cancer in his twenties, a new father. A dear friend, Scott Daily, the first executive director of a local grassroots community service and environmental organization, the Yaak Valley Forest Council, has been battling painful bone cancer for years now, and recently had an entire leg and hip removed. You can't build science from anecdote, but you can build story.

The cancer lodged in Scott's hip. Scott was a young man, only forty-one. Young wife, young daughters: the genius-dreamer, grand visionary, exuberant spirit behind that organization, on whose board I sit. A peace-and-granola gentle spirit, but a hell-raiser, once upon a time, too, a late-night devotee of the Yaak bars.

I remember a story Scott told me about a kind of Superman day he had, one summer. He had been out doing stream surveys all day, had come hiking down off the mountain with a full pack—a glorious day, one of the longest days of the year—and had been crossing the bridge over the West Fork of the Yaak, just downstream of the falls.

He stopped to look down at the beautiful riffling river, some twenty feet below, and leaned just a little too far forward, a little too top-heavy with his pack, and pitched forward, toward the stony riverbed: free-falling.

Without missing a beat, he allowed himself to continue falling, and though he had no gymnastics training whatsoever, he leaned farther forward, performed a midair somersault, and landed perfectly upright, midriver, on his feet, unharmed, heavy pack and all. The jolt smashed the heck out of his hips but nothing broke, not even an ankle: landing in the current amid all those slippery stones.

What could have been tragedy was just nothing, and he stood there, ankle deep in beauty, looked up at the setting sun over Waper Ridge, and continued on into the long summer day.

He kept his home in the Yaak, but moved to Sandpoint, started a native plants restoration business, growing seedlings to plant in disturbed areas harmed by roadbuilding, wildfire, excavation, mining. I don't know where he got the idea. Some slow genesis of values, intuition, observation, science.

A few years later, working on his house in Idaho, he fell off a high ladder, breaking his jaw, ribs, and incurring all kinds of stoved-up injuries. Not long after that the hip pain started. He stood it until it was unbearable, then went and got it checked out.

He's had ever-larger chunks of hipbone cut out—in March of this year the tumor returned with such vengeance that he had to have the entire leg and hip removed—and is pushing on, living each day with wonder and that other thing, the thing Gayla and so many others have—the thing that is blessing and curse, the extreme mindfulness of not just being alive, but living. His oldest daughter, Abby, had a school project to build an Amazonian hut, a rite of passage we all recall from grade school days: the thimble-sized little clump of thatch.

In typical Scott fashion, he and Abby cut some reeds from his nursery and built a life-sized hut, a Habitat-for-Humanity-sized bamboo *house*.

Tell me, writes the poet Mary Oliver, *what is it you intend to do with your one wild and precious life?*

Did the trauma of the bridge leap, or the ladder fall, stir to action some latent toxins, or allow them access to the very marrow of things, changing the chromosomal orders within? What do each and all of us—not just in Lincoln County, but as humans—carry within us, sleeping—not just the harmful, dormant poisons, but also, perhaps, the brighter burning ability to shine and do good?

Scott is nothing if not a do-gooder. Even after the most recent hip surgery, flat on his back in the bed, he's working on a big grant for the local independent radio station, these little islands or sanctuaries of resistance against the wave of what's coming.

———

I think about Scott's hip—the inflammation that might have occurred after his bridge jump, or his ladder fall. I think about the little needles of fiber lodging in the joints, hung up there in the cartilage and ligaments like iron filings, pausing in their migration through the body—passing through and between cells and helices like arrows fired relentlessly, daily, by a thousand or ten thousand archers—and causing further inflammation in the joints: lupus, rheumatoid arthritis.

I think about veins—rivers of blood—attempting to reroute around such piercements, trying to find new paths along which to ship and return the blood's oxygen to the rest of the body, particularly as the lungs begin to send subtle messages to the rest of the body that they can no longer do it alone. I think about Gayla's brother-in-law sitting up in bed screaming, with a cancer growing inside his heart. I wish I hadn't gone to the trial.

I wish I had gone for a walk in the bright sun on those days, wish I had gone to the ice cream parlor, wish I had gone to the library and checked out a book of poetry. I wish I had skipped rope that day, had sung a little song, had put on a blindfold and walked on further and deeper into the future.

———————

My observations are that those most affected by the disease tend to try their best to avoid inhabiting the territory of bitterness. Kathleen Straley, who worked in home health and hospice care in Lincoln County for many years, has noted that most of the dying don't harbor ill will toward the mine (though the spouses and children who are left behind after the dying certainly do).

Gayla—with the air drawing away from her breath by breath, each slow lung-hardening year—even Gayla, the fiercest of warriors—says much the same thing. "Let your vices kill you," she says. "Don't let Grace kill you."

Lesson One, maybe, is the hoary chestnut of living one day at a time. Lesson Two might be don't let the fox into the henhouse, and don't give corporations the power they ask for. Or rather, we've given it to them. We need to get it back.

————————

Our story, here in this green garden, is drifting slowly out to the rest of the world. It is the understandable tendency of human nature to not attach to stories that do not affect the individual directly, but a wise reader or listener will perceive and understand that this story is not able to be compartmentalized and walled off behind the mountains.

What if the unique assault our bodies are facing, here in Lincoln County—unstudied, and unprecedented—might be yet again a tip of the iceberg—and let's name the iceberg for what it is, species extinction—not grizzly bear or salamander, but *Homo sapiens, Homo gluttonous, Homo denialus, Homo corporatus, Homo whatever-we-are-quietly-becoming*?

Lincoln County is one of the only places in the world where the human immune system and central nervous system has become subjected to so much infiltration by such ultrafine fibers for so sustained a period. As our little mountain range is the birthing ground (or burying ground) of landmark environmental case law, whereby a corporation, for the first time, was tried for criminal accountability, so too might this newest garden on earth, only a few thousand years old, be ground zero for a demonstration of what happens when the drift of tiny particles are sucked into our airways, particles so small that they can penetrate cell walls and travel interstitially, clogging up the traffic of veins and slicing electrical lines in the nervous system.

Such are my worries about the impending approach of nano-technology. Perhaps there can be physical materials so small and sharp in the world that they knife through traditional, evolved defenses, are able to slice and sever, bend or bruise critical strands of DNA and electrical wiring, causing the body to spin out of control.

Can such a thing happen? I don't know. It can happen metaphorically and culturally, and it is. Who we once were is not who we are now. We exist increasingly as fodder or cultivar for the products that are generated by the corporations. Whether it's scientifically possible or not, the truth remains undeniable: tiny things are coming into us relentlessly in Lincoln County, and they are making a lot of people very sick. It's unprecedented, and I believe intuitively that anything and everything we can learn about this small valley will serve the rest of mankind—one of the newest species on earth—well.

How to survive? It seems so much that luck is involved. The monitoring that has occurred this far has broken sites down into "detect" or "non-detect." The Environmental Protection Agency has determined that a concentration below about 0.02 fibers per cubic centimeter of air is safe, but there's no one who is really comfortable with that number. Nobody really knows how clean is clean, nor which cubic centimeter of air in the big valley contains which percentage: the air tending to swirl around the way air does.

In the criminal trial, the defense attorneys made a big deal of how there were more non-detect sites than detect sites in Lincoln County! It wasn't all poisoned!

As if the defense truly expected that each of us should somehow identify those little refuges, and like hostages, hole up in one or another, or wend one's way, the rest of one's life, as if through a minefield, from one point that the government had deemed temporarily safe to the next.

Who gets it, and who doesn't? Luck—being in the right place at the right time, again and again and again—and maybe genetic or biological luck, too. Perhaps some immune systems have a greater vigor, or a slightly different response, to lower "pulsed" exposures. Perhaps two consecutive days on the toxic pathway has little if any effect, whereas a third consecutive day begins to elicit dramatic response.

With regard to multiple sclerosis, there's a phenomenon called "Clinically Isolated Syndrome," or CIS, where a patient presents with full-blown symptoms once, which then either never recur, or lie dormant, contained, walled off by the body's newly tested and adjusted immune system: almost like an immunization, an inoculation.

Why?

Could the self-immunized—survivors of CIS—somehow help either the non-immunized or the debilitated? We don't know.

Who's lucky, and who's not, in the face of ecological disaster, and in the surviving?

When Elizabeth and I first moved up here, in 1987, we spent a lot of time in Libby. I was in the gym more often than not, and she swam at the pool. We drove out to the Champion mill and loaded odds and ends of two-by-four short lengths into the back of our truck to burn in the woodstove, knocking the sawdust from them—industrial disarray, junk piles of this and that everywhere, but free firewood—and we went to the grocery store, and the Ben Franklin.

Within that first year, Elizabeth's knees and elbows blew up one morning—this lean, athletic young woman of twenty-nine suddenly possessing melon-sized joints that were painful.

We rushed down to the clinic in Libby, where blood tests couldn't find anything. Lupus, came one suggestion—there had been another local patient recently diagnosed with that—or maybe extreme rheumatoid arthritis, perhaps in response to some bacteria, or some environmental contaminant.

Elizabeth went on antibiotics even as the swelling was already beginning to recede; essentially, she got better on her own. It was a mystery. And had not returned since.

I think that in northwest Montana—and all along the rail lines, where the loose asbestos was shipped for decades—there are tens of thousands of stories like these. Something is stirring in the wind in all the communities along the railroad tracks.

———

Three years later, in 1991, I was hiking in the Brooks Range of Alaska when I developed a range of alarming symptoms that were initially diagnosed as either a brain tumor or multiple sclerosis. For some weeks beforehand I had been having what I considered neurological anomalies—misspelling simple words with which I was familiar, and mispronouncing words. Calling salad "saddle" and crust "crusp." Up in Alaska, my vision went haywire, flooding my line of sight with a shimmering, oscillating aura. No doctors could pinpoint what was the matter. Finally one suggested I take an aspirin a day—maybe the eyesight was the result of a silent migraine—and, eventually, the shimmering faded. I got better, though what the mispronunciations might have been about, I couldn't say.

———

What if our bodies are less static than we suppose them to be? What if there is constantly a roiling and shifting within us, a quivering, in which chromosomes and genetic templates that call for phenotypical expressions oscillate within a certain range of variability, second by second and day by day?

What if there are days when certain illnesses—including cancers—enter us, begin to take hold, then are sloughed away, defeated, with their losses—our victories—never known?

Perhaps we pass through a hundred such eyes of the needle,

or a thousand, in our mortal span. Maybe it becomes old hat to us, and, like some miracles, never even seen or known.

———————

What questions would a full-blown countywide epidemiological study ask? The primary exposure—the mine—is a no-brainer. The pathways of secondary exposure are becoming increasingly illuminated, as more and more fibers are detected in the day care, the schools, the gyms, the running tracks, the skating rinks, the yards and gardens, the mill.

What of the swirling, shifting tertiary pathways, glowing sometimes like the lit-up neurological circuitry of a brain in use, and other times silent, dark, clean and free?

We have one chance to study this well, from crisis of outbreak to recovery.

———————

Some people deal with the asbestos-related diseases by running. I don't mean metaphorically. Tony Smith—ironically, Gayla's next-door neighbor, growing up—is surely the most beloved teacher ever to work at Troy High School. Born and raised in Libby, he played in the first basketball game ever held in the now-aging Libby Loggers' gym. He has played or coached pretty much every sport available in high school, and is a member of the Libby High School Hall of Fame. His social sciences classes are the most popular at Troy High, year after year, ranging from U.S. and World History to History of Rock and Roll. He has steadfastly avoided getting roped into administrative duties in order to be more available for the students, and each year, in addition to being a longtime championship basketball coach, he also directs the hugely popular and much anticipated annual school play. He left Lincoln County briefly to go to college and then was in the marines before returning home to teach.

Troy, population 900—eighteen miles downriver of Libby, close to the Idaho state line—is, like much of northwest Montana, extremely poor. Some people live there because they can't get out, but some live there by choice, choosing the region's beauty over higher wages and amenities that are available elsewhere.

With his teaching awards and accolades, Tony certainly has had opportunities to work anywhere other than one of the poorest school districts in the nation. There's a tradition at Troy of teachers giving their lives to the young people there. Tony isn't the only great teacher who's toiled in Troy for decades, but he's definitely the exemplar.

If a small town is extremely lucky—and not many are any more, in this way—there might be a teacher like Tony Smith once every generation or two, with his or her influence touching, like the slow laminar accrual of sediment, thousands of lives, spreading far and wide in ripples from one epicenter.

Teaching is his first and greatest passion, but so too is music—he sings in a popular regional group, the Men of Troy, and plays piano, has recorded several CDs. He finally had to retire from coaching basketball for health reasons, and sometimes misses that, he says, almost more than he can bear.

And still another passion, his and his wife Peggy's grandchildren, and still another, the wild, beautiful mountains that frame the Kootenai Valley: the Yaak country to the north, and the Cabinet Mountains to the south, and, a little farther east, the magnificence of Glacier National Park.

Tony's got asbestosis, has been carrying it a long time. He probably contracted it from any of a dozen or perhaps a hundred well-established secondary pathways, though he never worked at the mine—but he just keeps on going. He and Peggy have bought a small piece of land up in the Yaak, where they hope to put a small cabin that will one day be a family place for their grandchildren, and when he's not doing his other activities, he's hiking, always hiking: ascending the steep slopes of the mountains to the high peaks and ridges that look down on the little bowls and valleys of this country, with the lowlands often hidden beneath smooth luminous billowings of silver-blue fog.

From those vantages, he looks down on a view that must surely be pretty much identical to how this country looked three or four hundred years ago, before the first roads entered.

The Kootenai and Salish would have been living in camps down along the river, following the fish. Once in a while—perhaps—a traveler on the game trails in the millions of acres of backcountry above the river might have encountered a lone hunter.

For Tony, the math is simple. Mentally, he must accept the illness, but physically he must run from it. If he keeps busting his old stiffening-up and shrinking lungs, keeps stretching them out every day, maybe he can hold at bay a little longer the tightening double-fisted grip that is trying to close them off. Maybe.

And in the meantime, he gets to see the most beautiful landscape in the world, again and again: for as long as his legs and heart will carry him.

To a man, it seems, the miners who died didn't hold a grudge against the company. The job of a man back then—the identity of a man—was to secure money: to pack up the lunchbox and go, to surge out into the dark and the snow, plowing through the hours, securing so many dollars per hour, so many pennies per footstep, and to keep pushing forward, head down, in order to help keep one's family secure and attached to the world.

It makes for an inelegant logic: as if such men, having already decided long ago to give up their hours and days in order to provide for their families, viewed the final giving up of their bodies as but one more extension of the continuum that began long ago when they first signed on for a job which, while not stimulating to them spiritually or mentally, nonetheless helped secure a future for their family.

The absolute worst, then, is the knowledge that when they came home dusty and dirty, they brought the poison back with them, and gave it to their wives, children, grandchildren. Testimony after testimony repeats this lamentation. It seems they can even forgive the company—that ethereal stock-driven blind gnawing investment vehicle—but they cannot forgive themselves.

Kathleen Straley's job as a home health care and hospice worker required that she enter people's homes with a hazmat uniform and spaceman helmet, to comfort and tend to them in their last months, weeks, hours. But that wasn't what they needed, wasn't what any of them—she or her patients—had signed on for, and so she just kept on going into her patients' homes without such indignity, providing aid and comfort as if to soldiers felled, lying dazed and bleeding on a vast battlefield, though with no enemy in sight.

———

They found the asbestos in the day care facility, and on the carpet too, where the little kids crawled around, shoving their hands into their mouths. The stuff got tracked in year after year. I don't know what concentrations they found. I know we took the girls there occasionally, for an hour or two, while we played tennis (another place they found it), or swam or lifted (they found it there too), or went to the laundry and car wash (the absolute worst possible places to go). When we visited friends: whose houses were safe, and whose were not?

The wind swirling down the dusty streets. Going in the bank. Going to the car wash. Where are the safe paths, where are the islands of refuge?

We can do a better job of measuring and monitoring. We can

establish better maps for a landscape laced with invisible mountains and epicenters of toxicity.

We know some of them but others are yet invisible.

This might be how it was for us when we first came into the world as a species, not in the least bit dominant, but vulnerable instead to almost everything in the world. Moving carefully through a savannah filled with lions, and possessing no more defense than a sharp stick and the fierce will to go on.

What paths were safe, which routes were more dangerous, and how to live, really, when each ticking moment was filled with significance?

———

All throughout Lincoln County, you see the orange safety ribbon around one property or another—the workers in their space suits working inside that orange plastic fence, while just on the other side, regular people come and go.

Portable generators growling, giant vacuum hoses throbbing, all day long, trying to suck out all of the invisible thing. Dump trucks groaning up and down the roads in the bright sun and wind, taking away one yard and garden after another.

When I ask Gayla where it is all going, she says, "To the Magic Place."

It's a long death. She's able to find humor in irony. "To the dump," she says, the landfill up Pipe Creek, above town, and above the river. The place where everything goes: back up into the mountains from which it came.

———

Scott was the Yaak Valley Forest Council's first executive director. After he retired from that position and became our grant writer, another member, Robyn King, stepped in and agreed to be the new executive director. It's a stressful position, one that requires not just the day-to-day management of the small grass-roots nonprofit organization, but also attendance at innumerable meetings, public and private. Often the meetings are contentious, held between opposing stakeholders, which can create a stress, an internal toxicity.

Over the years, after many such meetings, Robyn would be debriefing, and would comment to me that "at one point I thought the top of my head was going to explode!"

It turns out she was on to something. One day a massage therapist felt a bump on her skull and recommended she get it checked out. She did, and the tests showed a soft tissue mass that was diagnosed as a meningioma. She had brain surgery—the growth was attached to the underside of her crown; they scraped it all away; it was benign—and sewed her back up. Within a couple of weeks, she was back at work.

I'm simplifying it, of course, skipping over the gory stuff, the weakness, the dizziness, the fatigue—the cranial leaking, the swelling—and at the time, I didn't think her illness had anything to do with other asbestos-related diseases, which, again, are associated more commonly with lung and stomach.

But just a little digging into scientific papers turns up some interesting articles. An Italian physician, Dr. Paulo Zamboni, is reporting a link between MS and a phenomenon known as "chronic cerebrospinal venous insufficiency," or CCSVI. In Dr. Zamboni's study, "the team evaluated abnormalities of blood out-flow in major veins draining from the brain and spinal cord to the heart in 65 people with different types of MS . . . The investigators reported evidence of slowed and obscured drainage in the veins draining the brain and spinal cord of many of those with MS. They also reported evidence of the opening of 'substitute circles'—where the flow is deviated to smaller vessels to bypass obstructions, and these were often found to have reverse flow (reflux) of blood back into the brain."

Is this what's going on with Robyn's meningioma? Certainly, she hasn't been diagnosed with MS, just a venous tangle in her brain, in which those vessels—like a partially dammed or occluded river—seek an alternate route. Zamboni's study, it is noted, "has raised as many questions as it has potentially answered," one of which would further examine the link between CCSVI and MS.

There's a saying that when you're holding a hammer, everything looks like a nail. When so many around you are getting sick with rare and inexplicable autoimmune disorders, everything around you looks like, well, an autoimmune disorder.

Why would there be venous tangling in the brain? Is that like a settling pond for the fibers—a swamp, a magnetic lodestone for the fibers, a blood-rich marsh? Or do such venous tangles begin to occur everywhere, and it is only in the central nervous system where the tangling most dramatically manifests itself?

The authors speculated that the reverse flow of blood back into the brain—the body seeking alternate paths—"might set off the inflammation and immune-mediated damage that has been well described in MS."

It's interesting stuff, the way the body *does* repair itself—and the way the land tries to repair itself, as well. I'm not a researcher like Dr. Zamboni, nor a large-scale landscape restorationist like Scott Daily or Robyn King. I'm in the middle. I'm just walking around observing things, and watching all these trains go by.

As the body—particularly the front line of defense, the lungs—is absorbing these fibers, so too is the forest.

The largest private landowner in the world—and Montana— is Ted Turner, but the largest corporate landowner is, or was,

Plum Creek Timber, with nearly a million acres. During the timber wars of the 1980s, Plum Creek began selling liquidated, cutover lands as real estate developments.

Conservation groups such as the Yaak Valley Forest Council sought for years to purchase some of those lands to manage as community forests or restoration forests—local lands to be managed for a sustainable flow of timber, rather than used for gated communities in the distant backcountry.

In the Yaak, there were—and are—13,000 acres of such lands. After working with the Trust for Public Land (TPL) for years, we succeeded in convincing TPL to purchase those lands and deed them to a sustainable timber production model, only to have that phase of a larger statewide landmark conservation purchase get put on hold, in the Yaak, due to attorneys' concerns that when Plum Creek transferred those lands to TPL, there might be an associated liability for asbestos exposure. Preliminary studies indicated that asbestos fibers were showing up in the bark of the trees; that the lungs of the land, the forest, were absorbing the exhalation of the mine and the dusty plumes of the ore's transit.

Are the leaves and needles of trees likewise absorbing the fibers, or only the bark? Might some species of trees and plants be more facile at absorbing the fibers than others? What happens when these trees—and the fibers—are burned, either in a forest fire, or as firewood? What happens when they're sawed down, or milled, and the sawdust whirs through the workers' lungs? Is it like working in the mine all over again?

Is the concentration of tree bark fiber located only in the immediate vicinity of the mill, or is there a more coherent pattern of such concentration and absorption, one that follows primary roads and wind currents?

Is the best remediation to merely let those trees continue growing, pulsing, breathing, absorbing more fibers for us—for those trees to then grow old, fall over, and rot, being slowly converted back into soil, with other vegetation covering up the fibers?

How long might such a cycle take? How clean is clean?

In her book *The Global Forest*, Canadian scientist Diana Beresford-Kroeger describes "a new violence in the world," one which "is measured in microns . . . The 2.5 (micron patricles) or less is lethal to the human body . . . Particles of 2.5 microns or less" go into the deeper passages of the lungs—the tiny bronchioles, where the body begins its oxygen extraction from the air. These bronchioles are paper thin and delicate. The lungs can produce free radicals to fix matters, but this in turn causes scarring of the lung tissue, a condition called fibrosis. The natural act of breathing becomes more difficult with fibrosis.

"The story for the heart is similar . . . These smallest of arteries deliver oxygen-rich blood to the local tissues. Such paper-thin walled arteries must relax a little further to complete their oxygen delivery. They do this by means of a dissolved gas called nitrogen oxide. But, in the presence of particulate pollution of 2.5 microns or less, the nitrogen oxide doesn't work, again because of irritation, and the arterioles cannot relax and deliver oxygen. This causes damage to the local healthy tissue . . . Nasal passages, too, break down, leaving areas of the brain open for contamination by brain plaques . . .

"Trees and forests hold the answer to particulate pollution in a way that is surprising. Many trees have leaves that differ from one species to another. The diversity is found in the leaf's anatomy. Some leaves have a waxy cuticle on their upper surface. These leaves repel water and attract particles that are water insoluble. The underside of the leaf is downy. This down is composed of thousands of fine hairs, all only a few microns in size. These hairs are multiplied in the full canopy into billions of fine hairs.

"This microscopic world of the leaf within the tree canopy acts like a fine-toothed comb for the air. The particulate pollution of the air becomes caught mechanically like dandruff in this microscopic world of hairs. Sometimes the particles, which hold a charge, can get grounded on the tree. This depends on weather conditions, and on electrostatic forces of attraction generated by the tree's leaves. The trees and the forest act as a sweeping brush or giant comb. The leaf hairs numbering in billions clean the air of these tiny particles. These particles get swept down the trunk by rain and are detoxified by the hungry . . . living soil."

––––––––––

Doubtless there are many in the country who are applauding the Supreme Court and this increased power and presence of corporations. The widening shift from a democracy to a corpocracy.

It's everyone's story, whether afflicted or not. More days than not, I find myself, at fifty-four, rubbing that slightly swollen, slightly bulging fingernail, as if rubbing a wedding ring. It's my home. But I've been so lucky. I'm just trying to listen, mostly. Laying out the puzzle pieces and trying to make some kind of sense or order.

I remain haunted by the trial. It would have been a lot easier to be all philosophical about this whole deal if I hadn't sat in on some of the daily sessions of the month-long criminal trial against Grace, held in Missoula.

Watching the defendants—former CEOs of Grace—appear with their phalanx of defense attorneys, mocking the plaintiffs and the asbestos survivors, as well as those who did not survive—mocking the guinea pigs, the rodents used in scientific studies to determine how much asbestos was required to cause respiratory damage, heart failure, and cancer—joking about the debilitation and ultimate death of those test animals, back in the 1960s—being present in the courtroom during these proceedings, witnessing this *banter* and ridicule, opened in me a revulsion not quite like any I'd ever experienced.

I understand that human beings are capable of just about anything, but never before had I witnessed quite such a depth of amorality—neither moral nor immoral, but instead, simply a vacuousness, a hollow bravado or swagger, the defense attorneys like blind hostages to evil, not acknowledging or considering the consequences of their servitude, other than the short-term treats of their sterling careers.

I had heard about such things but had never witnessed that phenomenon, and I had been totally prepared for the hollow, desperate, wheedling mirth and mirthlessness. The lead attorney was a small fellow, David—never mind his last name—and to say that I felt a new low, watching him try to bond with the jury with his jokes about the guinea pigs, isn't accurate; what I felt was a despair and bottomlessness, like looking down into a vast pit.

I felt sorrow and pity for the little man in his sharp suit, who was trying so hard—*Love me, be with me on this, jury—we're alike, you and me, laugh at the guinea pig joke, isn't life fun, isn't this all just one grand misunderstanding, darn it all?*—and I was reminded again of how the plaintiffs in this case—the survivors, and families of those who did not survive—were prevented in this trial from even being able to bear witness, due to the graphic and prolonged suffering of their illnesses and their deaths, which the court claimed could inflame and sway the jury!

For what to the best of my knowledge was the first time in the history of this country, an accuser was not allowed to testify at his trial.

Surely there was a greater loss of freedom and constitutional right in that censorship than any military tribunal for suspected terrorists or enemy combatants, and yet it passed uncommented upon, unnoticed.

And as such, it was a field day for the little lawyer. The part that made me feel sorry for him was that he enjoyed it, and began to think he was special, and then, worse than special, he began to think he was *right*.

It broke my heart open.

———————

Because the plaintiffs who had been harmed by Grace were not allowed to testify in their trial, it turned into a document case, one in which actions and consequences were not viewed, but instead, only written documents could be considered: letters, rebuttals, hypotheses, claims and refutations. The corporation turned in over a million pages of documents, which the jury had one day to examine, and which the prosecuting attorneys—the U.S. Department of Justice, representing the plaintiffs—had to condense into a two- or three-day narrative.

The government's attorneys tried. But every time they flashed a corporate memo onto the overhead screen, the defense countered with the response that just because Grace knew their product was toxic and sought to avoid financial responsibility didn't make it criminal, and that there wasn't a "conspiracy," but that instead such evasions were simply part and parcel of acceptable corporate culture—that evasion of laws was for corporations as natural and unquestioned an act as breathing.

It was awful. Department of Justice attorneys would flash on the overhead screen copies of notes from meetings in which the accused criminals would be talking about how to keep the Sierra Club or some other do-good organization from finding out what the executives *knew* about the toxicity of asbestos, and what to do if the news did leak, which it didn't.

Damning correspondence was flashed onto the screen—a culling of half a century of the conspiracy's greatest hits—wherein meeting participants, the very executives on trial, had in my opinion conspired on how to avoid turning over certain documents and test results they had run in which, yes, the guinea pigs died horribly.

There were documents, letters of resistance and obstruction, calculated evasionary instructions from Grace attorneys to Grace executives about how to stonewall EPA mine-site investigators *after* 1990 and the passage of the Clean Air Act—secret padlocks on the gates, canceled appointments, that kind of thing—but again, it was decided that such actions were not criminal but instead fell within the normal range of actions that were required to keep a corporation a living and breathing entity.

The closing arguments were particularly hard to take. If hypothetical witness testimony might have been able to be described as potentially inflammatory, then the replacement evidence—blurry overhead black-and-white transparencies of correspondence written on ancient Royal typewriters—letters written in sleepy 1950s lawyer language—was by comparison abstract and even narcoleptic.

The letters possessed no soul, they were just words on a page, and from long ago, hence how could there really be a crime, or even criminal proceedings? All the defense attorneys had to do was stand up and say "Did not, did not, did not," with a living, breathing human—a defense attorney—so much more personal and, well, *alive*, than any old sheet of paper.

Graphs, bars, charts, and tables showing the effects of asbestos exposure on lung capacity: so what? *Boring*.

The deeper the documents went, the wider became the separation between the defense and the plaintiffs, between pleasure and pain, between justice and calumny; in the end, the executives walked, they got away with fifty years of murder and mayhem—fifty down, and maybe hundreds still remaining.

Nobody knows where all the kegs and fuses are, and the better a job we insist upon being done to find out, the more it's going to cost.

In the meantime, Grace—having shape-shifted, vanishing for a while, but now reappearing—is working over on the East Coast; has fled Montana. Law professor Andrew King-Reiss, who participated in a post-trial forum at the University of Montana, reports that the newly reformed, emerging-from-bankruptcy Grace has just received philanthropy awards for its donations to those communities in the East.

Living a life amid invisible poison, and seeing so many of your comrades fall suddenly as if felled by an invisible archer, can be horrific, but again there can be a blessing. For many, there can be a subconscious effort to always have one's affairs somewhat in order. We've seen too many of our kind get that six-week to two-month call to arms, the shipping-out papers.

Gradually, I think, there might be developing in the populace the dawning idea of not leaving too many important things unsaid or undone. It's not exactly like everyone goes around living like there's no tomorrow. But I think it's fair to say that an awful lot of us don't take mortality—or the brief beauty of health and physical strength—for granted. If there's a mountain you want to hike, go ahead and do it this summer, not next. And again; and again.

My brother Frank was for many years a reporter for Associated Press, before that news organization, like so many others, went down in the flames and fallout of the Great Recession. He worked in New York, and covered the fall of the World Trade Center. He breathed the air of the burning rubble that authorities were saying was not dangerous, and three months later came down with an inexplicable fever, in excess of 106 degrees. The doctors threw him in an ice bath and he survived, though they had no idea what caused the fever. A year later, it recurred—again the ice bath, antibiotics, CT scans, MRIs, spinal taps, blood work, revealed nothing—and again, he survived.

Some years later he began developing numbness in his extremities, numbness alternating with pain, as well as extreme fatigue, to the point where he had to sleep more often than not—and doctors ran him through every test, it seemed, known to the medical profession, but found nothing. Not Lyme, not lupus, not malaria; not Parkinson's, no tumors, no virus, no bacteria. The new CT scan showed a little scarring, a little venous tangle, like burn marks, in one patch of the brain. They told him the circuitry would reroute around that traffic jam.

But what had lodged there? What had disrupted the currents to begin with?

The doctors theorized that it might be rough sledding for a while, as the brain slowly rewired itself in these areas, but that then he would get better; amazingly, that's what happened.

There's no proof yet. But there's another story developing, a pattern and similarity: the body, faced with initial exposure to a high pulse of the fibers, surges with an isolated major response by the immune system—reacting massively to the inorganic substance as it would to a plague or virus or bacterial invader—and some get lucky and survive, while the bodies of others cannot isolate or turn off the autoimmune response, but fall into a feedback loop in which the body keeps attacking itself.

No terrorist's calculation could have been more devious or cunning, no attack on the homeland more insidious.

Admittedly, I'm pretty good at finding things to worry about. Most environmentalists are. We're not always right, but we're right just often enough to perpetuate our cycle of worry.

Global warming is the big one these days. Oh, wait, that reminds me, I'm back in jail, I'm talking about Otter Creek again, and the Montana Land Board's idea to help convert the third world into a dirty coal economy—why do they keep coming to Montana for these things? What is it about us that draws them?—but once more I can't help but look at the coming of nanotechnology, and wonder how our bodies are going to respond to an infinitude of new particles, so small they can penetrate not just organs but cells, and the spaces between cells, causing the body to respond in the way it always has to foreign invaders.

I imagine I may be in the minority on this, but I worry that the positives of nanotech will not come close to outweighing the negatives.

———————

I worry about the Supreme Court even more than the embrace of nanotechnology and the unleashing of forty quadrillion sharp-edged nanomolecules glittering into the air every hour. I worry about the Supreme Court more than I do about rising sea levels and the rapid release of ancient mutagens currently trapped in permafrost and ice caps, or about the vanishing of free oxygen here on the blue planet.

Is this all a dream, that something as immense as this world can be erased by the utterance of one man or one woman in a decision that goes either 5–4 or 4–5?

How can a nation that separates church from state then turn and refuse to separate corporation from state?

I've never been a big fan of amending the Constitution—past screeds and lamentations aimed at tweaking or altering that living document to explicitly prevent ultraspecific activities typically abhorred by the right-wingers, such as flag burning or gay marriage, have always seemed ridiculous to me.

But this might well be the time to spend that one silver bullet. I fear that corporations already own the Congress too deeply—that already, insufficient independent representation exists, and that a congressional bill amending the Constitution on this matter might fail to even secure enough votes to be introduced or passed. I fear that already corporations have infiltrated the political lives of our leaders—like unseen narrow spindles insinuating themselves—to the point where if an elected official voted against corporate donations, the corporations would destroy him or her, would swarm his or her district with anonymous and unregulated donations, coalescing, like antigens swarming a foreign object in the body.

Fevers, chills, shakes, swelling; cancer, asphyxiation, death.

––––––––––

We want to believe the Constitution is a perfect, holy text, sent down from the Mount in a single act of divine inspiration. But it wasn't. Creating it was an awful mess, more than ten years in the making, and even after it was ratified in 1787, the founders acknowledged its imperfections, its continuing need for amendments. There were a lot of folks back then who were against the Constitution; they feared it would give government too much power. Fresh in their minds was the memory of the Southern states' violation of civil rights before and during the Revolution. These opponents demanded a bill of rights "that would spell out the immunities of individual citizenry." These opponents eventually ratified the 1787 Constitution with the understanding that subsequent amendments preserving—or securing—those immunities, those freedoms, would be offered.

We don't have to take up arms. We just have to petition for one amendment. But we need to do so quickly. The corporations become ever more powerful in their unaccountability, while those who would stand before them do so for but twenty, thirty, forty years before becoming old and infirm, and crumbling.

We worship the corporations even though we would deny it is worship, and when they fall ill, we pump our resources—our time and hopes and money—into them as if with prayer; and when they die, we resurrect them.

There's a screening program going on in Libby, held in a portable building such as the temporary structures in which one used to take driver's ed classes after school, in the long ago.

The program starts and stops according to funding and budget cuts, but whenever we get a postcard saying it's open again, and that it's our time, we go in and have the X-rays—so far, nothing—and blow into the little tube for the lung capacity test.

I always fail that one; I always have to take it four or five times, just to get to 97 percent, 98 percent capacity. It doesn't make any sense to me. Elizabeth always tests 110 percent, easily. Hiking, I never get tired or short of breath. It doesn't make sense. Maybe I'm used to delivering oxygen to my muscles in a different or more efficient manner, making more to do with what I've got.

Or maybe my lungs are larger, so that 97 percent of them sends out more than 110 percent of someone else. I don't know. It seems a crude test but I fret about slipping, always slipping; from 98 to 96, to 95, and so on. I fret about the quality of life—the burning—slipping away, the hot coals cooling to heavy gray ash.

And yet what answer is there but to try not to oversleep, and to get out and burn as often as one can? I think that I'm just getting older. I think that's all it is. Other times I roll my shoulders to help get those deep breaths, even while seated at a desk, not exerting myself, as my body tries to remember or summon that feeling. It's maybe like what a whale does before sounding. It's strange, these tiny threads that the Lilliputians throw across our chests, hour by hour and day by day. It's strange. Each one is so small and insignificant.

The last ice carved the mountains around Libby, in its leaving. Grassland came in—sagebrush—then cool dark forests. What happens when the forests burn in the coming, warmer world? How much smoke will we filter again through our pink-red lungs, and through our stomachs?

Maybe the burning—the rising tide of the world's fire and heat—will come all the way up here to the Yaak, but this will be the high-water mark of change. The high-flame mark. Then things will finally begin to get better, and heal. The burning will recede.

———

We should install those detect/non-detect sensors at every spot, every residence, where a meso case has occurred. They need to march the detect/non-detect monitors right up over the top of Vermiculite Mountain and into the Yaak. They need to place one on the house of everyone who died of meso or who has contracted ARD. They need to put one over Point's grave, to see if he is still exhaling the fibers from his body, from the soil, even in death.

This isn't about my dog. This is about science—or about science, and data, being willfully ignored. This is a data point being willfully ignored.

How many other data points are being ignored? Too often, we tend to find only the science we want to find.

———

I have hiked up the steep slopes of Rainy Creek, beneath Vermiculite Mountain, in hunting season, before I knew any better—watching the waters cascade down Rainy Creek toward the sprawling Kootenai River, largest tributary to the Columbia, bound for the Pacific—the waters crashing down through the forest like a current of electricity sizzling through the brain of the valley, with the lopped-off skullcap of the mine, just a little farther on, a little higher up, a little farther north.

As the biology of the affliction—slow suffocation—might be said to match the story of an isolated, rural community so afflicted—relatively voiceless, in terms of the ability to dictate terms of existence to a multinational corporation—so too might the biology of the affliction hold some clues to a recovery or restoration.

In the scarring of cells and cell walls from exposure to tiny foreign objects, perhaps a story of counterresponse might be found. Perhaps we can yet isolate and build protective covenants around the dangerous corporations—sealing them off, encasing them in the scar tissue of our hard-gotten experience, just as the scar tissue in a body seeks to isolate an infection, attempts to seal the pustulous wound.

It will not make anyone who is currently afflicted better, but it might serve the story of the future—the story of a do-over in the garden—to cover up the old sawed-off mountain, Vermiculite Mountain, with a cast of clay: to bury it, and to revegetate the surrounding area, to begin the slow hard work of filtering those deadly fibers not so much with tender human lungs, but with the green bark of living trees. Trees, perhaps, like the native larch, particularly the mature or old-growth ones, with thick crenulated bark that maximizes the surface area for such absorption, and which, being the world's only deciduous conifer, might even filter the fibers into its needles each year before shedding them, gold needles flying harmlessly through the sky each autumn, and back down, then, via the composition of the rainforest into the soil.

To identify the safe paths in our community through more testing, as well as the dangerous paths, and to have the cleansing lungs of plants—in gardens, flowerpots, planter-boxes—in every building and every room, every hallway; to move, like aliens in our own homeland, from one breathing station to the next, breathing the cleansed or cleaner air in the vicinity of the living plants.

Already, for years in Lincoln County, we have been seeing too many of our neighbors patrolling the streets in electric wheelchairs, oxygen bottles strapped to their sides, and moon-suited hazmat workers probing their giant vacuum hoses into one building after another, seeking to suck out literally billions of invisible micron-sized poisons.

Already, here in this new place on earth, this new start from where the ice went away, we have become like aliens yet again, cast out from paradise.

If this is a new world we are all entering, why shouldn't one of the first stories of that new world come from one of the newest and most injured, and yet also most pristine places in the United States?

The fact that there are not many of us who live here shouldn't matter. The fact that our story is new and usable by others is what should matter. And it is our duty to make it be.

———

It's far from an original thought, looking to the processes of nature to help determine the shape of a story. And maybe I place too much faith in the power of story to affect the coming flow of history and the course of events. But I don't think so. I think stories are a lens through which we view the world, and our responsibilities and parts in it: and that that affects everything, or almost everything, that is to come.

It may be a simple ceremony, as primitive as the first story, but in addition to a commitment to identifying safe paths and sealing over old wounds, I'd like to see religious and community leaders petition the greater spirit of the world for a third do-over: to place a blessing on the broad wide river, the Kootenai, that cleaves the valley, and into which all the veins of the surrounding mountains flow.

There are logistical proposals to restore our air, our health, our power and independence—political and financial fixes that are required, and environmental remediations—but I think a ceremony would be valuable too, as a cultural marker of Before and After.

In a perfect world, or perfect ceremony, we'd have someone like the Dalai Lama, and leaders of the region's tribes, in a boat, floating past Rainy Creek, bestowing a blessing of compassion on the river and the handful of people who live in the shadow of these mountains.

It would be an ecumenical ceremony, with political leaders, local churches. In a perfect world, apolitical, the president would be in one of those boats, drifting in the autumn with the mountainsides all around burning gold with the going-away—for the winter, at least—of the larch. And in a perfect world, for one day, much if not most of the world—even if just for a moment—would be listening to our story.

The intent is to help personalize the histories here, and to learn from them. The trouble is that Grace's—and any corporation's—goal is to depersonalize those stories, those voices, those bright-burning powers of the individual within.

Still, my goal here is to bring honor to the afflicted: not to waste my breath haranguing an invisible thing.

I don't think all of Lincoln County has been examined or repaired. I think there remains work to be done. As bad as the asbestosis and mesothelioma is, I don't think that's all there is. I don't think it's that neat. Would that it were so.

In the meantime, there remains work to be done.

Who gets lucky, and who does not? Every morning I wake up feeling lucky. I would not go so far as to say every morning I bound out of bed with a spring in my step and joy in my heart, but every morning, I realize my luck that any of us are here, and the implicit obligation—the mandate, the inalienable duty—to make our lives count, in some fashion or another, even if only to one's self.

It's cliché stuff, but living amid death or perhaps even more so the shadow of death helps bring a greater clarity to such thoughts.

Nobody I know of goes around redlining it, thinking, *What if my six weeks begins today?* But speaking only for myself, becoming middle-aged in a land of illness, I am aware with every physical exertion, every glorious lung-bursting short-of-breath hike up a steep slope, of the glory of being able to stagger around in these mountains, the glory of being short of breath as opposed to possessing no breath at all. And while I wouldn't quite go so far as to say I'm compiling a bucket list—I hate that idea of looking down the mountain, to descend, rather than seeing skyline and new country beyond—I can't help but notice this year, particularly, with so many still falling ill, even though the cleanup is proceeding, that there are certain places I've been thinking about going for years, which I absolutely am going to visit this year, come hell or high water.

I have gone and seen them, but here's the thing: from those ridges, you see new places, and want more.

I think even if there had never been this dust, this invisible fiber, I would be feeling this way, at this age. It's just that the circumstances put a little finer edge on it. And while I have always loved such hikes, there is often these days an added emotion, the bittersweet complication of mixing pleasure with something akin to duty or responsibility; that it is in some way more important than ever for me to feel the full depths of joy possible on those hikes into such amazing backcountry, now that there are increasing numbers of peers and neighbors and friends who are unable.

The survivors have an obligation to survive, but more; there is more to life than just surviving.

In the old days, I ran marathons, triathlons, cross-country. I ran all day, ran up mountains. All my life, when I inhaled, I would take in a delicious and seemingly bottomless double-lungful of sweet clean air that made me stronger each time: taking in air as if it were a great meal, and with the oxygen igniting, combusting, feeding, and fanning a fire that burned away all impurities and weakness. Even then I did not take it for granted; even then, with every great breath, I recognized it for what it was—glorious. Soon I'll be going to court to testify why I wouldn't leave the governor's office, the capital, when asked. Soon, hopefully, I'll have an opportunity to present testimony about why I thought that was necessary, and about Otter Creek, and the Tongue River country, and open boxcars, and rail lines, and conspiracy and secrecy.

The prison is not the iron bars here in Helena.

In a little while my prescriptions will be produced, and my bail, and I will walk through the bars of the jail as if through a veil. The state of Montana may well soon be eradicated by Mr. Peabody's coal trains, black plumes may snake through all the sleeping towns and communities of the Northwest—but we'll all still be free, sort of. Only if you have lived and worked in Lincoln County will you be imprisoned in a kind of waiting, a kind of statistical limbo.

The corporations like it that way.

DESCENT, WITH MODIFICATIONS

WE SAW EVERYTHING, AND EVERYTHING WAS UNAFRAID of us.

I am not a churchgoer. If I am anything it would be a lapsed Druid. I am a geologist who likes to touch rocks. To hold them. To smell them. But there is no way to talk about the Galápagos without remembering one of the most powerful stories, and oldest.

Which came first, the Bible or the Galápagos? Who wrote the book of Genesis? It wasn't Darwin, though he'd read it inside and out.

I was there three weeks. I was there for a century. I was there for one breath—one inhalation. One day I swam alongside a ten-ton whale shark, and beheld the eye of the world's largest fish, chilled to the bone, and kicked like mad to keep from being swallowed: *Jonah, redux.*

Shearwaters, petrels. Tropic birds, frigate birds, the males with their fantastic red gulars; boobies: birds in outrageous numbers, but not yet so much the clamant diversity of other places; so many of the Galápagos are still in the first day, first morning, with everything still sorting itself out—the woodpecker finch picking up twigs to dig out insects from within the pulp of rotting trees. The little ground and tree finches, each of them beginning to specialize. Experimenting with the great bounty of this one place on earth, where the sun's presence is an unquestioned constant, delivering millennium after millennium the same amount of energy, and the rich cold-water currents delivering their same bounty, every day, to the doorstep of the creation.

As if the world was made not for the coming of man, but for birds. As if there once was or still is a Bird God. As if someday maybe there will be a Man-and-Woman God, but that here, in Day Two, or whatever hour it is, the world and its stories wheel around the axis of birds and their strivings and desires, not ours.

Will the story of the seven days be the same, again and again, for all species, no matter at what point they join the spectacle, the party?

Hardly anything eats anything else here, yet. There's one species of hawk, the Galápagos hawk, that hunts in cooperative packs. *Cooperation:* Darwin wasn't looking for that, so didn't see it, I think.

War has not yet arrived here. There's intraspecies strife, but between the nations of other species, barely yet at all.

I think Darwin saw evolution and initial competition because he wanted to see it—also because here, on this utterly new, just-made land, he could not miss it. But what we have done with that idea—hewing only to the idea that strength and domination is all, desperately all, that neither tenderness nor wisdom matter, nor, for that matter, luck, that only survival matters, rather than, say, the dignity of the moment—could he have suspected the brutal ideological shortcuts the coming world would make with what was once an elegant idea?

Yeah, the strong are going to kick ass, but is there not another and perhaps larger dynamic at play across the long term?

What is meeker than a turtle?

I also wonder if, in watching things move earnestly forward, Darwin missed a countercurrent of things going backward. I wonder if he sensed this. I find it interesting that his initial title wasn't *On the Origin of Species*, but rather, *Descent, With Modifications*.

Sometimes we overlook things most when we are staring right at them.

How did we get here, and why are we here? We know in our heart of hearts that we are neither all-powerful nor, really, all that smart.

Is it chance, or something else? It is surely not natural selection. If anything, unnatural selection. We defy evolution. Are we ourselves descending—sinking—while other species—the Galápagos mockingbird, for instance—are quietly, meekly, continuing to ascend?

We can understand the spots on the whale shark and the beaks of the little finches, and the marine iguanas that dive beneath the sea to gnaw on the steady equatorial bounty of tidewater algae. Anyone can understand the flightless cormorants of the Galápagos, giving up their gift of flight to remain evolutionary homebodies, diving for fish all day long. Each morning they hold their stubby wings to the morning sun to warm themselves before plunging back into the cold rich currents—and it looks absolutely as if the cormorants are beseeching the sun, *praying* to the sun, *hurry up, get rid of these wings, I don't need them and they're not working out.*

The islands are so new. The islands are still on Day Two or Three, I think. Darwin's science was dead-on for a new garden, but I'm wondering, and hoping, that he might have missed things.

Other questions I would have for the young captain: Why do we love beauty—why does beauty exist, and what, oh what are we going to do, if anything, about any of it?

Day One, there's a big old ocean, and the lake o' fire beneath us makes a seam, comes roaring up in the precise middle of the earth, builds a little garden—so little—on the equator. Let there be land.

Things start drifting in. Iguanas clinging to driftwood, holding their mouths open to the sky during the rainy season.

Tortoises, bobbing along like coconuts, until they make random landfall. Were they the fittest, or did they just float well? They'd have been lost without the guidance of those equatorial currents. Day Two, a multitude of fishes, and fowl in the skies by the tens of thousands. The drift of seeds and insects.

I forget how the rest of it goes—every creeping thing working its way to the garden. I may be mixing stories now, about the lamb lying down with the lion, but you see a significant absence of predation here, in this garden that is younger even than we are; some of the islands are only 30,000 years old, while we, at 180,000 years, are like teenagers.

I wonder if we humans are as if at Day Seven, compared to the islands' still being Day One or Two.

I don't blame Darwin for seeing only evolution, not devolution; he did the best he could, in only a few months. He came to these islands with an idea, at the end of a long journey, and, still a young man, saw what he wanted to see, and maybe he saw too what he did not want to see. His wife was worried that what he was proposing was blasphemy, and that consequently he might not meet her in heaven. He fretted about it, tried to sit on his suspicions, until another scientist, Alfred Wallace, clued in to the same idea and made plans to publish his same hypothesis. Spurred by competition, Darwin released his idea, and the rest was history.

They say that Darwin was never quite the same: that he'd lost his faith, reasoning that a truly omnipotent God would have made only one finch, not five or six, and certainly not seven or eight. As if that God could barely make heaven and earth, and a sprinkling of inhabitants, but then, exhausted by His labors, could go no further.

Is there an evolutionary path for faith?

It seems so strange to me: to think that the Grand Designer could make or dream or nurture only one kind of bird, or tortoise, or anything, rather than making many rooms in the mansion, for as many as cared to dwell, sought to dwell, yearned—in the brief, clamant condition of life—to dwell.

I wish I could ask Darwin what he was really thinking.

———————

The return to an earlier hour of Day One or Two—another great inundation—might be a long way off. It might be another forty or fifty years before the last of the world's sweet ice is gone, and gardens such as the Galápagos sink back beneath the warming sea. The Galápagos—birthplace of one of the biggest ideas that ever got into our heads, treasure vault museum-place for who we are and how we think about the world, and ourselves—will hit *reset* in the story, will return as if to Day One, *Ocean*—and, in a planet gone suddenly all soft and watery, like an unboiled egg, the earth's rotation will no longer be quite as taut. It's possible that the variance in precession will cause us to wobble slightly, canting us one-trillionth of a degree away from the sun's steady gaze, resulting in the great sheets of ice and hard-heartedness, misery, casting themselves over the green world, where once—once—we had bounty . . .

I'm a good worrier.

What does it mean, that we are wrecking yet another of our little gardens—maybe no more or no less important than any other garden—and yet, from a historical perspective—the unnatural history of us—maybe the most important shrine to our strange intellect and worrisome consciousness of self?

———————

The Galápagos aren't the only thing that will go underwater from the melting ice. And not all of the islands will be submerged. The iguanas and tortoises can climb to the highest peaks of the volcanic cones and calderas. But the islands will be smaller. Much that is still being made here will be lost. Those cute little penguins, zipping around underwater, chasing sardines—the world's only tropical penguins—won't like the warmer ocean currents; they'll be at risk of baking in their own exertions, like fat little sausages. And it's true, if we survive the new burning, the coming fire, we can study evolution—or devolution—in other places: newer places, older places, larger places, smaller places. This will just be one more loss, among so many. The doors to this museum, this cathedral, will be lost, covered over with sand and algae, moss and barnacles. But we can still tell stories about what we lost.

It's all there, in the Good Book, is the thing. Noah's ark—one and two of everything—came down the gangplank here, after clinging to the life rafts of driftwood. There are even poison apples in the Galápagos, brought here from the mainland in the bellies of iguanas, apples which only the tortoises can eat. Man must not bite into them.

Mr. Darwin: How did we get here, and why do we love beauty, if not to nurture in us stewardship for all the other places and beings around and beyond us?

I don't think we earned it. I think it was given to us. What are we going to do about it?

A LIFE WITH BEARS

I GREW UP IN TEXAS, WHICH MIGHT BE SEEN AS PART OF the problem. Football was the deity, whiteness was dominant, and guns were the answer, the final punctuation to any disagreement.

I want to make something beautiful. I believe these are the very words spoken by the earnest and nerdy playwright-turned-screenwriter Barton Fink in the eponymous film, a movie in which—atypical for America—I recall no handguns appearing for the simple matter of a sagging plot. Perhaps because the Coens are good writers and in no need of guns, save for a weird dream sequence that spoofs private-eye noir. (And now that I think more about it, the devil, as played by John Goodman, does make a brief appearance with a machine gun. Ah, well.)

We see that today in all forms of cinema—the two cultural media of our times, guns and film—and I wonder how we can regulate cigarettes, nudity, and alcohol on the airwaves but not the most dangerous of our many addictions and distractions.

Relax. I have turned my back on all that stuff, while the rest of society goes to opera and ballet openings and binges on *Game of Thrones*. (I don't know what it is but hear of it often, so that I imagine it lies somewhere between electricity and the precise origins of World War II as yet another thing I don't understand, will never understand, and really don't need to understand.)

I am of no help to society, even as—sedated, happily or unhappily—distracted, we pile sandbags against the rising waters that are the manifestation of the self-fulfilling legacy of self-destruction that follows from biting the apple in Eden's Garden.

As a novelist and essayist, *I just want to make something beautiful.*

I've been working on a novel, I can feel it in my blood and see it in my mind, can access its interiority on a few ghostly occasions when I'm walking at dusk and it's just me and the novel, with time to inhabit it as a fly, strangely, might be said to inhabit a spiderweb. I want it so badly, and while I've known logistically that the day was coming, the wall where time and energy begin to become finite (where previously they were not), I am in no way eager for nor prepared for its arrival. My yearning for the novel, thirty years of dreaming, rises steadily, slowly, still growing—increasing maybe 2 to 3 percent a year—but now the focus, and on good days the incandescence, the burning that hollows you out and fashions you anew, sends you forward, is harder to reach. It always requires at least as much a physical act as mental—the two are not separate—and, for the first time, nap taker that I have become, in times of stress, I find myself only able to do one or two things in a day, so that my choices seem to matter more. They always mattered. There were just more of them available.

Relax. In addition to avoiding a discussion of gun control, this is not going to be an essay about fiction writing, or about the abstract concept of time—though as a geologist, how I would love to wallow in that ore for an hour, a day, a lifetime. Nor is it even about the burden of activism, which has become, somehow, in a way I still haven't been able to figure out, both an indulgence and a necessity in my life.

I want to focus on bears. On knowing them, and on what they need. Which is—let's be honest—what I need. Where I live, the Yaak Valley of northwest Montana, only about two dozen remain. Twenty-five, tops. Three or four breeding-age females with young.

I guess this makes it an essay about activism after all. But is not everything we choose to do, then, activism—in the sense that living a life of direction and action is, over time, a form of activism—an expression of one's self and values, for better or worse? Of course it is.

———————

This isn't even an essay about global warming.

It's never lost on me that the things I am most passionate about are things it seems almost all the rest of the world knows nothing about, so that I exist as if on the tiniest of rafts, floating, lost in a vast sea but stroking, paddling, nonetheless, though with the currents—Humboldt, equatorial, Indonesian—so varied and powerful. I know and care about Paleozoic sedimentary point bars buried a mile beneath the surface in the Black Warrior Basin of north Alabama. I know, and care, again passionately, that a quarterback can pump fake to get a cornerback to open his hips while running in deep coverage with a wide receiver; I know half a hundred ways a defensive lineman can entice an offensive lineman to flinch, particularly on a passing down.

I know and care about the names of plants and trees and birds in the Yaak Valley, and know and care about the intricate human politics of my home, my immense state with such a tiny population: Jeannette Rankin, the first woman in Congress; Jon Tester, the last farmer in the Senate; Ted Kennedy's progressive schoolteacher pal, Pat Williams . . . I know and care about the tribes, the Indigenous communities that were first here back in the old days, and that remain. These values and ideas and images are what I hunger for when I spend too much time in my head fretting about the future, or about ideas.

The one thing a person needs to understand about a grizzly is that it's powerful. And indeed, that's people's main impression. A grizzly inspires awe and fear. And what a great word, *grizzly*.

Not *toad* or *pig*, not *butterfly* or *hippo*. There is no fear wrought in the name of the lovely little ocelot. *Armadillo* is uttered with the whimsical Latinate flourish the animal deserves. *Swan*, elegant.

It's hard, being an environmental writer. If one puts on one's blinders, gets in a canoe early one cool, sunny summer morning, and paddles solo, or perhaps with a pup, down a lazy winding river—say, the Bull River, in northwest Montana, or for faster waters, choppy little whitecap rapids on the Yaak River—lovely runs of clean water funneling in a long tongue, then splaying into broad still stretches with high cliff banks on one side and rich green meadows of grass that's already shoulder-high, and not even the solstice yet—

—it is easy then to write of the bald eagles perched along the river in the tops of towering cedars, their snowy heads bowed to watch with a fierce intensity and perhaps judgment of the paddler or paddlers below, on that lazy stretch of river, plates of sunlit green water spinning in radials, drifting past giant boulders mid-river, and feeling as a traveler might not have felt in a very long time—suspended in water, with only the thinnest membrane between one's self and the body of water, and the water moving forward, past eddies and riffles, being pulled along: blah blah blah blah blah.

So an environmental writer can write about those kinds of things, and change very little, if anything.

Or one can go to war, can beat the drum and preach to the choir, can run one's traps, call in favors, agitate, riot; can pen *Lamentations: The Sequel*. Gone are the brief days when this high-adrenaline scorched-earth accounting, though it would not be inappropriate, was effective. We ourselves are a different species these days, overstimulated and constantly adrenalized—essentially inhabiting a toxic soup of nonstop worry and fret and fear, for which plenty of short-term distraction exists but no true cure. After only 180,000 years in this world, we have lost our way, if ever we had a way. I am not optimistic about our chances for emerging reunified and graceful, which is one of the many reasons I think I am all in with the bears. They still are unified, still graceful. And they're incredibly endangered, and in this, as in so many other things, we share a great similarity, so great as to sometimes resemble familiality. Natural historian Douglas Chadwick reminds us that grizzlies and humans share 88 percent DNA.

———————

The second and other thing one needs to know about a grizzly is that, in all place-based cultures of humankind, bears have always occupied the level of deity or, in the case of contemporary Christianity and secularism, of demigod, which is what passes for deities and worship in these days of money-as-God, in which commerce or business is godlike, as is the decidedly unpoetic word *entertainment*. Vancouver Grizzlies, Grizzly ATVs, Grizzly chewing tobacco, Grizzly Car Wash.

Irony went extinct a long time ago, and it's hard to say what moved in to occupy its place. Nature abhors a vacuum. Something less complicated than irony, I'm almost certain. Maybe something more elemental, like pain or sorrow.

———————

Let me tell you what a grizzly is first.

A local reporter has been asking me what good are they, why do they matter. How are they different from any other nature? The questions elicit a sinking feeling in me, not unlike the one I had when I was first charged by a grizzly, a mother with young, up here in the Yaak.

There was a *tiny* bit of slow-motion quality to it, but for the most part it pretty much took place in real time. I would have *loved* a little more of a slo-mo aspect. I'd been watching the young bear, a sub-adult I'd spooked up a tree. He was having a hell of a time getting up it and staying up—it kind of looked like it was the first tree he'd climbed in his life, and his mother stood up from behind the hill, kind of Godzilla-looking—how could a bear be that tall?—then galloped down the hill toward me, from maybe thirty-five yards away.

Things I saw clearly: her long, straight dinnerware claws; dust rising from her as she ran. Had she been dust bathing? The sagging old radio collar on her, placed by the U.S. Fish and Wildlife Service to track her movements—it wasn't berry season yet, so she was still lean.

And though I didn't panic, I had the distinct thought, *Ah, I'm fucked now.* That a thing had been initiated that could now not be undone. It was—cliché—a decidedly sinking feeling. Falling, floating, descending to a place and a situation, a predicament, where one did not want to be, with not enough time remaining, and not enough space. A situation, it occurs to me now, that mimics the bears' own existence.

Obviously, it turned out okay for all of us. I drew my bear spray, discharged it even as I was pretty sure she was starting at the last possible moment to veer away. It was tense as hell but not quite terrifying—in part, I think, because it was so beautiful. These days when I see other hikers in the hills, whether hunters or not, their hips bristle with dual canisters of bear spray—good—but more often than not they also have strapped to their chests, in a weird sports-bra kind of contraption, some thick, ugly, blue-chrome-and-black thousand-dollar pistol. And if they'd seen that mother stand up, presenting such an easy target, I have little doubt they would have unstrapped (the barrel pointing disturbingly toward the shoulder as they hike uphill) and discharged the bullet rather than the spray. Such a tempting target.

The reality of a standing bear ("She *reared*," in the parlance of purveyors of magazines filled with sagas of blood and matted fur) is that, while intimidating to behold (one of the evolution-ary elements of the bears' and our coexistence), it's essentially a get-out-of-jail-free card for a hiker. She's only standing up to get better scent details, to see better (their eyesight, by the way, is excellent, better than our own), and to gauge your response. She's buying time. This is a very good thing for both of you. So long as you don't do something stupid to change the dynamic or force the issue—like shoot a gun—you're already home free; it just may not yet feel like it, in the moment.

The bears who don't stand up are the ones that'll bite you. Those bears' charges are not of considered meditation but of blind fury. A standing bear, however, has pretty much already made up its mind not to initiate conflict. All you have to do is sign on the dotted line. Still, they can be really tall.

Why do bears matter, and in the Yaak? The fact that someone can ask such a question makes me feel—again—that we're sinking. Let me tell you a little bit about a thing I love while it is still here on the earth.

Famously, they hibernate. They climb high into the moun-tains, drawn to a northeast slope, often at the base of a steep cliff, where snow piles up deepest and stays longest. Sometimes they go into a cave or den they have dug themselves—it's almost im-possible not to think of Christianity's borrowing of this ancient saga—and pretty much stay there until spring.

Their cubs are born as the mother sleeps, a snow astronaut, in January, each cub small enough to balance in a soup spoon. There is no other animal in the world with so great a disparity in size between birth and maturity. You tell me, god or demigod?

Their relationship with time is beyond profound, so aligned with and fitted to the landscape they inhabit as to expose our crude notions of time—sixty seconds in a minute, sixty minutes in an hour—as the mathematical abstractions they are. In hibernation, their heart rate slows to three or four beats per minute. Call it four beats; between each heartbeat, an entire dream, of an entire season. Winter, spring, summer, fall. Winter, again. Four months per breath. Timelessness not in their dreams but in their living.

There are five subpopulations of grizzlies in Montana: in the Northern Continental Divide Ecosystem, which includes Glacier National Park, and in the Cabinet Mountains, the Yaak, the Greater Yellowstone Ecosystem, and the Selway-Bitterroot, currently extinct, though with a few bears sensing it's out there and trying to get back home. No one subpopulation can reach the other, however. Even in Montana, a matrix of logging roads, highways, railroads, towns, cities, and villages prevents them from connecting with each other. "Blood knowledge," wrote D. H. Lawrence, in *At Home on This Earth*. "Oh, what a catastrophe for man when he cut himself off from the rhythm of the year, from his unison with the sun and the earth. Oh, what a catastrophe, what a maiming of love when it was made a personal, merely personal feeling, taken away from the rising and setting of the sun, and cut off from the magical connection of the solstice and equinox. This is what is wrong with us. We are bleeding at the roots."

They don't live quite as long as humans or parrots, but quite a bit longer than most animals on this hard continent: into their midthirties, if no one kills them. A big one in these parts is six hundred pounds. The bulk of their diet is grass. Every subpopulation has adapted and evolved to depend on the specificity of the particular landscape of its residency. Each subpopulation has negotiated, over the long course of its existence, something quite a bit more elegant and sophisticated than what Darwin saw in the far more recent, even nascent, economies of the Galápagos, which was termed, mistakenly, survival of the fittest. (In reality, what Darwin was witnessing was a brief hierarchy of the luckiest—the ecological equivalent, perhaps, of white privilege.) For example, the famed Galápagos tortoise. Having gotten a leg up by sheer luck, not cunning, and having made random landfall on a patch of bare ground so new in the world as to still be smoldering, the tortoises pretty much had it made from the beginning. It was not through cunning or wile or strength that they found the Garden of Eden that was the Galápagos, newly made Day One, blossomed from fire, but instead the grace of the equatorial currents that guided the tortoises—tossed overboard when no longer needed for sailors' food on long voyages. And it wasn't the tortoises' cunning there, either, but more luck, that a lighter-weight sailor, one who ate less across the long seagoing journey, resulted in a few tortoises—possibly the weaker, more infirm ones, at that—being spared.) Whatever it was, grace or luck, it definitely wasn't survival of the fittest. *Chance* is as good an in-the-middle word for it as any. Luck and chance are far and away the greatest drivers of evolution, not the more dramatic elements of strength and cunning. Cooperation is the greatest tool, and the hardest. Darwin didn't see it because it wasn't there yet. It wasn't needed yet.

What if we ourselves, now inhabiting what was once a much larger garden, nonetheless arrived here under similar circumstances—once to have been briefly useful to a god or demigod, or even a single great creator, only to be cast aside, no longer a necessity, the creator's journey—the farther shore—in sight, leaving us to drift and align wherever we landed, which is *here?*

And, still so new to this world, we struggle. Even so, we ourselves are capable of exuding, at times, a kind of primitive grace, leaving here and there patches and residues of it in our own small travels, a pattern or trail that glints gold in certain conditions of light, like the glittering sheen a land snail leaves on stone—visible perhaps only to the eye of whoever cast us out of heaven, or aside, and then visible only under certain conditions. Still, we, and all living things in this slightly larger garden, this earth-island, struggle, with the most successful and enduring inhabitants surviving not by brawn but by the connections to all others: establishing complex and numerous interdependent points of attachment within the ecosystem, the garden that they—we—inhabit.

(In fiction and nonfiction, these points of attachment are what allow a reader to enter and inhabit the dreamscape of the story. Specificity: it's what keeps us out of our heads and in our bodies.)

Along the coast of British Columbia, grizzlies grow larger on diets of oceangoing salmon returning to lay eggs in the headwaters of the rushing snowmelt rivers discharged from the flanks of glaciers. It seems a simple case of the bears utilizing bounty, and it is that—bears line the shores and scoop salmon out of the narrowing creeks' rapids, farther inland, gorging until they can eat no more, in the period of hyperphagia as they prepare for the nearing of hibernation. (Dr. Barrie Gilbert calls bears lipophiles—fat lovers—because, even after they can eat no more, they open the skulls of sunken spawn-ravaged dead salmon and pull out the salmon's brains neatly with their teeth, unable to resist that sweet protein-rich delicacy.)

So it's a utilization of bounty, horn of plenty. But the bears are also the firmament on which all others stand within their ecosystem. Without the bears redistributing the marine-rich nitrogen from the oceangoing salmon in their spoor, the granitic soil of the inland mountains would be too sterile to grow anything, much less the old-growth cedar forests that shade and cool the water to temperatures that the salmon depend on, the forest without which the bears and salmon would not exist. Who among us would not be forgiven for wondering if such a relationship of symbiosis exists in our spiritual lives, between a creator and the created?

Similarly, in Glacier National Park, the bears aerate the alpine soil, rototilling it to just the right depth with their daggered claws as they search for roots: gentle farmers furrowing their fields, away from hikers and campers. In Yellowstone, where the high-elevation whitebark pine is the ecological driver of the ecosystem—each seed the caloric equivalent of a little bomb of butter—an elegant evolutionary cooperative agreement exists in which the Clark's nutcracker, with its specialized bill, pries open the tight clutch of the pine's cones, and squirrels cache the left-over cones, which bears then raid and, again, redistribute in their spoor, as do the nutcrackers, at the highest elevations, which are favored by female grizzlies with young.

The bears' attachment to high places, wherever they are still found, is nothing less than mythic.

If I consider them a deity, it is not so much in the traditional sense, in which one offers up an irregular stream of prayers that are at least partly, if not most or even all of the time, aimed at de-livering products or desired outcomes not for the god or demigod but for the supplicant. A sort of calling in of goods and services. How fucked up is that, instead of giving, as some long ago have advised, unceasing thanks for being allowed to be here?

So no, it could not be said that I worship bears, nor do I find myself in conversation with them; I neither thank them for my existence nor lobby and beseech them for favor and fortune. I do, however, find my days filled by service to them. Pretty much unceasingly, now that I consider it. In the mornings I campaign for their protection, and the protection of their habitat, and in the afternoons I try still to get out and take a little walk through their woods. Only on occasion now do I go up to their mountaintops. They need the rarest thing now, rarer even than time: space.

Increasingly, I dream of them: never dreams of violence, and never of lambs-and-lions unification with them. Instead, between us there is always a slight distance, one that is enforced by them, not me. Often in the dreams I am with another person or persons and am acting as a guide, and in the dream I am worried not for myself but for the other travelers.

When I'm not dreaming I prepare press packets, a pamphleteer waging a war of rhetoric against state-sponsored reassurances that the bears are recovering, have recovered, everywhere, and that all is good and that, in the words of the primary agency tasked with their protection, the USFWS, global warming is not a threat to them now nor is it anticipated ever to be so in the future. How different am I, really, from any other true believer who leaves copies of *The Watch* or *The Watch Tower* or *End Times* in phone booths, or Gideon Bibles in the drawers of hotels throughout the West, or, depending on location, *The Book of Mormon?* (The last grizzly in Utah, Old Ephraim, caught his foot in a trap and was chased down in 1923 by a Boy Scout scoutmaster, whose scouts pelted the bear with stones. Some fun.)

One by one the bears have been blinking out. This is the fate of all small and isolated subpopulations. David Quammen's excellent book *The Song of the Dodo* details the mathematical reasons for this phenomenon. With each grizzly subpopulation in Montana cut off from all others, they are having to wander farther, as if lost in the wilderness, seeking one another, and through an increasingly complex maze of fragmented environment. And as with everything, global warming is taking a blowtorch to their old world: scorching their old food supplies, forcing them to travel farther, risk more to find less. Immense and magnificent creatures that were once far more intimately fitted to the intricacies of their home than any citizens to a civilization of humankind. As fitted to place as the proverbial Swiss watch is to itself, with every piece, no matter how tiny, fitted to every other piece. A bounty of attachment points. Naturalist Doug Peacock says that grizzlies hold down the skin of the earth with the weight of their four paws.

I hate to be the evangelical in the room, but now that they are on the move, forced to expand their territories as the resources within grow thinner and more scarce—the book of Exodus—and as they encounter record and unsustainable mortalities in their globally warmed peregrinations, what might that mean for us? When, in our shallow past, have we too been forced to get up and move, abandoning our homes—our gardens, our forests, our prairies, our hilltops—forsaking all and wandering, equally lost, searching for any of the three basic requirements of our own identity—food, water, shelter—and, if we are different, requiring one more of the softer necessities, love or compassion or even beauty?

———————

This summer I received an Apple Watch, the function of which breaches, then breaks down whatever tenuous firewall existed between one's brain and the coming thing called artificial intelligence. Let me disclose here, in the requirement of full journalistic transparency, that one of the things I love, perhaps worship, about art is that it is an avenue by which one can present the self one wishes to explore—to celebrate or, conversely, purge. Short of the slicing and splicing of genes and the nip and tuck of various sun-blasted chromosomes, art's the best way, still, to remake the human mind, the human being, into something different from the individual who emerged from the womb.

We do change, over time. We do assume different genetic identities, picking them up simply from living proximate to, in the same environment with, others. A yew tree growing next to an aspen absorbs aspen DNA through the soil and from the shared atmosphere, from its respiration, its breath. The world is *complicated;* life is more connected that we have been taught or led to believe. I'm sure there's a Bible verse somewhere that reinforces this truth, but I don't know it offhand. If I had time, I'd go back and reread it to find it.

I don't have time. The last twenty-five grizzlies in the Yaak Valley don't have time.

The Apple Watch receives texts, profiles my pulse rate in blue EKG mountains and valleys of sweet "good" sleep, etches in red the terrifying peaks and troughs of nightmares—even identifies for me, for them, what articles I've read, and what I reread. Whether I am agitated or becalmed, where I go, what I buy, what I sell, what I like, what I don't like.

How much stuff, really, do I need to know? How much do any of us?

Is there a more marvelous feeling known to a writer than the condition in which the lawn mower's buzzing down the street falls away, and the thrumming of one's heart becomes even bigger in the writing of the scene, next word by next word, than it would be, could possibly be, even in the living of it? Which is to say, those moments when the dream transcends and towers above even the miracle of the living, and the body, the brain, the soul are transformed, and one becomes a better, fuller person—a real person rather than just a regular person.

The *Los Angeles Times* newsfeed, Instagram, Accuweather—it all comes pouring into my blood now, the three tiny sensors tapping my wrist, buzzing, searching for a connection, seeking to send their electronic blossoming of facts into my veins, the clutter and detritus of our times surging up those blood rivers toward my brain, where—in a finite space crowded and cramped with plaque, the geologic signatures of concussions and time—those facts collide, as if in bumper cars, with a lifetime of carefully and also sometimes randomly curated events; a smattering of facts, their perimeters fraying and disintegrating as they shape-shift into something less than full or accurate and become instead metamorphic amalgamations of time and place as if everything is living: stones, grizzlies, memory. As if memories, isolated, yearn to get up and travel sometimes. As if, buried, they reemerge in later seasons with many of the old characteristics of their predecessors but also modified, transformed.

Life is this way, across the span of almost any amount of time. Perhaps the abstraction of time, beyond its sixty-second/sixty-minute paradigm, does not even exist, the truer measure of what we are seeking when we try to speak of time being instead the degree or amount of alteration, modification, or transformation any one thing experiences—so that *time* might exist not as an abstraction but indeed as a physical presence, sometimes erosive and corrosive, and at other times creative, generative.

The fancy Apple Watch: It tells my average resting heart rate as well as beat by beat. It monitors me when I read articles from Fox News, when I read the *NYT.* I am a tiny, extraneous, outlaw part of the forming of the one-brain, the brain that always makes sense, is always predictable, sterile, insensate, dead, doomed.

When I was in my twenties, still playing football and doing marathons and triathlons and all that youthful stuff, my average pulse was low forties; there was a measuring cuff, a rubber sleeve, at the YMCA where I lifted and worked out, where, on occasion, I could and did descend to the dream state of thirty-five beats per minute. Good writing territory.

That's no longer the case. This is an essay about grizzly bears and why they matter—not just to me, but to keep the world spinning for all of us, which, as I understand it, is one of the main duties and responsibilities of the gods—not the false gods we've created to serve as vessels for our needs and desires, but the real McCoys, the ones who were here before we arrived, and who I would hope will be here after our departure.

I cruise around at seventy heartbeats now. Discouraging, when forty came as easily, and miraculously, as each next breath. And yet: even now, an old man, in search of late-spring and early-summer morels, I take my first step into the old forest that I have loved for decades, and a glance at my watch shows the sweet plummeting of love, back down into the midforties, as if descending into the lovely orange mulch I will soon enough be rejoining. It's where I most want to be, and a place from which I have been too long absent.

At other times the pulse-o-meter drops wonderfully, precipitously, into the deep thunk of the dreamscape of a story—in the words of George Plimpton, recalling Muhammad Ali's description of boxers' concussions that cause them to envision "the Near Room"—a dungeon in which alligators play trombones.

It doesn't drop quite as far—the mental journey—as it does in the real and the physical. In the writing dream, it only gets down into the low fifties. I take this to mean that the difference between the real and the virtually real is about 10–20 percent. The more you know of the real world, then—the more there are of these anchor points of attachment—the more recklessly you can inhabit your dreamscapes. Eudora Welty was onto this, I think, when she wrote, "A sheltered life can be a daring life."

Still.

———————

I don't like writing, someone—maybe Dorothy Parker—said, *I like having written.*

It was Flannery O' Connor who said, when asked why she wrote, *Because I'm good at it.*

Bears are really good at living where they live. They used to be great at living where they lived—in at least the western half of North America, and maybe all of it—but our species has killed their species, either by killing them outright or, more recently, by converting their habitat into unnatural and essentially unrecognizable fragments of ruin. There is nothing about a logging road that is replicated in the wild nature in which bears evolved. There is nothing in nature, other than a volcanic blast, that replicates a clear-cut. We have killed bears steadily, wherever we have encountered them, so that now they live within less than 1 percent of their former range. They are essentially invisible.

Sometimes a careful hiker will see clues that they are still there, proof that such a being is still out there, if no longer in our midst, no longer in our memories or in our own hearts and, who knows, maybe one day no longer even in our dreams. There are still clues, and rumors of sightings. A few twists of hair caught in drops of sunlit amber, where the animal has rubbed its back against a fir tree. Sometimes they do this because they have an itch and at other times—scientists can never be fully sure—to create a signpost for other bears and, I suspect, for humans also: that one has now entered the last homeland of bears, and is advised and encouraged—strongly requested—to behave accordingly.

On the island of Hokkaido in extreme northern Japan, emigration or immigration requires a bear to make but a short swim or walk, depending upon the presence or absence of ice, to reach Russia, and from there another short jaunt, no more taxing than a subway transfer, to North America. On the island of Hokkaido, the Indigenous people—the Ainu, of whom there are still a few dozen remaining—used to make statues of standing bears, deep in the forest, particularly along the Ainu's own territorial borders. Other peoples around the world used to do the same thing, carving them out of wood or chiseling them from the stone where, I suppose, they were worshipped, reflected upon by solitary hunters; so far back in the mountains, the place where bears are safest and least likely to be killed by interactions with humans. I myself have never come upon such a statue in our forests and mountains—the bears were here before the humans—but wonder if, should our species persevere long enough on this continent, we might one day think to place one or two statues in some special place—maybe not in the heart's center of their territory, for we have already taken so much from them, but perhaps at the edge of such wild country, as a signpost or other signal that we would welcome their expansion, would welcome their recolonizing their old territory, and that this time we will behave better, will be better neighbors. That we support their need to reconnect with one another. That it was a mistake to set them apart from one another.

God or demigod? I don't kneel in their presence, but I never move as carefully, or with so much reverence, as when I am breast-stroking into the sun through rain-drip blazing green alder up above five thousand feet in June, the heated breeding season, and the path before me is impressed with their fresh prints and their grass- and deer-fur-wrapped scat, deposited hours or even minutes ago.

———————

I come close to praying. But maybe more than praying, I work. There are so many threats to my valley's last twenty-five grizzlies. Global warming, and a copper and silver mine proposed beneath the Cabinet Mountains Wilderness Area, which is located in the mountain range to the south, through which Yaak bears would otherwise be able to reach Yellowstone and central Idaho. Also inhibiting bears' ability to connect is the Burlington Northern Railroad (BN; now Burlington Northern and Santa Fe), with increased traffic hauling coal—coal too dirty to burn in this country—from eastern Montana's Tongue River Valley to the ports in Seattle and Tacoma, where it is then sold for a penny on the dollar and shipped to China, in the hope that investors can lure Chinese manufacturers into building new coal plants to utilize this subsidized largesse from the United States. (Karl Rove's Carlisle Group owns the largest reserves of coal in the world, beneath the West's public lands.) Once China builds their new coal plants, the price of that penny-per-ton dirty coal will, of course, escalate—ka-ching! And in the meantime, there's a correlative uptick of dead Yaak grizzlies on Warren Buffett's BN line, should any bears be peppy enough to obey their ancient territorial imperative of dispersing into new country—traveling south to the Cabinet Mountains and Idaho, or north, from Yellowstone and the Bitterroot, up toward the Yaak. (Also correlative, let it not be forgotten, is the rise in pulmonary disease and fatalities in China.)

What is the price of that sweet yellow sweater, that Captain Marvel lunchbox? More than we would be willing to spend, I have to believe, if only the true accounting could be known. More than we could afford. Instead, a great roar of white noise drowns out even the ability to ask or wonder if the cost is greater than the advertised sale. Pick apart any one thing in the universe, wrote John Muir, and find, always, it is inextricably hitched to all else.

So there are a lot of threats against those last twenty-five. But the most imminent threat is a dark-of-the-night legislative rider that authorized, without debate or committee hearing or consultation with the Montana delegation, a high-volume through-hiker trail that would act as a spur trail, a link and connection, between the immensely popular Pacific Crest Trail (PCT) and Continental Divide Trail (CDT). For thirty-two years, the two land management agencies in charge of our national forests and our threatened and endangered species—the U.S. Forest Service and the U.S. Fish and Wildlife Service —opposed the hiking club's proposal, recognizing it would be expensive but more importantly against the law, in that the proposed route would bisect almost thirty miles of designated core grizzly bear habitat.

There was an independent grizzly bear biologist working in

northwest Montana at the time, a big old friendly Santa Claus–looking guy with a surprisingly high voice, Dr. Chuck Jonkel. Let me tell you a little about him. He was a man on fire, a big old roly-poly four-season ball of passion. He changed lives when he was alive, and now from beyond the grave his work is still helping protect a thing he loved perhaps more than all others: grizzly bears.

I have drifted far from one of the early exploratory premises of this essay, that we can change one another, even across interspecies barriers, just by being in close proximity, as if through the heat of our ideas, our dreams. I'm exploring the idea that our dreams can intrude upon reality, can edge into the territory of reality, can come to occupy the territory of reality, like a big old boar grizzly hip-checking a cub away from a moose carcass. For a little while, I got down into the stinkweeds of public policy, down into the sterile limbo land of politics—but Chuck's passion, which took place out in the field, is still having this effect of transformation, every bit as profound as genetic splicing or procreational mixing.

What a fireball, what a force. He served as on-the-ground ambassador for the bears, the shadow bears that pass back and forth across the international border between Montana and British Columbia. He once cut six hundred pounds of fresh grass from the banks of the Flathead River to rush to a bear being held in a zoo in Seattle, detained there for one bear-ish crime or another. He wanted to use the opportunity to study digestibility coefficients—a chance to feed a bear its native foods and measure calories in and calories out. Chuck Jonkel was a scruffy-looking field guy—there never seemed to be time to shave—and when he passed through the customs gate just before midnight, bleary eyed and salt stained from his day's labors, and the agent looked at the camper shell on the back of his truck and asked what was inside, Chuck didn't miss a beat, said, "About six hundred pounds of grass." The agent stared at him for a moment—Chuck stared back, deadpan—and then the agent waved him on.

———————

Chuck Jonkel started the Wild Parade in Missoula, now an annual street festival where children and adults alike, little pagans all, dress up as their favorite wild animal for one day each year.

He developed bear spray. This in itself would have been more than a lifetime achievement. How many hikers' lives—how many bears' lives—have been saved by pepper spray? And how revolutionary is that—to circle back to the topic of Americans and our guns, a nation of pistoleros—to subvert the fucking dominant paradigm, to *not* shoot and kill a thing of which one is frightened, but to instead preserve it: to send it away, changed, altered, and with both human and bear better for the experience.

He taught wildlife biology at the University of Montana for decades. He took students up to Canada to see polar bears.

He held a bear honoring every spring, when the bears were first coming back to life after their long sleep.

He walked the suburbs at night in Missoula, picking up loose apples that might otherwise lure grizzlies into people's yards: the reverse of Johnny Appleseed.

Native cultures call the grizzly the real bear. I'd say Dr. Jonkel was a real human.

Best of all, to my thinking, or most pertinent to my home, back in 1978—forty-one years ago now!—Congress directed Dr. Jonkel to make a report assessing the proposed Pacific Northwest Trail. He did, and found that the route the hikers desired would be the absolute worst route for Yaak grizzlies, but—as if knowing, even as a young man, that no work is ever wasted, and that despite being in his prime he would someday grow old and die, which might severely limit his future effectiveness—Dr. Jonkel recommended a scenic southern route that would still please high-volume through-hikers while keeping the bears safe.

When, in 2009, a hiking club finally succeeded in getting Senator Maria Cantwell (D-WA) to authorize the trail nonetheless—with the senator evidently having been misled into believing there was no science arguing against that route—it was the thin imaginary line, the dream, of Dr. Jonkel's that endured, giving us hope even now that we can convince Congress to correct their oversight, their mistake.

We pour money and time—our lives and livelihoods—into fighting to move this trail. We've hired attorneys, traveled to D.C.—our staff of seven, our board of six volunteers—thirteen people working for five years now, the equivalent of one full human life, sixty-five worker-years—to try to correct something as innocuous and dangerous as a line on a map drawn by a long-ago hiker who did not live here and who chose to ignore or hide the science, for whatever reasons. To try to protect these last twenty-five grizzlies.

There is no end to the shit going on in the world.

I need the dreamscape of fiction.

I also need a wilderness with grizzlies still in it—to wander off-trail on certain days, not in a floating cloud or bubble of trail buddies, a roving pack of others of my kind with nicknames, trail names, ten or twenty strong, but moving quietly, slowly. Noticing every breath of breeze, every molecule of scent. Praying, I guess you could call it. Listening. Looking. Knowing—believing—knowing—that the thing you most need and yet cannot see is out there, nonetheless. (Developing such a mind, such a spirit, is probably very good training for becoming a writer.)

It's the summer solstice. The mountains are flooded with light. Snow remains at the highest elevations. I continue to feel wracked by my biological and neurological destiny—to write stories, tell stories, inhabit dreams—which is in conflict with my heart, my desire to serve a greater good and—I believe this—a greater being. Beauty incarnate; beauty in motion across a beloved and singular landscape. Twenty-five beauties.

What good is a grizzly? Even if years or decades hence scientists do discover that the germination of huckleberry seeds requires ingestion by the very grizzlies that, like gardeners, broadcast those seeds in the most favorable locations for the berries' survival—those curious and just-right places on the landscape with the thus far immeasurable differences between pockets of cool air and warm, and a certain geometric arrangement, like a composition between shadow and sun, at a certain time of year, and a certain soil chemistry, a certain enzyme in the guts of grizzlies, which they each and all twenty-five of them carry around within them like a fire in the horn—even if all these things and more are discovered, I would say they need no reason; for if we judge them thus, how can we avoid asking ourselves the same question? And what would our answer be? Surely to make beauty is all we really have to offer—and thin soup, that, against the majesty of what is already here, was already here before us.

The fight has gotten into my head. I read all the self-help articles that come into my watch—the silent counsel of Siri and Alexa, who listen to my own silent turmoil as they chart the wild metrics of my pulse, my sleep and my sleeplessness, my self-medication, my binge-hikes back into the wilderness. Indeed, the frenzy of my activism is destroying my inner capacity for wisdom or even peace. The peace that is wisdom. I know too much to be calm, or if not too much then more than I want to know or need to know, to be a good writer.

What does one really need to know, to be a good writer? Definitely, less is more. I was born into the tribe of Welty, Munro, Cheever, Updike, and of Wolff, Beattie and Moore and

Carver—but have allowed myself to be seduced, brainwashed, recruited by anger, fear, fury: all waste, right, when the dirt is piled atop one—the dirt from which there will be no springtime reemergence.

I've trafficked in novels but what my brain and being were made for was, still is, short stories and novellas. *I want to make something beautiful.* I don't want to be a soldier. Because I love what I love, I'll be the best I can be. But approaching the age of sixty-two I am beginning to be keenly aware of what a waste it is. Or what a waste it seems. I do believe no work is ever wasted. *Wasted* is too strong, too bitter a word. Still: this is the first year of my life in which I have to honestly say, I have left stories un-written. I have given away much. Youthful time is cheap. I would encourage all young writers to write like there is no tomorrow.

And yet, like a life possessed, a life squandered can be won-derful also. In the Yaak, it's exquisitely lonely. No help is coming. There are twenty-five of them, and I fear in a perverse way that my fate and theirs are strangely connected. If we lose even one female every other year—not every year, but every twenty-four months—the Yaak subpopulation will be extinct within twenty years.

"Lord, let me die," writes the American poet James Dickey in "For the Last Wolverine," "but not die Out."

The closing in and connecting of full circles. In college, in Utah, I studied wildlife science and geology; took one essay elective, and one Appreciation of the Short Story class in which, to give a sense of how undialed-in I was to writing, whenever the prof waxed rhapsodic about Flaubert, I thought—this was in the strange new western landscape of Utah, mind you, not Texas, where I'd grown up—he was speaking of a highly revered but intensely local Native

American chieftain and evidently consummate storyteller, with the curious name of Flow Bear.

My professor in wildlife science was Dr. Barrie Gilbert—then a young man who in 1977 was attacked by a female grizzly with cubs in Yellowstone. Over nine hundred stitches and two quarts of blood and one year later, he was teaching me and now—where have forty-plus years gone?—has written a singular and revolutionary book, *One of Us*, about his experiences with grizzlies, and specifically about how some populations learn to move quietly and unobtrusively, becoming smaller, living up high in marginal habitat. Nocturnal secretive nonconformers who, though being much like us, and vice versa, survive by staying away from us.

———————

The Yaak is nothing if not a landscape constructed of dreams and ghosts. The Yaak, like a bear itself, once rested beneath two or more miles of thick blue ice pressing down on the bowl of this low valley, this garden-to-be, even as the rest of the West, far above, clattered and groaned and shrieked with the retreat of the last Ice Age. Glaciers screeching and carving the most amazing peaks. The high winds of the cordillera scrubbing the newly exposed cliff faces. Hawks and eagles wheeling in circles, in sky-sentences, above the blue ice that remained, trapped, like a lake of blue fog, a lake of blue ice: the land that would become our home.

Finally—a couple of thousand years later than the rest of the West—the Yaak emerged from its den. Bears that had been walking above the thinning ice now moved through its then-nascent old-growth forests, flipping logs and boulders still cold from the ice, looking for beetles, ants, tiny rootlets of grass. Fire would eventually come to the valley, in flickers and tongues, but mostly it was rot. And the fuel for rot: a riot of life.

Glacier lilies, yarrow, hedysarum, angelica: a vegetarian's

feast. Berries. Buffaloberry serviceberry huckleberry chokecherry kinnikinnick. The bears tended to the garden. Nothing exists long without the support of another thing.

Then came the roads, then came the schools—then came the churches, then came the rules. To the best of my knowledge, native cultures never lived up here year-round, but instead lived down along the Kootenai River, a fish culture, coming up into the valley in the summer and fall to hunt woodland caribou, in the old forests of larch and cedar, and mountain goats—all gone now, ghosts.

The Forest Service, my nemesis in war and in peace, bulldozed ten thousand miles or more of logging roads on the Kootenai, clear-cutting so fast to feed the mills—ghosts themselves, now—that they couldn't remember which places on their maps still had trees and which did not. Phantom forests, the legal experts called them. Picture the old filmstrips showing calendar pages flipping past in a fast-motion whir. Under pressure from the courts, the Forest Service put up gates to prevent people from cruising those ten thousand miles of roads with guns, shooting at bears and other wildlife and in general disrupting what had always before been a pretty quiet place, the wilderness.

Many of the grizzlies fled north to Canada, where they met a fate no different than had they stayed. And the gates were easy to drive around—ghost gates, protecting ghost bears that inhabit ghost forests.

When I write, I inhabit the dreamscapes of fiction, comprising ghosts and ideas, and yet even when I emerge from that lowermost place and run to join the fight above, I find myself still amid ghosts. Even the names of things in this newer, younger place—the Yaak Valley—are the names of the often invisible or unseen, described in a lexicon that suggests they might not even really have a true identity, residing instead in artifice and otherworldliness, or diminishment. False azalea, false morels. False hellebore. Lewis's mock orange. Least weasel.

One thing is not false or invisible or ghostly or lesser, yet: the presence of those last twenty-five grizzlies. I often suspect our two species, bears and humankind, are linked in ways we don't even fully know, but again so much so that one might as easily ask, *What good are humans?* For surely the answer veers quickly to the spiritual, rather than the economical or even what is termed *ecosystem services* (filtration of air and water, recycling and redistributing of carbon and other nutrients, etc.).

Grizzly bears help define us as a species. In Montana, they have the opportunity to help shape us as a culture. It is good to have other sentient beings in the forest, beings that are more powerful and more deeply established than we are. What else is this but a primary lesson in humility for us, the most recent experiment and offshoot of the ancient and still-living tree of life?

I have a secret, wrote the poet H.D.; *I am alive.* The writer or person who knows something has a secret: she or he is alive.

Sally Matsuishi, the executive director of Next Generation Scholars, says of writing that "radical care is a form of wildness. It is all we really have to break the reader's heart." She says there is no more radical political act than to inhabit the life of another being. Inhabit, please, in your minds and hearts, a race of grizzlies living on the island of the Yaak—one of the last places where the ice remained during the last episode of global warming, even after global warming had come and gone.

Slowly, the Yaak stirred: loosened boulders that clattered like dice thrown by the retreating flanks of that cold ice, blue as an old man's or an old woman's eyes. The Yaak slept still, as if in hibernation, holding the last of the ice, the bowl of the Yaak being compressed, metamorphosed, transformed, beneath all that weight. Finally, however, it too emerged, as the last ice melted and flowed to the Pacific, to the north and west, following the trail of the Kootenai River, to the Columbia.

Down from the north, a unique clade of grizzly bears tumbled into the valley where they find themselves now surrounded. Their alpine meadows, the tops of bare ridges in the Yaak, are only a few acres in size—sometimes little larger than the lawn of a rich person's home in a gated community, or even in the burbs. The mother bears with their young rototill and aerate these small gardens for each day's sustenance; afterward they sleep with their noses pointed to the wind coming from those tiny meadows. They hear no hikers, no bells; they scent no campfires. They exist, and wait, for a radical act.

NEW
ESSAYS

FIREBUILDER

WHO KNOWS HOW WE COME TO ANYTHING? HE WASN'T
the first writer I read, once I decided to become a writer myself,
but he certainly was formative. Helpful. I had picked up his work
on a suggestion. An insistence; a celebration. The book I picked
up, *Desert Notes*, was a marvel in its thinness and in what it contained. My first introduction to his work—the first page—was a
description of someone driving a van through the desert, not on
any road or trail, just kind of magic carpeting along, and stepping
out of the van while it was idling forward, and running around to
the other side and climbing into the passenger side, and continuing on. He did not present it as metaphor, but as truth: the truth
of a landscape without boundaries and an imagination likewise.
This was valuable to me. I had always suspected—believed—that
was the way the world was, but it was extraordinarily valuable to
me to have that belief validated. Encouraged.

He did this thing a lot, where he helped us see anew—usually
deeper, but sometimes broader—things we'd been looking past,
or looking at incorrectly: with a flawed set of assumptions, or
with faulty logic. He helped us look at landscape differently. A
classic example is in his celebration of the photographer Hoshino
Michio, who was revolutionary at the time for photographing the
grizzly bears of Denali and other wildlife not with nature porn

close-up head-and-shoulders portraits, but images where enormous herds and individual animals were tiny against the landscape they inhabited.

Barry Lopez questioned pretty much everything. I think that might have become exhausting at times.

Something else he taught me, or rather, in which he served as exemplar: he made it easier for me to make hard and stubborn, even obstinate choices with regard to what some might call art, and the artist's relationship to the rest of the world. He helped remind me—with the unquestioning insistence of his intensity—that art was *different*. Different from everything. And a way through. A way through everything.

He did not die a rich man. This is nobody's business, certainly not the future's. I bring it up only to verify to the reader, and to other writers and artists who will follow, that his decisions—as they always do in a life of meaning, which is to say, engagement—were not based on finances but rather artistic and personal integrity.

He was a man who in some ways was very aware of limits—unusual for either an artist or a philosopher—yet certainly he had access to both imagination and one of imagination's unavoidable fruits, hope. I believe that, being mortal, he had doubt. I think one of the primary doubts was his view of contemporary humanity's ability to grow and change. Of its ability to not be seduced. And yet to not despair.

I think it was his doubt that made him fierce. It was his ferocity that brought the fire.

Of course he lived in the rainforests of western Oregon. Sea fog, mist, and the broad red backs of salmon. And yet of course the fire eventually found him. Each seeks its own. Each seeks our own. Our kin, our kind, our community.

———

Because he understood science as perhaps only a poet can, he was unafraid to move in directions that seemed opposite to science. Spirituality and storytelling were his foundation. The facts mattered to him as much as they would to a journalist, yet at the end of the day I think he was most ardent-hearted about magic. He had seen and felt enough of it to be comfortable trusting its presence. Whether Crazy Horse actually flew up onto his horse like a bird, never touching it; whether Moses parted the Red Sea—one must consider that the things we call miracles might once have been almost commonplace. That somehow we lost the ability to summon or even receive them.

They still happen, now and again, but on a scale that feels muted. We tend to call them coincidence. We tweeze them apart and try to use our always incomplete, always inadequate science to explain.

You might think at this point that I am going to tell you a story about a coincidence, or magic. As if to prove a point. And I will tell you the first time I met Barry was at Edward Abbey's memorial, outside of Moab. And that when Barry walked up to make his remarks, out in the orange cliffs, beneath an April-blue sky, a raven followed him above, like a pet, then flared away. And that before Barry could speak, the wind picked up the American flag and hurled it to the ground.

But there are a lot of ravens around Moab, and it is true also that in the canyonlands country there can be sudden gusts of wind. And it is possible too, I suppose, that we are each alone and all we have in the world and forever is each other.

———

He was a leader—along with Richard Nelson, and others—in helping white folk appreciate certain Indigenous teachings not just as an abstract way of listening, but as a sometimes deeper learning that comes from curiosity. In an era when not many were listening to First Nations and Indigenous people, it was instructive to see him and a few others asking questions and listening, rather than presuming, or not thinking about such things at all.

He knew from the beginning, as Robin Wall Kimmerer and others remind us, to be unafraid of creating our own rituals and ceremonies; that gratitude is or once was and can be again an underpinning of our species and our route, our path, to connecting back to the tree of life from which we fell, like an apple. Or from which we were cast.

_____

He still visits me in dreams. Not a lot. But he checks in, now and again. I fill Debra in on what he was up to. To say that she misses him—that she and Amanda, Stephanie, Mary, and Mollie miss him—is the wildest of understatements. What he gave was huge; how then could what he took with him, or rather what went away, not also be immense? Grief upon grief upon grief becomes—what? Water? Enough water to extinguish all fires, if for but a while?

She kayaks. She paddles a lime-green kayak on a blue lake beneath a blue sky. She still lives in Oregon, on the rainy coast. The fires from the Southwest have found even this place. She was born into a time of rot and lives now, as do we all, in a time of burning.

_____

In one dream, I was at a campfire in the woods and he came from out of the forest with an envelope he said he wanted me to have. He said I would need it. The envelope was unsealed and when I looked in it there was some paper money—ones and fives, adding up to about ten dollars. Maybe a little more. I thanked him, but thought, *How far is* this *going to take me, and how am I going to make this last?*

Another one. There was a war going on, as there have been in so many of my dreams these last few years: in the bombed-out Gaza Strip, in Afghanistan, in Ukraine. And in this one I had of him, he was young, thirty-five (I don't know how I knew this exact number) and was running toward, rather than away from the active war; toward the smoke and rubble and collapse. He was looking back over his shoulder at me with a look of wild exhilaration and fearlessness—more than that, the delight of meeting a destiny—and he was a journalist, with camera and notepad and flak jacket, and the look on his face said clearly that he was doing what he loved and he was good at it. It was the happiest I'd ever seen him.

Still another—he was driving at night, trying to get somewhere. A big old low-to-the-ground four-door gas-hog sedan. Belly-scraping, really. Big old goggle headlights. Fins. A Detroit relic. Not a Cadillac Eldorado, I don't think; some kind of Oldsmobile. And it was snowing—a blizzard, a whiteout. He was in a hurry to get somewhere and had been driving a long time. I was riding with him, and we went off the road just as he was coming into sight of the place he was trying to reach. Down in a ditch. Out onto a sagebrush prairie—a night blizzard, us snowblind from the rooster tails of snow thrown up by the car, just the shushing sound of snow all around us as we plowed through it, an occasional feathery scratching of sagebrush against the sides and belly of the car. It looked like the end of things—there was so much snow—but I reached over and took the steering wheel and aimed the car back up toward where I thought the road was and accelerated, gave it all the power it had rather than braking, and the car muscled up out of the snowy prairie and miraculously found the road again in all that blizzard, and all was well. We continued on into the falling snow—following that one road that led straight and deeper into the storm.

––––––––

I ragged him about his inveterate habit—a commitment, really, the way a monk or nun might commit—of writing a response to every letter he ever received. And I don't mean with a postcard, nor by the brain-scrambling wires-crossing miasma of email. He'd type out a thoughtful and generous response on the butter-colored parchment of his notepaper, sign the letter with his calligraphic flourish, then fold the letter neatly and, from a special map drawer where he kept an extraordinary volume of specialty stamps—butterflies, Artic explorers, constellations, flora and fauna of New Zealand, what have you—the map drawer housed in the sunroom of his and Debra's beautiful home just above the sun-bright riffling waters of the broad McKenzie, in the dappled sun and shadow of cedars—the light falling upon his hands, his face, as he opened one or another of the long flat drawers and pondered his selection, in conjunction with the recipient and the missive's content—he would choose just the right stamp, or stamps.

This act had all the elements of art. Art gives. Art is selectivity. Art is creative. It was unhurried. It was slow.

A story he told more than once—not so much agreeing or disagreeing (and he would do that so often; take into private counsel some thought or idea to examine, and worry over, as they say in the South, the way a dog worries a bone)—was of how he came to be a writer.

In grade school, he'd read a book (I can't remember whether novel, biography, or natural history) by some local/regional writer—I've forgotten the name, if ever I knew it—and written a letter to the writer. Sixty-plus years later, Barry still marveled that the writer took the time to take the child's letter seriously and write back to the child without condescension, but instead with direct intellectual engagement, and gratitude.

To hear Barry describe it was to imagine that for the child, the boy, it was the first time he'd ever felt heard; that, as he had always desired, holding out hope in the darkness that the one ray of light he saw could be something good, someone good, decent, kind.

As if his prayers had made a thing into reality, had then summoned the thing—kindness, and intelligence. Meaningful connection.

Still, I pushed the opposite thought: you don't have to answer every letter you get, from so many thousands of strangers. *You've more than paid back your debt, your gift. Enough's enough—it takes you away from the here-and-now. You have a duty to the moment, too,* I wanted to say—not just the past, and not even always to the future. But who was I to counsel an elder? By this point he had married my dear friend, the writer and fantastic mother of four incredible young women, Debra Gwartney. Her daughters—in time, they became his, too, in the way of such meldings, and he spoke of them as daughters—and then, from the oldest, Amanda, and then from Mollie, a profusion of sweet and indefatigable grandchildren.

He encouraged me to write what I wanted to write—a slim fine arts book about a mythical logger. A book about a caribou hunt. An extended essay about this, that, or another, when no market for such exists, or existed. To spend a month writing an introduction to a photo book, or a week or longer on a band's album liner notes. A week on an op-ed, or an essay for an obscure publication in some foreign country where my people—all five, six, seven, ten, or however many of them there are—do not live. And with my back turned on the hours with them. This awful fire; this awful light.

I do not answer the letters of strangers. By ragging him about his prolific letter-writing, I think I was able to pretend I was in control of my own relationship with time. With the burning.

———

He could be daunting. As W. S. Merwin wrote of John Berryman in his poem, "Berryman"—

"his lips and the bones of his long fingers trembled
with the vehemence of his views about poetry"

He was a smart son of a gun. It couldn't have been easy, holding so much in his mind—in his body. Edward Hoagland writes that Turgenev's brain was the heaviest ever measured—approximately four pounds. I have heard it said also that of the brain's mass—so many coils and loops and folds, going who knows where—we generally only use about 1 percent. So then where does the other 99 percent go?

I don't know how much he used. But he could be daunting. He seemed smarter, and maybe he was, but mostly I think he just went deeper. "Just." The hunter-gatherer, always giving readers more when they asked for it. Needed it, or even just wanted it. It seemed to be a terrible pressure, a terrible burden, in some ways little dissimilar from our own these days, of placing a four-year-old on a balance beam, or a football into a seven-year-old's hands. He gave. That old fellow he wrote the letter to as a child—it's hard to say what might have happened, if he hadn't. Maybe all of this, nonetheless—unstoppable, roaring like a long fire. Or maybe none of it. It doesn't matter, does it? He was not wrong to write the letters; he wanted to write them, he needed to write them, and so he did. He gave. He gave, and gave.

———

One of the great tenets of Christianity is the necessity of waiting. The Sun Dance and prophecies of seven generations out address better times ahead. Christianity certainly is founded on the faith of a savior's return. But Barry was not much of a waiter. To the best of my knowledge he worked every day, and as he grew more ill—he was sick a long time; Debra and the girls' caretaking of him, across those years—he worked harder.

It's understandable; there can be a terrible urgency for any writer with things still unsaid. I've always marveled at my old heroes for this—the way they push harder near the end, in the way of the female shark injured in the trawl-net who, upon being extricated and tossed onto the deck, gives sudden birth to all her live babies, which skitter across the deck and over the edge, back into the sea, even as she herself will never return.

The way pine trees, under stress of drought or beetle infestation or fire scarring, or the gash of a bulldozer, will generate an extraordinary volume of cones in that same year, a last-gasp pulse of life in the dying.

This would be the opportunity for a writer to talk about Barry's last book. But I don't want to talk about *Embracing Fearlessly the Burning World*, or any of his books. What I wanted for him—when he and Debra knew, really knew, the transition was near—was for him to slow down and live. I wanted him to choose. I wanted him to feel at peace with what he had given to strangers, and to pull in tight. I want that for all of my heroes—they who have sacrificed so much time away from the world, for so many years, decades. Desk-anchored, while this bright world does not slip away but rather the five senses with which they engage it. I wanted him to step away from the desk for himself, but also for Debra and the girls.

Even as I, entering the first of the gray territory, where vision begins to fail and one must look more closely with that light fading, find myself anticipating each next day's work. As might a prisoner, the night before, fall asleep considering his next day's workout in the gym. Might awaken and hasten to it for two-a-days, even before breakfast. As if to a wedding.

What I was thinking, when he'd write those deeply engaged letters to strangers—to utter strangers, I'm tempted to say, even though one thing the pandemic has helped teach or remind us is that we are a global community, all eating the same food, drinking the same water, breathing the same air—that the fires burn and the seas rise whether we are Hindu or Christian, Democrat or Libertarian—

—What I was thinking was of how he and Debra and I would go on walks through the old forest that had not yet burned, the ancient light that left the sun so long ago falling softly now down through the fronds of the overstory like a kind of unheard music, unheard song. On those walks through the old forest behind his and Debra's house, through ferns ankle high and higher, across spongy green moss and the orange vibrant wet duff of the forest floor—through vertical columns of old-growth sunlight sliding off the feathers of cedars, with the creek trickling beside the trail, sounding not as small creeks usually gurgle but instead somehow like chimes—he would point to one giant fallen tree or another and tell how that was a place where he and Debra and Owen and Ezzie, Amanda's son and daughter, would picnic. Point to a bend in the creek and tell of how he and Harry, Mollie's young son, liked to sit in the tiny plunge pool on the hottest days and tell stories that it seemed even the trees were listening to.

You can't put one second back. Yet you can pass forward a pebble of green sea-glass, a curl of turquoise polished by who knows what relentless journey. You can pass forward an image: Barry sitting in a chair next to Debra at Stephanie's wedding, on a hot August day, in the shade. Out in the country. The scent of horses.

He and Debra holding hands at the candlelit dinner table for a meal my daughter Lowry, Erin Halcomb, and I prepared for them, when he was sick, a long time ago; but not yet too sick. Elk backstrap, chocolate ginger cake, dry-rubbed king salmon. Cornbread pudding. A bottle of really good Bordeaux.

You can pass forward an idea. One that is the opposite of greed, or rage, or fear. You can pass beauty forward; kindness, too. Though it is not unnoticed by me that while his and Debra's home was spared somehow, in the center of the great burning, the library where all the maps and letters were kept—tens of thousands?—is now not even ash.

And yet, what we carry from the fire remains real. It all remains present. It is just different; changed.

He was a devotee of sports, particularly that most old-fashioned and nonviolent of games, baseball—what used to be called, in an earlier era, America's pastime. Picnics on the lawn, straw hampers, a blanket spread for all to sit on. He could be boyish. I think that as with so many boys, the statistics of the endeavor intrigued him. A safe harbor, a ferocity of control in the precision, down to the thousandth of a percentage point. Al Kaline's batting average. Willie Stargell's. Pete Rose stealing 198 bases. Juan Marichal's 2,303 strikeouts and 2.89 earned runs allowed in 3,507 innings. And so on.

Something changed in him at the Fire & Grit conference hosted in Washington, D.C., by *Orion* magazine in 1999. We'd been on Capitol Hill to lobby Bruce Babbitt for national monuments, including one in the Yaak Valley. It didn't happen; I forget the reasons why, now. There are always reasons. A quarter century has gone by, the reasons are gone, the need is still there, and now they have come up with new reasons, all of which have as their common denominator one word, *cowardice*. Mike Dombeck was chief of the U.S. Forest Service, beginning his drive to protect all of his agency's roadless lands: a major policy victory, and one of the last I can recall.

We were seated in some conference room in Interior and had been granted maybe twenty minutes with Secretary Babbitt. Hardly the week-long camping trips of Muir and Roosevelt. Bill Kittredge was with us to lobby for Steens Mountain in Oregon, which passed; Terry for Red Rocks Wilderness, which didn't, though later President Clinton, in a somewhat defiant gesture toward Senator Orrin Hatch, passed Grand Staircase–Escalante National Monument.

The Yaak, alas, with all its timber, is not yet protected. (The annular growth rings in the old-growth forests there—centuries-old giants—might be a quarter of an inch thicker, while the mountains above them, also still growing, are *perhaps* a quarter-inch taller, in places.)

Barry wasn't there to lobby for a place, but instead for an idea. Straight out of the gate, before any of us had begun to describe our native landscapes and the passions we held for them, Barry leaned across the table, both elbows on the table—flat, low, as if to minimize wind shear; as if preparing to lunge—and asked, *Secretary Babbitt, when you close your eyes and sleep, what are your dreams?*

I do not remember the secretary's answer. Barry was never one to talk about the weather.

———

I do not know what he dreamed about. We were friends but not that kind of friend where you share your dreams. Your waking ones, sure—aspirations. But not the ones when you sleep. When fears come skulking in.

———

I don't remember all the specifics, at the Fire & Grit conference, only that we were reading on a hill—some park. I read a story about wilderness, and grizzly bears, and bear spray. About what it's like to be sprayed by it—self-inflicted. The mood was light, humorous. Another era. I won't say it was better or worse. It was just a long time ago.

Then he read. He read a story about a boy hiding in a closet. A story about a boy hiding in a closet knowing the man was coming to molest him again. The boy seeing a tiny speck of light outside, from the darkness within, and then the man's shadow. The terror.

It was dark, there in D.C., even in summer. The evening had gone on long. Lightning began to flicker to the north—heat lightning at first, but then real forks of it, seeking and searching: the sky on fire. It's so hard to write about fire. The lightning splitting the darkness. The way the light scorches whatever it falls upon. The way we can be frightened of it, with an awe that—in that quick blink—is not at all dissimilar from joy. Then the dark again.

He had never before told anyone that I know of. People were only just beginning to speak of such things. I'd never read or heard anything of his remotely like it. The piece—"Sliver of Sky"—was in the first person, but at the time I believed it was fiction, and I went to find him. To congratulate him, for fuck's sake. I didn't know. I thought we were there for art, and that it was a short story. I thought we were there for activism. I didn't yet quite understand there can be no difference, no matter how much one wants to believe otherwise. That the dark calls for that scorch of light.

Something changed in him, I think, after writing that story and reading it aloud to his friends, family, and fans in D.C. that night. I went up to him and said "What the hell?" It was so unlike anything he'd written to that point; so unadorned by intelligence or any aspect of his intellect that I felt sometimes he employed almost as a shield.

He looked at me as if he had no answer and was somehow—almost—frightened of the place he had gotten to. The place where he was. But determined. And I still thought it was a short story, and an amazing one, for the empathy he had with the character of that boy.

"I have to go off and be by myself," he said and drifted into the night. There were no cell phones then. I do not know if he called Debra. I do not know where he walked. I never asked.

What I think changed for him was his willingness to trust— to ask for help, in the form of support, understanding, respect, empathy. Fifty or sixty years later, to ask or communicate once again, as he had to that long-ago forgotten writer who'd answered his letter.

———

How can a river summon fire? How can a salmon become a raven, or a cedar tree, or a grizzly? The system is closed—the energy flows where it will flow, assuming in its passage different forms: earth, sky, water, fire. A salmon is a salmon for a while, then it is a raven, then it is a river, then it is a cedar tree, or a grizzly. There is no waste, just as there is no gain. And yet how we grieve and mourn the passage of things, just as we celebrate and exult in the arrival of things. These are not new lessons. But there is great service, I think, in finding new ways to tell the old stories. This is how life itself—evolution or, as Darwin once wrote, "descent, with modifications"—proceeds, or does not proceed.

Proceeds.

———

There's this thing all writers know, where the words, working their way across the page, access something deeper, or higher. A different plane, where understanding—first emotionally, but from that, intellectually—comes surging in. *Metaphor*: we're not just talking about wolves any more. And then—stay in the burning, ride it out—transcendence, or sublimation. The solid becomes a gas, the ether becomes a solid. The metaphor burns away, leaving only the thing, pure and irreducible. And we can carry it with us. We do not have to leave it behind, or be left by it. We are taught otherwise, but that is not my experience. A letter, or a book—a story or a poem—no matter; I am not speaking of symbol or metaphor, but the physical thing, held in your hands, and connecting you to the physical thing—the grove of aspen, the gray wolf on the hill, across the ravine, looking over at you—you are connected, and finally escaping the abstract cage of your emotions and beliefs, foursquare now in the land of the specific—that which many would assert is the proof of a god or greater being, proof that the abstract rattlings in the mind are not simply lost disconnected madness or unbearable loneliness. The book or poem or letter is like the mycorrhizae beneath the surface of ancient forests, connecting all trees and preparing the way for the aging and strengthening of that forest.

The forest has been made real for us. We are allowed a glimpse, touch, taste, scent, sound of the green burning, whether we can see the flames yet or not—for what else is rot but slow burning? The letters, poems, stories give us entry into the fire. And once it is in us I believe it can never be extinguished.

We speak of our footprints—of being mindful. Of trying to travel lightly and minimize our impact. But even the lightest and best of our kind leave enormous prints, we all leave prints, and it seems to me that our feet are burning, that we ignite the ground now wherever we pass.

I do not mean metaphorically but instead actually. The ground beneath our feet is buckling in the heat and the heat is coming up through our shoes. Places where we step are igniting. Places here in the Yaak where I have hiked: Gold Hill, Lick Mountain, Davis Mountain, Caribou Mountain. Thrice when I have been camping a helicopter has flown to a lake where I camped, a different lake each time, and dipped water to go fight a fire just on the other side of the mountain. All trees burn, even when they are being kept in captivity—even as they are in the mill, awaiting their next journey on the way back to sky and soil. John Brown's little lumber mill in the Yaak. The Stimson mill in Libby. This year, almost, the IFG mill in Moyie Springs. The West is burning and the world is burning and there is no longer any metaphor and perhaps there never was. Perhaps metaphor was simply a device by which we avoided looking at things the way they really were and chose instead to compare them, slantwise. To contrast them rather than to really see.

He tapped deep. He was practiced at the art of the descent into the steepest ravines and finding his way back up and out. He read a lot, and felt a lot—quivered, incandescent—and, like a boy memorizing the statistics of various players—not just batting averages or strikeouts, but on-base percentages versus the shift, percentages when facing left-handed pitchers versus right-handed, and so on—he connected various conduits and cables of knowledge, of light. Sometimes with a bit of obstinance, I want to believe, which could also be called faith—he dug his own trenches through the jungle and unspooled his cables, with great effort and exertion.

He wasn't always fully present, I noticed sometimes, but when he was, it was an incandescence. I don't know where he went, exactly, whenever he'd step away.

As Mary Oliver writes, "Said Mrs. Blake of the poet/I miss my husband's company/he is so often in paradise."

We got him when we got him. The rest of the time, he was somewhere else. It is not fair to say he was never here, not fair at all.

He was just not always here. Nor are any of us. Nor are all and each of us. We cannot see what he left behind but it is as real as a stone or piece of colored beach glass. Some days, as the years blow past, we might even think we have misplaced it. But then—on a walk through an old forest at twilight, the light leaving the forest so suddenly it seems taken, yet with other things seeming to glow for a moment—the carpet of butter-yellow arnica blossoms, like an expanse of miniature sunflowers or, later in the year, the entire forest floor stippled with yellow aspen coins, or the orange-gold needles of larch carpeting everything, so that every shape, every inanimate object draped with that gold, seems in that twilight to have been briefly animated, awakening finally if briefly stunned with the wholly unexpected gift of life and surging quickly— before the dark—toward joy.

There are moments when it comes back to us, the gift—the beach glass in the palm of a hand; the elk ivory in a medicine bundle; the stone on the windowsill. He was here. He is here. We were here. We are here. A nation, sometimes above ground, other times below, our tendrils and roots reaching blindly in the dark for one another, our hours and centuries punctuated by bursts of extraordinary light.

HEMINGWAY AND NATURE

I BELIEVE THAT HEMINGWAY'S NATURALIST'S EYE—THE sharpness required to have such sensitivity to detail—helped wire his brain toward becoming the writer we recognize and admire. I would even go further and say it is from this wiring that his best sentences emerge. His best writing.

Art is selectivity. In learning to hunt trout in northern Michigan, or birds, he was training his brain to choose: to see, and then select. Much of hunting is about being careful—about moving slowly. The wind has to be quartering just right. Clues are generally small. Often, instinct is paramount. To hunt is to be immersed in a sea of the specific. *No ideas but in things*, wrote William Carlos Williams. In learning to hunt and fish, Hemingway was learning, in every step, to be a writer.

I believe that the hunter's eye, heightened by a desire so ancient it could be said to be the founding principle of our essence—how we got here, and how we survived, and still do—*eat or die*—was so developed in Hemingway that it not only shaped his craft, but for a while became it. He entered each day's work like nothing but a hunter, or an angler. His days in the woods directed his pen: where to turn, when to go downhill or uphill. Where and when to lift his head to better take in the scent. When to pause next to a tree and grow invisible, and watch. Being in the forest, with the quarry hiding or moving away, is truer to the iceberg that

Hemingway described—the unseen and unannounced, the story just beneath the surface—than is an iceberg itself.

There are moments in all hunters' experience when, after a long and arduous journey, they come into the country of game, whether one sees the animal or not. You *know* it's there. This is the same neural blossoming—the epiphany—known to the writer who, after traveling long and hard in the landscape of the story, happens upon the thing long searched for, as if beneath the surface, but not yet seen. The brain is a cathedral, the brain is a map, and because of his time in the woods as a boy and then a young man, Hemingway was being made into a writer before he was a writer.

Nobody needs to be told that Hemingway was a tortured soul in battle with himself. Or that anger is essentially the same thing as fear. One of his first stories, "Three Shots"—written in a style so clean it appeared to have been transcribed from the stone tablets of a different time, a different world—confronts this fear, the fear of fear, from the very beginning.

> "Last night in the tent he had had the same fear. He never had it except at night. It was more a realization than a fear at first. But it was always on the edge of fear and became fear very quickly when it started."

None of us need to be told that in Hemingway's daily self-generated internal battles, greatness was created. Genius flowed up like a plume of rock dust, bits and glints of ice burning phosphorescent, friction-ground and glowing, supercharged.

(It makes one wonder: what hope is there for us ordinary folks? What is to become of us, we, the untortured?)

But I don't want to belabor his fear, or the luminous residue of his soul's battle, phosphorescent as the tips of the sharks' fins at night, slicing the water as they feast on an old man's swordfish, eating everything but the sword. (How wonderful that in the old man's ever-battling delirium he considers sawing off the sword from the ravaged fish and using it as a spear to continue his struggle against the sharks. "Fight them," he says to himself, even after there is no fish left to fight for. "I'll fight them until I die.")

Instead of exploring the battles, however, I am more interested in the balm of the woods that he sought instinctively. A wounded animal will always run downhill, he reminds us. (Well, almost always. When Hemingway shoots and wounds a couple of eagles, he provides us with the curious piece of natural history—indeed, how else might any of the rest of we non-eagle shooters have known this?—that a wounded eagle is perhaps the sole exception to this rule, or tendency, in that it will scramble madly uphill—as if trying to find a launch site from which to hurl its crippled self into one last attempt at flight, and escape.)

We see the hold that the woods have for him in "Big Two-Hearted River," where nature—a nurturing if not loving nature—has the young protagonist in its full grip. The world does not need another essay on this story, but one never tires of reading or re-reading a great classic, and this one illustrates to me again how the secret heart of nearly every story lies buried just beneath the surface of the best prose. In "Big Two-Hearted River," to switch analogies, we find the mountain the writer has been moving toward—perhaps led or urged toward, seeking. Hunting. This is the flat-topped pure white mountain of Kilimanjaro with the frozen leopard lying in the snow, rising nearly four miles above the sea.

The best writing is almost always the most specific writing, with the writer so close to their quarry—in Hemingway's case, contentment or relief, if not the deeper treasure, peace—that the abstractions of grand ideas are not needed.

"Big Two-Hearted River" is, like most great stories, about more than one thing; one of the things it is about is the battle, or rather the inextinguishable relationship, between fire and water. The fire or animus of the living, propelling all things forward while consuming them at the same time; the refuge and healing quality of water.

In "Big Two-Hearted River," the young Hemingway, not yet debilitated by the world and his wars, has discovered the mother lode of peace, and we read it for this. Here, in the Nick Adams stories, he is a hunter-gatherer, selecting trout from the river as he would individual words and images in other stories—"the heat-light over the plain"—"There were four crows walking in the green field"—"The sunlight shone through the empty glasses on the table."

Here, the object of his journey has already been reached. Here, it is not a struggle for fire or water to triumph but to locate and then inhabit for a little while that place of dynamic tension where the two move against and then with each other. A condition we would call a temporary peace.

"Nick sat down against the charred stump and smoked a cigarette. His pack balanced on the top of the stump, harness holding ready, a hollow molded in it from his back. Nick sat smoking, looking out over the country. He did not need to get his map out. He knew where he was from the position of the river.

"As he smoked, his legs stretched out in front of him, he noticed a grasshopper walk along the ground and up onto his woolen sock. As he had walked along the road, climbing, he had started many grasshoppers from the dust. They were all black. They were not the big grasshoppers with yellow and black or red and black wings whirring out from their black wing sheathing as they fly up. These were just ordinary hoppers, but all a sooty black in color . . . He realized that the fire must have come the year before, but the grasshoppers were all black now. He wondered how long they would stay that way."

Nick rises, loads up the weight of his pack, his burden in that blackened land, and begins walking again, toward the distant river and the distant hills. He picks sprigs of the heathery sweet fern and places them under his pack straps so he can smell the crushed scent of it as he walks. He travels through the fern, which grows ankle high, and through the pines—"a long undulating country with frequent rises and descents, sandy underfoot, and the country alive again."

Fire and water. "Nick tucked two big chips of pine under the grill. The fire flared up. He had forgotten to get water for the coffee . . . he walked down the hill, across the edge of the meadow, to the stream . . . The water was ice cold . . . [He] put some more chips under the grill onto the fire . . ."

It seems Nick's lighting a match on nearly every page. The temptation to tear down is strong. There is a part of him that is already charred and blackened. Maybe it will heal but likely not. "He did not feel like going down into the swamp." He did not want to engage in that battle, the one of healing or accepting himself. Better to fight.

Back and forth Nick goes, hunting an internal curling-up place—drawn always to the fire. In his tent, a mosquito hums close to his ear. Nick sits up and lights a match, moves the match quickly up to the mosquito. The mosquito makes a satisfactory hiss in the flame. This is troubling to those of us gifted with the more accurate vision of hindsight. There are, already, boxers, and guns, throughout these woods—even in the idyll, the refuge. They are in his head—but so too is the nature that feeds him— wild trout from a wild river—even as he's eating crap food from can after can.

He is poised at an edge. I think because of his hungers, Hemingway makes a misstep here and begins to equate hunting with killing. It was a common enough perspective of the times. Still is. Nature was doing its good work on his burning mind—imprinting in him deeply, indelibly, the power of the specific—no ideas but in things. Lying there in his tent, however, he—or his protagonist, Nick—turns away from the balm of a non-game nature and toward battle, and those damned guns.

In "Fathers and Sons," we see "the shotgun loaded and cocked," we see Nick "looking across at his father sitting on the screen porch reading the paper and thought, I can blow him to hell. I can kill him."

(This comes at the very end of the Nick Adams stories and as all writers know, what we put at the end of things matters a great deal. Just preceding "Fathers and Sons," in "Summer People," we see again, through the luminosity of prose, one of the secret hearts of the story in these woods-wandering, seeking tales.)

> "Halfway down the gravel road from Hortons Bay, the town, to the lake, there was a spring. The water came in a tile, sunk beside the road, lipping over the cracked edge of the tile and flowing away through the close-growing mint into the swamp. In the dark Nick put his arm down into the spring but could not hold it there because of the cold. He felt the featherings of the sand spouting up from the spring cones at the bottom against his fingers. Nick thought, I wish I could put all of myself in there. I bet that would fix me."

"Ten Indians" contains more of the balm of the non-game, non-hunted nature that he recognized he needed but left behind in his rush to be needed and useful—a provider, a village hunter.

> "When he awoke in the night he heard the wind in the hemlock trees outside the cottage and the waves of the lake coming in on the shore, and he went back to sleep. In the morning there was a big wind blowing and the waves were running high up on the beach and he was awake a long time before he remembered that his heart was broken."

No, his heart was not broken, or he would not have forgotten. He was so close. He was mapping in his mind the paths to relief and even peace. He had it—contentment and, briefly, balance—right there in the palm of his hand.

Hemingway was a hunter, probably long before he knew he was a writer. Step by step, far from academia, in the cooling shade of the forest, he built and then polished his brain into the generator—creative and destructive—that would power the vessel of his body and his craft. He was always looking for something. This is what hunters do. There is an absence, a need, and they move toward it. Sometimes hugely.

Having never hunted in the manner Hemingway did once he got to Africa, and certainly having not lived in the context of the 1930s, '40s, '50s, when all the lead was flying, I yet cannot help but wonder if Hemingway himself did not feel a great ambivalence with regard to Africa's roving artillery, this caravan of the group hunt, with gun men, trackers, spotters, drivers. Much of *True at First Light* involves him trying to talk Mary out of her lion-killing lust—even though we know the lion is going to die, else it would not be in his work. That would be a different writer indeed.

There is another aspect in which hunting and fishing (and nature) likely informed the writer. Death, and learning how to end a story: again, the woods made him into a writer. I don't know what he would have been, without the woods. A boxer. A football coach. A fishing or hunting guide.

Death, and learning closure as a writer: we can see, again and again, how in being so versed in death—drawn toward the thing he feared, and with death the logical terminus of hunting—Hemingway built his brain to serve him as a writer of good endings. Of learning—training, calibrating himself—to be sensitive to and recognize the stillness when a thing is over. This is a more organic and better way of achieving an end—far better than trudging as if on a forced march toward a long-ago predetermined ending. Instead, the recognized or happened-upon ending has more vitality, is more natural, and has greater durability—it permeates one's body with the five senses. It resonates with the unsuspected, the unknown now known. Even the craftiest writer who tries to hide a predetermined ending will carry into it some element of trickery, and hence some separation from, some superiority over the reader from whom he or she has been trying to hide it. Often a sophisticated reader will sense this, even without quite knowing what's up.

When you go hunting, you don't know quite what you'll see, and you don't know when or where you'll see it. You know only what you want. You walk—quietly, carefully—until you see the quarry. You come quietly into a clearing and there it is. *The End*, after a lot of hard damn work.

The guns and alcohol are so overwhelmingly present, in *True at First Light* and elsewhere, as is death, all manners and ways of it, things crashing down around him. Hunting equals death for Hemingway, and closure, finality, control—the closest space and condition he could find to peace, or contentment. For many of us, nature and even hunting is life and searching, not death and closure, but for Hemingway death *was* the face of nature—a nature he loved—and in this intimate relationship, Hemingway and nature, as with the relationship between Hemingway and himself, he was on the fence, on a high knife ridge; it could have gone either way. He went into the woods as he went into his prose each day, desperately, fully intent and present, and from the beginning, this shaped the brain he would use later, and through his various batterings and concussions and other debilitations, all his life.

Again, we see it at the very beginning in "Indian Camp"— the bliss and wonder of the artist's innocence, and the child's contented innocence, with death nonetheless just beyond. This is an early innocence; the score is still tied essentially zero to zero. It is an innocence that labors like a boatman rowing ever forward.

———

Even his little writing rules were like a hunter's: first and foremost, be aware of the wind. Don't spook one's quarry. Pay attention to the periphery of things—the calls of birds. (In *True at First Light* there's a splendid brief description of Hemingway hearing the alarm call of some small bird and knowing the bird was not scolding at them; that something else, just a little farther on, was on the move.)

His famous blue flame advice about a writer leaving off work each day when you know where you'll pick up the next: this is the mind of the hunter who, the night before, studies his or her maps intently, dreaming where he or she will set out to the next morning.

And, most famously, the iceberg. To a hunter, it is exactly this way, too, if not more so. Everything is unseen, until finally some one small thing becomes visible. The hunter imagines his or her quarry so intensely that it is like a mix between prayer and dream. The hunter inhabits deeply the landscape of the quarry, just as the good writer inhabits deeply the terrain of the story.

In Africa, the killing had to have been wearing him down. In *True at First Light*, he calibrated it, punctuated it, with drinking and reading. He continues to justify it by the need for meat, or an animal's villainy, or even its plain ugliness. An elephant has knocked over a tree. A lion has eaten a goat. An eagle eats a guinea, or a kongoni is old and unattractive, and needs Miss Mary to dispatch it. In midlife, Hemingway changes over to the village hunter. Is it coincidence that his doubts about his writing blossomed as he saw the wearing down of his bloodlust for killing—his reason for being—and sought to find new rationale?

"The time of shooting beasts for trophies was long past with me. I still loved to shoot and to kill cleanly," he says, as if arguing with himself. "But [now] I was shooting for the meat we needed to eat and to back up Miss Mary and against beasts that had been outlawed for cause and for what is known as control of marauding animals, predators and vermin. I had shot one impala for a trophy and an oryx for meat . . . which had a pair of horns worth keeping . . ."

Any middle-aged hunter knows how next to impossible it is to sustain the drive and hunger that once burned so hot in the younger hunter. It is a mystery of biology, that a thing that was ever once so bright can dim, but it does. Almost always, it does.

Reading *True at First Light*, it would be easy for many readers to be turned away, to say the least. I myself find pity for the animals whose paths are crossed—Miss Mary's lion, certainly, with its various four shots—and by all the driving around, looking. More than once, more than twice, Hemingway mentions the American West, as if homesick.

His fire is going out. One of his main reasons for being is

deteriorating. His relationship with a nature that invigorated and might have sustained him a bit further—not forever, but further—is faltering, and he knows it.

> "Now here in Africa there were beautiful birds around the camp all of the time . . . I could not think how I had become so stupid and calloused about the birds and I was very ashamed.
>
> "For a long time I realized I had only paid attention to the predators, the scavengers and the birds that were good to eat and the birds that had to do with hunting. Then as I thought of which birds I did notice there came such a great long list of them that I did not feel quite as bad but I resolved to watch the birds around our camp more and to ask Mary about all the ones I did not know, and most of all, to really see them and not look past them.
>
> "This looking and not seeing things was a great sin, I thought, and one that was easy to fall into. It was always the beginning of something bad and I thought that we did not deserve to live in the world if we did not see it."

Nobody needs to be told that Hemingway drank.

> "I tried to think how I had gotten into not seeing the small birds around camp and I thought some of it was reading too much to take my mind off the concentration of the serious hunting and some was certainly drinking in camp to relax when we came in from hunting."

But in *True at First Light*, there *is* a lot of drinking, even for Hemingway. Beer for breakfast; beer at first light. Gin for anything that ailed anyone, and something, always, was ailing someone. I am not the first reader to wish we could go back to the Nick Adams stories, before the war that was within Ernest Hemingway began to get the upper hand. There were not enough hours in the day to combat this enemy within: not enough drink, not enough killing, not even enough oh so carefully constructed sentences, fragile crystalline latticed structures of other worlds where all was controlled and things were done a certain way and there were fierce ethics and codes and manners designed to keep those worlds just the way they had been crafted. There were not enough sparring partners to box. Again, even in *True at First Light*—an attempt to purge, it feels like, one last long killing spree, punctuated by rest and contemplation—he casts about in brief spare moments of boredom, asking if there are any boys he can fight.

The secret heart of any story lies almost always beneath the cleanest prose. When Hemingway is coming back to camp in lighting too dark to kill, he approaches, yet again briefly, his truest and briefest quarry, peace. He writes that he goes for a walk at night with no gun, only a spear, in soft moccasins.

> "The spear shaft felt good and heavy and it was taped with surgical tape so that your hand would not slip if it was sweaty . . ."

He describes the stubble beneath his feet.

> "Ahead, on the plain, I could see something asleep in the moonlight. It was a wildebeest and I worked away from him . . .
>
> "There were many night birds and plover and I saw bat-eared foxes and leaping hares but their eyes did not shine as they did when we cruised with the Land

Rover since I had no light and the moon made no reflection. The moon was well up now and gave a good
light and I went along the trail happy to be out in the
night not caring if any beast presented himself . . . I
looked back and could . . . not see the lights of camp
but could see the Mountain high and square topped
and [it] shone white in the moonlight and I hoped I
would not run onto anything to kill . . .

"So I walked along in the moonlight hearing the
small animals move and the birds cry when they rose
from the dust of the trail . . .

"I could hear a leopard hunting in the edge of the
big swamp to the left. I thought of going on up to the
salt flats but I knew if I did I would be tempted by
some animal so I turned around and started on the
worn trail back to camp looking at the Mountain and
not hunting at all."

He could have been saved. Surely something could have kept
such a life force going a little further, a little farther. But what?

———

That was the African hunting. But what about the American
West, which Hemingway so loved, but which, even in his day,
he felt had gotten too small? The West even then was being
cleaved by roads. (Ironic that in Africa, he scouted so very many
animals from cars and gravel roads.) I too believe the West is
getting, has gotten, too small, but I love it. We love it. Just
because a thing becomes diminished does not mean one stops
loving it.

In addition to Hemingway's love of the West, there was a
larger need that sent him to Africa, and to the boundless ocean.
As if such spaces represented a hole, an abyss, that would not,

could not, be filled. In closing, I want to leave us with an image and an idea: What if Hemingway had looked a little longer at the other side of the divide, at the other view? Nature is not all and only death. What if he had looked harder and longer at the side that is nurturing, creative, generative, nonresistant, flowing? I'm not asking him to put on a happy face here—he came into the game scarred and scared from the very beginning—that deck was stacked against him—but what if Idaho, Wyoming, and Montana had been enough? If he had found larger country—call it wilderness; call it the American wilderness—he *might* have produced even more and even finer work. But things, as we know, got in the way. There were so many things.

What if he had taken more time to investigate the other side of that divide, to be nurtured and nourished—fed—still using his hunter's eye to select images, but more frequently searching for, and selecting, the elements of peace? What if those things had found their way more often into his creations—and therefore, into him—in earned and natural fashion?

His gaze was pretty fixed. Now and again Nature tempted him with the peace he sought. And he saw it, he noted it. It is maybe his best writing. But then he turned away and trudged on, marched on. He wanted the appearance of order, not the appearance of chaos. We breathe still the fine white dust raised from his passage.

And the country he left, then returned to, at the end of his middle age, to begin the first days of his old age—a country he himself might have described as being middle-aged and diminished? There's certainly nothing to be done about it now, I think, except to protect and preserve as much of the West as is possible; to work to restore it, where possible, to a wilder and fuller state, and away from its reduced and damaged condition. We all have hungers and needs for such a country. What side of the divide each of us decides to look down into, and travel into, is our choice, but we need a fuller and wilder West—more wilderness—in order to be able to even have that choice. The freedom of that choice.

I regret and lament that Hemingway felt he had to go to Africa. I wish we had had enough here, even then, to keep him here. I wish it for him and I wish it for myself, and I hope that, with work, we might all yet see that again and more some day.

LETTER TO AMERICA

WHEN I WAS A CHILD GROWING UP IN TEXAS, IN THE 1950s and '60s, time capsules were a big thing. We made one every year in grade school. There was a quaint, almost querulous child-like quality to them. Preserving things, the way they used to be.

But folks had been burying things in Texas for a long time. There was a famous horned toad named Rip who was buried in the concrete poured in the foundation of the Eastland County Courthouse in 1898. When the courthouse was torn down thirty-one years later, the foundation was broken open and Rip was still alive.

This idea that things, even the past, can stay the same is not uniquely Texan, but there was certainly fertile ground for it back then.

What I want to say now already has a time capsule quality to it—a few months from now, all manner of dramatic things will have happened and no small amount of them will be heinous. And since this is to be a letter to my country—a nation founded on genocide, which rose to economic power on slavery—we've already read *that* letter. We could recite it with every hangdog step as we are carried into our future.

Now, I could chat with America about the long-standing fetish for guns. Again, not a peculiarly Texan affliction, the idea that might makes right, and that whenever a conversation lags, just whip out a gun and fix whatever's inconveniencing you.

It could be mild fun to call Donald Trump a grotesque idiot, a bloated manifestation that has nothing to do with our country's soul—an unwitting Trojan horse foisted upon us by Russian oligarchs.

It would feel okay, to say something like that.

But the truth is, things could get worse; in a year, this railing could be as antiquated as a time capsule.

If America were a person—and it occurs to me, in this fast-evolving speciation where we are willingly abandoning our individual voices for corporate-proxy voices, that plausibility seems ever more remote—I really don't think I'd write a screed about what's wrong. It feels too much like telling a sick person you're afraid they're dying.

I think if America were here at the table with me, on this porch, at the end of summer and beginning of fall, with the rich green scent of marsh grass flowing up toward me, and no birdsong, no frogs, just stillness (later tonight, there will be wolves), I'd fix her a meal. It would be elegant and heartfelt—potatoes and meat—elk backstrap cooked in an iron skillet with a dash of cream and sautéed morel mushrooms picked from last season's fire and then dried, stringing them on this same porch with thread and needle to twist and dry in the summer sun and breezes, before rehydrating.

I wouldn't feel the need to preach or complain. Being sentimental, I might even tell her I'm grateful to her for much. Later in the evening, as we got near the bottom of the wine I'd opened—a Côtes du Rhône or Bordeaux—I might read some poetry to her. American poetry; American art, created in hard times, leaning hard on those old crutches of beauty, creativity, imagination.

We'd save room for dessert, because even though I think there's going to be a tomorrow, one never knows. Huckleberry rhubarb.

We might talk about what makes a great American. Great ones we've known. Teachers would be thick among them, and older people of integrity we've been lucky to know. My grand-parents. My parents.

Artists are my heroes, too. I'd talk about Berger, and Merwin's poem, "Thanks." We'd stay up late. I'd plug in the porch lights.

The pie would be pretty great. She'd want to know the recipe for the crust, but I wouldn't give it to her, not yet. I'd want to keep her coming back.

And after we caught up on her last 10,000 years—*Say what you want about global warming,* she'd say with a laugh, *but I was pretty excited at first, when that last ice sheet started to go away*—she might ask what I've been up to.

I'd tell her. While all the other shit's going on, I've been living like a hermit here in this little bowl of a valley on the Montana–British Columbia border—this island, separated from all other mountain ranges—fighting to protect the last twenty-five grizzly bears that are hanging on here. It's the most endangered popu-lation in North America. You see one family unit of four, you're seeing 15 percent of the entire population.

But you don't see them. They live deep in the woods, in this low-elevation swampy rainforest garden. They're ghosts.

Why do they matter? she might say. *With all that's going on, do they really even matter?*

I've thought about that, I'd tell her. I'd shake my head. They're beautiful, I'd say. Just because there's so much going on, that doesn't allow us to extinguish them. Doesn't allow our gov-ernment to extinguish them. *Remember,* I'd say, *haven't we seen this story before?*

I love the bears for what they are: ice-bound astronauts, sleep-ing five months of the year beneath the ice, their hearts beating two to three times a minute, dreaming in slow motion. I love that they're largely vegetarian, eating hundreds of pounds of grass and berries. I love how the adults slide down the ice with their cubs and splash each other in the lake. I love how they will protect their young with a ferocity not seen elsewhere on this continent. I love that they possess the greatest growth disparity between newborn (teaspoon-sized) and mature adult (six hundreed pounds or more). I love that they came over the land bridge and lived on top of the ice—that they were the first thing here, when the ice left. Waiting.

I love that Native people call them Teacher or Grandfather. I love that theirs is a maternal culture, that the female takes her cubs all over their territory, showing them where to catch fish when the berries are dry, where to go when they hear rifle shots, where—

You don't like being around people much, do you?

Do I have to?

No. There is plenty to love about America other than people. Just curious.

I like people but I don't like being around them.

How can I help, she'd say, leaning forward. *You're right: a country that can't protect its last twenty-five grizzlies . . .*

. . . doesn't deserve them, I'd think, but neither of us would say that.

Write Senator Tester, I'd say: www.tester.senate.gov/contact. Write Senator Daines, and Governor Gianforte. Read about it at www.yaakvalley.org.

All right. Good night, she'd say, getting up. *I have to be up early. Thank you for the pie. Thank you for the elk.*

Thank you, I'd say. *Thank you.*

But we wouldn't be finished talking.

ACKNOWLEDGMENTS

THE PAST IS NEVER PAST, TO PARAPHRASE FAULKNER. There's a powerful amount of truth in that observation, but it's also true he never anthologized his nonfiction. What was, no longer is. This is the dual and dueling truth. When I look back at these collected essays, I'm struck by their earnestness, the in-the-moment quality that suggests a writer who—how could this be?—had no idea that such a thing as the future might exist.

I don't know how many books I've written. They are not each "like my children." Good God. They're just *books*.

I still like to write. But what I really crave is the physical world, in this bright moment of life. Moving rocks, gathering firewood, hiking, swimming in cold lakes. Puttering, beneath an immense sky.

The author of these essays was a writer, on his way to becoming someone who would one day be asked to look back. It's an interesting enough view, but I don't feel the need to stare too long upon it. For there are still days, and miles, ahead, until there aren't.

I'm so grateful to be welcomed into the Counterpoint family. Not an angle of repose, but a dynamic, living ecosystem of literature, ideas, passion, craft. Thank you to Jack Shoemaker, Dan Smetanka, Tajja Isen, Laura Berry, Nicole Caputo, Farjana Yasmin, Rachel Fershleiser, Wah-Ming Chang, Yukiko Tominaga, Megan Fishmann, Vanessa Genao, Katherine Kiger, and Barbra Rodriguez. I'm grateful to my family and friends who have somehow always accepted and even understood the solitude a writer craves, needs, and fears, and have helped make a space for it: my parents, brothers, cousins, aunts and uncles; my daughters, Mary Katherine and Lowry, their mother, Elizabeth; and my sweethearts Carter, Sissel and Siri. What heaven is this, to be embedded into such a matrix of love, intellect, and passion?

Thank you also to the University of New Mexico Press, publishers of my previous book of essays, *Fortunate Son*, which contains two of the essays reprinted here. And to the countless editors, publishers, editorial assistants, copy editors, factcheckers, and proofreaders of journals, magazines, and books that have handled these essays over the years, turning them over and over in their hands, polishing, smoothing, stretching, trimming, sanding, clarifying. Thank you.

PUBLICATION ACKNOWLEDGMENTS

"Into the Fire": First published in *Men's Journal*, September 1995.

"The Rage of the Squat King": First published in *Best American Sports Writing 2015*, *New Nowhere 2014*.

"Whale Song": First published in *Tricycle*, Summer 2011.

"The Beauty That Wills Us On": First published in *Tricycle*, Fall 2013.

"Ice Fishing": First published in *Narrative*, Stories of the Week 2014–2015.

"The Hunters": First published in *Virginia Quarterly Review* online, July 10, 2010.

"Border Patrol": First published in *Narrative*, Winter 2017.

"The Larch": First published in *Orion*, September/October 2012.

"Wolf Palette": First published in *Orion*, June 2003.

"Whale Shark": First published in *Narrative*, Spring 2016.

"Moon Story": First published in *Fortunate Son: Selected Essays of the Lone Star State*, 2021.

"The Stamp of the African Elephant": First published in *Tricycle*, Winter 2011.

"Hearts and Bones": First published in *Sierra* online digital excusive, June 3, 2016.

"Fifteen Dogs": First published in *Narrative*, Spring 2019.

"With Every Great Breath": First published in *Whitefish Review*, Winter 2012/2013.

"Descent, with Modifications": First published in *Audubon*, November–December 2014.

"A Life with Bears": First published in *Narrative*, Spring 2020.

RICK BASS is the author of over thirty books. He is a winner of the Story Prize, the James Jones First Novel Fellowship, a PEN/Nelson Algren Award Special Citation for fiction, and a finalist for the National Book Critics Circle Award. He is a recipient of a National Endowment for the Arts Fellowship. He has served as contributing editor to *Sierra*, *Tricycle: The Buddhist Review*, *Big Sky Journal*, *Amicus Journal*, *Outside*, *Orion*, *Field & Stream*, *The Contemporary Wingshooter*, and many other publications. He currently serves on the editorial board of *Whitefish Review*. He was born and raised in Texas, worked as a petroleum geologist in Mississippi, and has lived in Montana's Yaak Valley for almost thirty years. Find out more at rickbass.net.